WHAT IT MEANS TO BE FIGHTING IRISH

ARA PARSEGHIAN

AND NOTRE DAME'S GREATEST PLAYERS

EDITED BY TIM PRISTER

TRIUMPH
BOOKS
CHICAGO

Library of Congress Cataloging-in-Publication Data

What it means to be Fighting Irish : Ara Parseghian and Notre Dame's
    greatest players / edited by Tim Prister.
        p.   cm.
    ISBN 1-57243-640-9
        1. Notre Dame Fighting Irish (Football team)—History.   2.
University of Notre Dame—Football—History.   3. Football players—
United States—Anecdotes.   I. Prister, Tim, 1960–

GV958.N6W53   2004
796.332'63'0977289—dc22

                                                    2004046099

This book is available in quantity at special discounts for your group or organization. For further information, contact:

Triumph Books
601 South LaSalle Street
Suite 500
Chicago, Illinois 60605
(312) 939-3330
Fax (312) 663-3557

Printed in the United States of America
ISBN 1-57243-640-9
Interior design by Nick Panos.
All photos courtesy of the Notre Dame Sports Information Department
unless indicated otherwise.

CONTENTS

D'Juan Francisco, Tony Rice, Scott Kowalkowski, Raghib Ismail, Rick Mirer, Kevin McDougal, Aaron Taylor, Pete Chryplewicz, Derrick Mayes, Marc Edwards, Melvin Dansby, Ron Powlus, Bobby Brown, Jarious Jackson

FOREWORD

What It Means to Be Fighting Irish

WHEN JOE KUHARICH STEPPED ASIDE at Notre Dame after the 1962 season, I didn't think anything about it. We had a big season at Northwestern in 1962 [7–2] and had a lot of players returning. We were picked by the Big 10 Skywriters to win the conference in 1963, so we felt good about where we were.

We started 4–1, but then lost three straight before defeating Ohio State. We didn't fulfill the preseason expectations. A writer for the *Chicago American* really began getting on me. He printed an article that said that 1964 was the last year of my contract—which was true—and then Northwestern would get rid of me.

I took the article to my athletic director [Stu Holcomb] and asked him, "Stu, what is this?" His response was, "Well, Ara, you can't expect to coach here forever." That was it for me. I said to myself, "If there's no respect, I'm not staying where I'm not wanted." I told him I was going to make every effort to find another job.

We finished the season early [November 16] in 1963, so I had time to look around. The first job I inquired about was Miami [Florida], where Andy Gustafson had left, but I noticed the interim status at Notre Dame with Hughie Devore. I didn't get a hold of Father Joyce until later because they still had a game with Syracuse [November 28]. I made the initial contact with Father Joyce and said, "I've noted you have an interim coach, and if you're contemplating a change, I'd like to throw my hat into the ring." Father Joyce said he appreciated the call and he would get back to me.

I didn't think I had much of a chance for the Notre Dame job. I look back now with pride at what we did at Northwestern, but at that time there were some who thought I was doing a lousy job. We never won a Big 10 title, which was a goal, and I had a reputation that I couldn't coach in November. Yet all of a sudden, the four straight games we won over Notre Dame [1959–1962] became important.

It was at the Army–Navy football game [December 7] when Father Joyce approached Stu to inquire about my availability and for permission to interview me. The next week there was a Notre Dame Club of Chicago dinner. Since Northwestern is near Chicago, it presented us an opportunity to convene in private.

When I drove down to Notre Dame for the announcement of my hiring, the campus was dead. The students had left for Christmas vacation and there was nobody on the campus. Father Hesburgh, Father Joyce, and I had dinner at the Morris Inn. After I took the job, I had some trepidation because there was a lot of talk and some stories about how I was the first non-Catholic, the first nongraduate, to take the job since Knute Rockne.

I discussed it extensively with Father Joyce and he said, "We have a broad spectrum of people here. We're not all Catholics in the faculty. We have people of the Jewish faith, Protestants. . . . We hire people based on their capabilities, not religion. We're a Catholic institution and it would be nice if it happened that the coach also was Catholic, but we don't make that our principal intention."

When I went to Notre Dame, the talent was already there. It was a matter of putting people in the right positions, motivating them, and giving them direction. At Northwestern, the talent wasn't near what Notre Dame had, and we didn't have the tradition, facilities, or exposure either. Add in the incredible spirit at Notre Dame with its history, and we felt we could have something special.

Maybe it sounds strange or you might say it was exorbitant overconfidence, but I really believed it. After our first year when we started 9–0 and won the MacArthur Bowl, Father Joyce wanted me to sign a five-year contract. I said fine, but not because I thought it was necessary. I've always felt if things aren't going well and you aren't doing the job, you shouldn't be there. After the five years expired (in 1969), I did not have another contract that went beyond one year. I did not ask for a lengthy contract or an extension. I respected Father Joyce and Father Hesburgh, and they respected me.

The 1964 season was special because there is a euphoria that comes with turning around a program. You can't duplicate it; you don't *want* to duplicate it. What I mean is you don't ever want to be 2–7 again and have to try to do it all over. That's something you can—and want to—experience only once.

I would agree with the statement that 1964 was my most fun season as a coach because of the unknown variables heading into the year. When you come into a program that hasn't had success, you have everything to gain and nothing to lose. Once you win, then you become a victim of your own success and you can't ever recapture that renewed invigoration. Climbing the mountain is easier and more fun than staying on top of it.

The best time of my life, for my family and me, was the 11 years at Notre Dame. My family was in the formative stage where our three children were being educated. Plus there was a lot of excitement around the Notre Dame family that football was resurrected.

We didn't belong to a conference and we didn't even go to bowl games when I arrived. You throw those dimensions in and it was really tough because there was no way you could recoup from an early season loss to win the national title. If we lost the second game—which we did several times in the sixties to Purdue—all of a sudden we fell in the rankings, we couldn't make it up with a conference title or go to a bowl game, and we had to fight our way back up the ladder.

That's why one of our proudest accomplishments was the fact that in 11 years, we never lost two games in a row during the regular season. That was a pretty impressive achievement considering how deflating and devastating just one loss could be as far as ending the main goal you work toward.

I found it unfair at times when the games we lost were often classified as the "big ones." How do you determine what is a big one? Going into 1964, Notre Dame had lost eight in a row to Michigan State, five of its last six to Purdue, three of four to Navy, and four of six to Pittsburgh. We won against all those teams in our first year. Were those "big games" or not? When we lost to Southern Cal in the final minute after going 9–0, that became "the big game."

So we beat Southern Cal the next year [28–7] and lost to Michigan State—the team that became the national champion—and now that was "the big game." In 1966, we beat USC [51–0] out there to clinch the national title, but the 10–10 tie the week before at Michigan State was "the big game." From 1969 on, we played five bowl games and four of our opponents were undefeated and ranked No. 1. We won three of them. Were those big games or not? If you won, great, that stigma of "not winning the big one" goes away temporarily, but you're never better than your last game.

One of the things I swallowed often was we would have players not admitted to Notre Dame, but they were accepted at other schools we competed against. When this particular recruit would excel at another school, we would get letters saying what a bum job we did in recruiting, how we didn't recruit this guy, how could we miss him, and so forth. We swallowed hard because we did not want to hurt any kid by saying he couldn't get admitted. Just because he was not academically qualified didn't mean he couldn't be a great citizen and achieve great things. A lot of marginal students have done exceptionally well.

There was one incident where I almost came forward with it because the individual involved became very critical of me and very critical of Notre Dame for not having pursued him. But we never, ever pointed the finger at anyone or publicized who was not qualified to come to Notre Dame.

Another issue we had to swallow hard was what was termed our "lily white" backfields in the late sixties and early seventies. We were an all-male school [prior to 1972], so there was almost a military academy atmosphere with the strong Catholic religious affiliation. There were a lot of outstanding black athletes we couldn't compete for because there was an academic issue sometimes or there was an issue where they didn't feel their social life would be equivalent to that of a state school. Those variables made it very difficult for us to bring in the black athletes until Father Hesburgh intervened.

It was early in the 1972 football season when Father Hesburgh approached me in private during a postgame party. He asked me, "Ara, why don't we have more black people on our team?" He had always been a champion of civil rights. I said, "Father, we've tried . . . but you better talk to your people in the admissions office."

Now, I didn't mean to be critical about admissions because they do a great job. My point was we had recruited a number of black student-athletes who qualified in all other ways, but they were just missing a credit unit here or there. Eventually exceptions were made with the help of Father Hesburgh. [The following spring, 1973, Notre Dame recruited its largest contingent of black athletes in one season, highlighted by Ross Browner, Luther Bradley, Willie Fry, and Al Hunter, among many others.]

Can somebody coach at Notre Dame beyond 11 years? That's a good question and I don't know if I can answer it. The answer probably is yes—but unlikely. The demands at Notre Dame and the expectations would have to be built around the physical, emotional, and psychological abilities of the person we're talking about.

In my case, I was emotionally involved. My very nature is emotional. While that probably helped me motivate the team, it also probably was a drain over 11 years. Some coach would have to have all these qualities to last a long time: emotional stability, great strategy, great motivating skills, great recruiting skills, a great relationship with the administration, a great relationship with the alumni, and great sentiment between the families of his players. To be able to do all those things and be balanced in all, that's going to take a very significant person. It's not easy.

I had two mottoes I lived by, and they were there to complement each other. One was for the success we achieved, and the other was for the adversity you face in life. When things weren't going well, it was: "Adversity elicits talent, which under prosperous conditions would have remained dormant." When you're down, it doesn't mean you have to stay down. It might stimulate you to be back on top.

For success it was: "Remember this your whole life through, that tomorrow there will be more to do. And failure waits for all who stray, with some made yesterday." That addressed the guys riding high. When you reach the high spot, you better recognize that somebody is trying to knock you off from there and a little humility might help you.

I didn't get tired of coaching. I enjoyed it and I missed being on the field and developing the techniques and game strategies. I was always a guy for today and tomorrow, and I'd let history speak for itself. I'd always tell my squad, "Last week's game against that opponent we beat badly has nothing to do with today or what we have coming up on Saturday. That day is for historians." I still felt I was creative and I still felt we were innovative. The demands to live up to the expectations were difficult. They became a burden in a sense. It was an accumulation of things over 11 years.

x

After I left coaching, I became amazed by all the eulogies people were presenting and the respect they had for what happened in those 11 years. I became more respected, more recognized, and more appreciated after I left coaching. I remember saying to [1949–1981 Notre Dame athletic director Ed] "Moose" Krause when he was retiring, "Moose, you're going to be amazed at how respected you're going to be and how honored you're going to be now that you're leaving." We both laughed about it because during his time, he took a lot of heat for his coaches and administration.

It's true that after you're gone, people have an opportunity to look back and they have measuring sticks: how did you do when you came in compared to your predecessor? How did you do compared to your successors? All of those things fall into place after a period of time.

The respect from accomplishment is not only from the alumni and people who were part of it, but the respect from the players, which has been very encouraging for the former coaching staff. What you feel good about is when they tell you how well prepared they were, how they never went onto a field sensing they were going to be surprised by anything. They knew what the opponent was going to do on both sides of the ball, and we weren't going to make glaring mistakes on the sideline to make it more difficult for them. That kind of attitude and respect has been prevalent since I've left coaching.

If people know me well enough, they know that receiving praise isn't what is most important to me. The word I most closely identify with is respect. The important things for me were to do the best possible job I could and to have a unity of team spirit and chemistry, a strong relationship with our staff, and respect for each other all around. All of those factors will lead to the successes.

—ARA PARSEGHIAN

Ara Parseghian took the once downtrodden Northwestern Wildcats to a 6–0 start and No. 2 national ranking in 1959 and another 6–0 start and No. 1 ranking in 1962. He was 3–1 against Woody Hayes' Ohio State Buckeyes from 1958 to 1963, whipped Bud Wilkinson's Oklahoma Sooners 45–13 and 19–3 in 1959 and 1960, and was 4–0 against Notre Dame from 1959 to 1962.

But because Parseghian's Northwestern teams lacked depth, they usually faltered in November. That made Parseghian somewhat unappreciated as he finished his eighth season at Northwestern in 1963 with a career record of 36–35–1.

Meanwhile, Notre Dame's football program was in the throes of its darkest days. From 1956 to 1963, Notre Dame was 34–45, including 2–8 in 1956 and 1960, and 2–7 in 1963. One head coach was fired (Terry Brennan in 1958), another resigned in disgust over the unrealistic expectations (Joe Kuharich in the spring of 1963), and a third was hired on an interim basis (Hugh Devore in 1963).

Unlike Frank Leahy in the forties and Lou Holtz in the eighties, Parseghian had no clause in his contract with Northwestern that expressed a desire to coach at Notre Dame. He was content with his position—until Holcomb verified after the 1963 football season that Parseghian was on the hot seat. The timing was ideal for Parseghian and Notre Dame to join forces, and the dynamic 40-year-old head coach made an indelible impression on the university president, Reverend Theodore Hesburgh C.S.C., and the vice president, Reverend Ed Joyce C.S.C.

Combining Notre Dame's spirit and tradition with the charismatic Parseghian's fire and football acumen, a new dynasty was forged at Notre Dame. From the 2–7 debacle of 1963, Parseghian transformed his first Irish squad into a 9–0 unit before losing a controversial 20–17 decision at USC in the season finale. Still, the Irish were awarded the MacArthur Bowl, emblematic of the national title.

In 1966 and 1973, Parseghian's Irish won consensus national titles. In 1970, the 10–1 Irish finished No. 2 after defeating No. 1 Texas in the Cotton Bowl.

Under Parseghian's direction from 1964 to 1974, Notre Dame was 95–17–4 (.836) and finished in the nation's top five during 8 out of 11 years. Ultimately, he became a victim of his own success once again and retired from coaching at the age of 51.

His impact on Notre Dame football, however, is everlasting.

EDITOR'S ACKNOWLEDGMENTS

THIS PROJECT NEVER WOULD HAVE reached completion without the dedicated efforts of three Notre Dame historians.

Joe Doyle has told Notre Dame's story for nearly half a century. He has been the main source of information to millions of Fighting Irish football fans and an inspiration to those of us who dreamed of one day following in his footsteps and paying our respects to the school we cherish.

Lou Somogyi, my partner for more than two decades at *Blue & Gold Illustrated*, is truly one of our era's most gifted writers. His dedication to covering Notre Dame football, his tireless commitment to his craft, his selfless and team-first attitude, and his unconditional support are some of the great gifts God has bestowed upon me.

A third contributor, Pete Sampson, has only just begun his journey through the Notre Dame experience. Remember the name. You will read it again. His talent is unmistakable.

On behalf of these talented and dedicated writers, we humbly offer the story of Notre Dame football through the eyes of some of the school's all-time greats. When it comes to the Notre Dame experience, there's no story quite like it.

To the wonderful men who took the time to share their Notre Dame experience, my respect for you and your accomplishments fills my heart, like yours, with gold.

To the University of Notre Dame, my beloved alma mater, thank you for the blueprint of how to live one's life like a Notre Dame man.

To my wife, Terri, and my son, Eric, you are my inspiration, my driving force, and my strength. I'm looking forward to spending the rest of eternity together.

And to my mother, Mary Ann Prister, who saw the vision, made the ultimate sacrifices, and continues to inspire the Notre Dame dream in all that I do. I owe everything that I am to you.

INTRODUCTION

"FRANK, ARE YOU STILL THERE?" There was a gap in the phone conversation. Had we been disconnected?

"Yeah, I'm still here, I just had to collect myself for a moment," said Frank Pomarico, tri-captain of the 1973 national champion Notre Dame football team, as his voice cracked.

Pomarico was the first player I had called after agreeing to edit a book chronicling the experiences of dozens of Notre Dame football players from as far back as the 1930s to the present. Pomarico was explaining how he had idolized Notre Dame offensive guard Larry DiNardo through high school, followed in his footsteps at Notre Dame, how he began wearing DiNardo's number [56] after DiNardo graduated, and how he stepped into the starting lineup in the exact same spot DiNardo had occupied for the Fighting Irish.

Pomarico had to take a moment to collect himself. Some 30 years after the fact, he still got emotional relating his experiences as a Notre Dame football player. I smiled to myself as I hung up the phone. I knew I was the right choice to present the story of Notre Dame football in *What It Means to Be Fighting Irish*. I was getting emotional too. I'd done that a lot through the years.

I remembered the first time I put on a Notre Dame baseball uniform in the spring of 1981. I looked down at my chest and saw Notre Dame scrawled across the top of the button-down shirt. What a remarkable feeling of pride, what an overwhelming feeling of responsibility. I had grown up, taken a huge stride toward manhood. I had not only become the first college student in my family, but I was fulfilling the unthinkable dream by wearing a Notre Dame baseball uniform and starting at third base for the Fighting Irish.

Pomarico had good reason to be emotional, and I completely understood how he felt.

My first recollection of watching a Notre Dame football game is from the rectory of our parish priest on November 19, 1966. It was the day of the Notre Dame–Michigan State game that ended in a 10–10 tie. I was six years old. Looking back now on my life in Notre Dame football, that was the first sign that this was the way my life was meant to be. Notre Dame football would be more than a passing interest. It would be the avenue by which I would become known. Little did I know at the time that not only would Notre Dame football become a family passion, but that beginning in 1982, upon graduation from Notre Dame, I would spend the rest of my adult life covering Fighting Irish football.

Beginning in 1986, with Lou Holtz's first game as head coach of the Fighting Irish, I began a streak that no other living human being can claim. I've attended and reported on every Notre Dame game since the 1986 opener against Michigan. That's 217 straight leading up to the 2004 opener against Michigan. The last Notre Dame football game I didn't attend was the 58–7 loss to Miami in 1985 to conclude the Gerry Faust era.

My attendance has included a whirlwind visit to Dublin, three trips to Hawaii, numerous excursions to some of college football's most venerated venues, and, of course, more than 100 Saturday afternoons (and a couple of evenings) in the most famous college football setting of all—Notre Dame Stadium.

So I felt a bit humbled yet eminently qualified to be selected as the editor of a book recapping the Notre Dame football experience through the memories and words of the former Irish greats. Interviews conducted with the headline makers and legends of Notre Dame proved to be a fascinating journey that always led back to the focal point—the University of Notre Dame. It is the thread that ties these people together. It is the emotional bond that inspires us to be something special. It is the ideal that directs our lives.

Each story had its own unique twist. Some of the Irish greats grew up just as passionate about Notre Dame football as I was. Ned Bolcar remembers the bus trips that ran from his town of Phillipsburg, New Jersey, to the mecca of college football in South Bend, Indiana. Joe Theismann, Aaron Taylor, and

xvi

Jarious Jackson knew from the moment they saw the lights on the Golden Dome against the backdrop of the falling snow that Notre Dame wasn't just the school they wanted to attend; it was where they had to be in order to be complete, to feel whole, and to be fully challenged. Raghib Ismail remembers waking up at a friend's house one morning to the strains of the "Notre Dame Victory March." Mike Golic still gets a chill down his spine thinking about running out of the tunnel in Notre Dame Stadium, and he hasn't done it in 20 years. D'Juan Francisco changed his dorm room so he could look out his window each morning and see the Lady on the Dome that his head coach, Lou Holtz, talked about. All Joe Montana needed to hear was that Notre Dame had a scholarship waiting for him. For many, the opportunity to play football for Notre Dame was a calling, a preordained event, a lure almost beyond their physical and/or emotional control.

And then there were those who didn't grow up with the Golden Dome casting a shadow across their baby crib. In fact, some Irish greats didn't even know where Notre Dame was located until much later in life. Paul Hornung wanted to go to Kentucky and play for Paul "Bear" Bryant. His mother had another idea, so Hornung went to Notre Dame, where he won the Heisman Trophy. Marc Edwards admitted to disliking Notre Dame as a kid because they won all the time. Joey Getherall grew up wanting to play for, shudder, Southern California! When Lou Holtz began thoroughly recruiting the South upon his arrival in the mideighties, a whole new section of the country was introduced to the tradition of Notre Dame football. Jarious Jackson, Bobby Brown, Kevin McDougal, Jeff Faine, Courtney Watson, et al, are forever grateful.

xvii

But regardless of locale or background, from Tupelo, Mississippi, to Santa Ana, California, from sunny southern Florida to frigid New England, from upper class to working class, regardless of race or family background or religious affiliation, a common thread runs through the stories of the Fighting Irish football greats. It leads to a place like no other in the world, battered and tattered at times by failures on the gridiron and human frailty, yet still unscathed in the ideals it will always represent.

People on the outside relate everything regarding Notre Dame football to a number or, rather, a set of numbers. The year 1966 elicits the numbers 10–10, as in the famous tie with Michigan State. The 1988 season is remembered by 12–0, as in 12 victories, no losses. A few 5–6s and 5–7s have leaked in there, especially in recent years. But from the inside, a won-lost record cannot sum up the Notre Dame experience. It is the feeling of putting on the gold helmet, hearing the "Victory March" at a pep rally, walking onto the field in hostile territory, and being booed simply because you represent Notre Dame. It's the personalities and lifelong friendships developed in the legend-filled Notre Dame dorms. It's representing the Blessed Virgin whose replica sits atop the Golden Dome.

Make no mistake, being a Notre Dame football player has been and always will be about wins and losses. There have been too many wins for it to be otherwise. Let's hope that never changes. But it's also about blending in with the rest of the student body, being held in the same esteem in the classroom as a non–football player who, more likely than not, was the valedictorian or salutatorian in his or her high school class. It's about learning different cultures, being exposed to varying ideas, and experiencing the full gamut of social situations that is made possible by the fact that your three roommates are from Redwood City, California, Baton Rouge, Louisiana, and an unpronounceable town in Sri Lanka. Whatever someone's background or path to this slow-paced town in northern Indiana, it all leads to the same conclusion. There's a bit of magic on these grounds, and if you've ever been there, you know it.

Ultimately, this book is about the experience that is the University of Notre Dame, where young people try to better themselves and experience the best of all worlds. In the end, whether or not they arrived so inclined, they walk away changed forever with a heart that pounds to the beat of the "Victory March" or "Notre Dame, Our Mother."

If you've worn the Notre Dame uniform, what pounds in your chest is a heart proud to represent something so special that you'll spend your life on earth sharing the experience with others. What you have is a heart of gold.

—TIM PRISTER

The
THIRTIES AND
FORTIES

BOB SAGGAU

1938–1940

M Y FATHER, HENRY, WAS AN AUTOMOBILE DEALER in Denison, Iowa, and one of his franchises was with Studebaker in South Bend. On one of his trips to the Studebaker plant, he met Knute Rockne, a part-time representative of Studebaker interests.

So you could say my dad had a Notre Dame connection with coach Rockne right from the beginning. In addition to my father meeting coach Rockne, my mother had two brothers who attended Notre Dame. But we also grew up listening to Fighting Irish games on the radio. We used to get the *Chicago Tribune* each day in Denison, and I grew up pulling for the Bears, the Blackhawks, and Notre Dame.

One of my fondest memories as a teenager was the famous "Game of the Century," the Notre Dame–Ohio State game of 1935. I remember the radio broadcast, and later I would get to play with some of those Notre Dame players.

Recruiting was a lot different back in those days. It was very limited. After Rockne died, most of the contact by the Notre Dame coaches was done by mail or word of mouth from the Catholic schools.

I didn't make any real recruiting visits, although I did go to the University of Minnesota during my junior year in high school. Dad was on a business trip, and we got to meet coach Bernie Bierman. He talked to my dad and seemed to ignore me.

So in the fall of 1937, my father took me on the 600-mile trip from Denison, Iowa, to Notre Dame. He dropped me off at Bronson Hall (a freshman

Notre Dame finished No. 5 in the Associated Press poll in 1938, the year Bob Saggau paced the Irish in rushing.

dormitory) and then had a conversation with some of the priests. So my early days at Notre Dame were spent literally under the shadow of the Golden Dome. Bronson Hall was where Rockne lived when he was a student at Notre Dame.

Knute Rockne, All-American was made during my time at Notre Dame, and they actually shot film of our freshman workouts. We had a small coaching staff then—Joe Boland [line], Joe Benda [ends], Chet Grant [first assistant], Bill Cerney [B-team]—and freshmen didn't play any games then. Elmer Layden was the head coach.

We were the "hamburger squad" for the varsity, and back then a couple hundred freshmen would try out for the team. I received scholarship aid—room, board, tuition, and books—in exchange for a job in the dining hall, the stadium, or somewhere else on campus. My job was in the cafeteria, although I had to switch jobs when I came down with an infection.

After a year in Bronson and a year in Carroll Hall, I got a regular room in Dillon Hall, which was one of the new dormitories at that time, and it was close to the dining hall too.

We were 6–2–1 in 1937 with stars such as tackle Ed Beinor and end Johnny Kelly. In 1938 I had to wait my turn at left halfback behind Harry Stevenson and Benny Sheridan.

We were undefeated in 1938 when we played [No. 12] Minnesota.

I'll never forget hearing coach Layden in the dressing room before that game. He started listing the lineups and when he got to Steve Sitko at quarterback, he then said, "Saggau at left half," and I was really elated. It was my first start, so I remember that game well.

I was a left-footed punter as well, and I had prepared our team for Bob Fitch, who was a very talented left-footed punter for Minnesota. We were outplayed that day, but we won [19–0].

Years later I was trying to sell some equipment to the Gophers' hockey coach, Johnny Mariucci, and I said, "Johnny, I played football against you in 1938." He said, "I know, I know. We ran all over you guys, and you didn't even get a first down, but you beat us on punt returns and interceptions!"

That 1938 team [8–1] was the best one I was on at Notre Dame. We lost to Southern California [13–0] in the last game of the season. I was one of the "S boys" that year. We had Steve Sitko at quarterback, Harry Stevenson at halfback, Benny Sheridan at halfback, and myself.

We lost to Iowa [7-6] with Heisman Trophy winner Nile Kinnick [in 1939], and then USC beat us [20–12]. In my last year [1940], Iowa [7–0] and Northwestern [20–0] beat us. But at least we beat Southern Cal [10-6] out there in our final game.

My folks came for every home game during my four years at Notre Dame. It was a long drive, but my dad also had the Chevrolet and Buick agency in Denison, so he always had good cars.

After Notre Dame I was sworn into the navy and went into flight training with Nile Kinnick. I was in the navy and Nile was in the marines. Kinnick was killed in a plane crash, and I went all over the Pacific flying bombers, including the first big navy operation at Guadalcanal.

There were all sorts of former players in the Pacific, but when I was eligible to get out in late 1945, I jumped at the chance. I thought about flying commercial airlines as a pilot, but I decided against it. Now I think back about it, and I would have had a nice pension.

When I was a bit younger I went back to the annual Monogram Club golf outings and attended two or three home games a year. I was amazed one time, a few years after graduating, when Reverend Theodore M. Hesburgh, who was the university's president then, not only recognized me but was well aware of my playing days.

That's Notre Dame for you. It's a place you can never forget, and they do not forget you.

5

Bob Saggau from Denison, Iowa, arrived at Notre Dame in the fall of 1937 and led the Irish in rushing in 1938 with 353 yards (on just 60 carries), despite being listed as the number three left halfback behind Harry Stevenson and Benny Sheridan. Listed at 6'0", 185 pounds, Saggau was as big as many of the Irish linemen during that era.

JOHN McHALE

1940

As a nine-year-old watching the dedication game of the Knute Rockne–built stadium in 1930 [a 26–2 victory over Navy on October 11], I became a Notre Damer.

To this day, every time I visit the Notre Dame campus, I am at peace with myself, with my family, and with my God. It means everything to me. I grew up with Notre Dame year after year. My father was a real follower of the Irish. He watched dozens of games when Rockne was the coach, and we followed his lead.

I saw many games at Notre Dame as a young person. I watched [fullback] George Melinkovich [1931–1932, 1934] star in a game at Notre Dame, and then years later, in 1944 when I was a V-12 navy cadet, I would get to know him as an assistant coach to Ed McKeever.

I was an all-state player in high school in Detroit. There were at least 20 schools that sent me letters, asking me to come play football for them. But I hadn't heard from my favorite team. Then the Notre Dame basketball team played a game at the University of Detroit, and my dad and I went to the game.

The only person I really talked to about getting to Notre Dame was the old trainer, Scrapiron Young. He was on the trip and talked to me about coming to play. He really encouraged me.

I was a freshman at Notre Dame in 1939, and I fell in love with everything about Notre Dame. Elmer Layden, one of the Four Horsemen, was the head coach, and he had a great staff with guys like Joe Boland [line], Chet Grant

Although he's known more for his exploits as a baseball player and executive, John McHale played for Elmer Layden's final Notre Dame squad in 1940, which finished 7–2.

[first assistant], and Bill Cerney [B-team]. They really worked with me to make me a better player. I made the travel squad, and I backed up regular center Bob Osterman, who was a senior and also was from Detroit.

I really got to play a lot, but my real love was baseball. I felt that was my best sport. But the football under Layden was great, too. In 1940, I started against Army [a 7–0 victory] and played 59 minutes in Yankee Stadium.

I have to admit, however, that I was anxious to see Yankee Stadium for another reason. That was the home of Babe Ruth, Lou Gehrig, and all those great New York players. It was a thrill for me to be on the same turf where they were such stars.

I remember my last game as a player for Notre Dame. It was the last game of the 1940 season against Southern California in Los Angeles [10–6 Irish victory]. I had to make a block against their star, Al Krueger, and I hit him with everything I had. When I came out of the game a bit later, coach Boland congratulated me on that great block. It made me feel great that I had helped my team.

But I said to coach Boland, "Why did you take me out?" and he replied, "Son, I know you want to be a great baseball player, and you could wreck your shoulder with a block like that." That was Joe Boland, always thinking about the player and not necessarily his sport.

In the spring of 1941, I was playing baseball for the Irish, and I had some major league scouts watching me, particularly from my hometown Tigers. Because I was there on a football scholarship, I thought it only fair to talk to coach Layden about possibly quitting football and turning pro in baseball.

Coach heard me out, and he didn't try to talk me out of leaving for baseball. I thought I was pretty good as a football player, but Layden didn't try to persuade me to stay. That disappointed me a little, but a few days later, it came out that coach Layden was going to the National Football League as the commissioner. Then I knew why he didn't try to persuade me to stay.

I ended up going to the Tigers, but when World War II broke out, I became a V-12 navy cadet. My navy service ended with a medical discharge, and I got back in baseball almost in time to play for the Tigers against the Cubs in the 1945 World Series. That was the year of the supposed Billy Goat curse, and the Cubs are still trying to get to another Series!

I ended up returning to Notre Dame in the off-season to complete my work for a degree that I earned in 1947. I had a big Memorial Day for the

Tigers, and that also was the day I graduated from Notre Dame in absentia. I also was married at Notre Dame—where else?—in 1947, so 1947 was a great year.

When my playing days were over, I moved into the front office with the Tigers and then Milwaukee, which eventually moved to Atlanta. When the Braves were sold, I joined the Montreal Expos. All this time, however, I never lost touch with Notre Dame.

I was appointed to the advisory board of the College of Arts and Letters at Notre Dame, and while I was in Atlanta, my son, John, enrolled at Notre Dame. He was a tough reserve linebacker and special-teams player for Ara Parseghian in 1970. John eventually became the president of the Tigers, and now he's the deputy commissioner of Major League Baseball.

Notre Dame has meant so much to me. Everywhere I have gone in baseball and in life, I am known as Fighting Irish and Notre Dame. And when I get back there, I am at peace.

I went to school there, I played football and baseball there, graduated from there, and got married there. What more could I want? It's just the greatest place.

Growing up in Detroit, John McHale became a Notre Dame fan at an early age, and his love for the Fighting Irish has never waned. Although he is known more for his baseball skills and administrative work in Major League Baseball, the 6'3", 201-pound McHale was a hard-nosed backup offensive lineman for Elmer Layden's squad in 1940.

BOB LIVINGSTONE

1942, 1946–1947

I WAS INDOCTRINATED INTO NOTRE DAME lore at a young age. At my Catholic grade school in Hammond, Indiana, the "Notre Dame Victory March" was played at recess almost every day. And so I grew up wanting to play for the Irish.

My first contact was with coach Frank Leahy's backfield coach, Ed McKeever, and I was happy that he wanted me. Other schools such as Northwestern, Purdue, and Michigan State showed an interest. I was even the ball boy at the Chicago All-Star Game because I visited Northwestern during their training camp.

In my freshman year, we were still using the Notre Dame shift formation, and in that first fall practice under Leahy, things were pretty tough. There were plenty of new players, many of them from the East because Leahy and his staff had been at Boston College.

When Notre Dame switched from its classical box formation to the T formation in 1942, I was ready. And when Angelo Bertelli, a great passer, became our T quarterback in 1942, I was ready to be his number one receiver.

When we switched to the T formation, I was as surprised as everyone else. The fans were asking, "How could [Leahy] switch away from the Knute Rockne formations? Doesn't he know about tradition?" But times change and some adjustments in our style of offense became necessary.

With Sid Luckman and Bob Snyder from the Bears on hand to work with the quarterbacks, it became easy. But for the halfbacks and fullbacks, it was a new game, too. Getting the ball on handoffs was different, and our blocking patterns sure changed.

We had some good backs for that 1942 season. Military service hadn't taken too many players away from us yet. At fullback we had Cornie Clatt, big Gerry Cowhig, and Jim Mello. At right halfback, there was the great Creighton Miller, Bill Earley, and Pete Ashbaugh. I was the number one left half with Tom Miller and Dick Creevy behind me. Dippy Evans figured to be number one, but he was hurt in the preseason and played in only one game.

Big Wally Ziemba, one of our Hammond players, was our center, and our captain, George Murphy, and the great Bob Dove were the ends. Big Lou Rymkus, Jim White, Bob Neff, and Ziggy Czarobski were at tackles. We had some great players. Harry Wright, a quarterback the previous year, and Bob McBride were the guards.

Things didn't turn out as well in that season, at least not as well as we had become accustomed to. We finished 7–2–2. We played to a 7–7 tie at Wisconsin, and then Georgia Tech spoiled our home opener [13–6]. Then coach Leahy came down with some severe back spasms and had to be hospitalized at the Mayo Clinic. McKeever took over, and we made some changes.

Angelo Bertelli had been a halfback and had never called plays before that year. So we switched back to having Wright call the plays and we got into a much better rhythm after that. With Leahy away, we won over Stanford [27–0], Iowa Preflight [28–0], Illinois [21–14], and then both Navy [9–0] and Army [13–0].

Leahy came back, but we disappointed everyone by losing to Michigan [32–20] and eventually finished with a 7–2–2 mark. I was the leading receiver with 17 catches for 272 yards and three touchdowns.

In 1943, I was in the Pacific and could only listen to the games if we could get them on shortwave radio. We were involved in the fighting on New Guinea and then taking back the Philippines from the Japanese. I was still in the Philippines as a staff sergeant when the A-bomb was dropped on Japan, but I didn't get home until the spring of 1946, three years after I had enlisted.

There was great competition on the Notre Dame team in 1946. Young guys like Terry Brennan, Ernie Zalejski, and Coy McGee were battling the older players like Cowhig and me. And of course, we had John Lujack back. He had been a freshman in 1942, and I knew he would be good. He finished out the 1943 season after Bertelli was called into service.

We had a good season in 1946 [8–0–1]. The 0–0 tie against Army rankled us, but we did finish as national champions again.

My final season in 1947 was another good one [9–0]. We won all nine games, and only Northwestern [26–19] was even close when the Wildcats made a late comeback.

My longest run and still a Notre Dame record was that 92-yarder against Southern California in the Coliseum in my final game for Notre Dame.

Years later at a team reunion, Lujack told his young daughter that his name should have been in the record book for the longest run, alongside mine. "But that was Bob Livingstone who did that," she argued. "Who do you think handed him the ball?" John responded.

Bob Livingstone still holds the Notre Dame record for longest run from scrimmage, a 92-yarder against Southern California in 1947.

We get together for reunions regularly, and those are the times when all the good memories come back. We know we played hard and won a lot of games, but it was a lot of fun, too.

I went into pro football for three seasons with four different teams in the old All-American Football Conference and finished up with the Baltimore Colts. Then I hooked on with LaSalle Steel and was there for 25 years.

I'm glad we live so close to Notre Dame. It's a great place, and I'll never forget those wonderful days in the forties.

Bob Livingstone holds one of the oldest records in Notre Dame football history. His 92-yard run against Southern California in 1947 capped his varsity career with the Irish, which was interrupted when he answered the call to serve in World War II.

The 6'0", 168-pounder arrived from Hammond, Indiana, as a freshman in 1941. After the 1942 season, he volunteered for army service and spent three years in an infantry division in such places as New Guinea and the Philippines.

He played in 24 victories, 2 losses, and 3 ties in his three seasons with the Irish. He went on to play professionally in the All-American Football Conference for two teams in Chicago and in Buffalo. He ended his pro career with the Baltimore Colts.

JOHN LUJACK

1943, 1946–1947

WHEN I WAS IN GRADE SCHOOL in Connellsville, Pennsylvania, I would never miss a Notre Dame game on radio. Players such as Andy Pilney, Bill Shakespeare, and Wayne Milner were our heroes, and we listened every Saturday in the fall.

It was my dream to play for Notre Dame someday, but after high school, I really didn't think I was good enough to play there. Many schools contacted me, but I didn't hear from Notre Dame.

My congressman had an interest too, and he got me an appointment to West Point. But I didn't want to play football for Army, just Notre Dame. My dad couldn't understand why I wouldn't accept an appointment to Army, but I had absolutely no interest in becoming an Army man, even though World War II had started.

Finally, a man by the name of Henry Opperman decided he would help. He contacted his friend, Fritz Wilson, who ran a men's clothing store in Pittsburgh. Fritz had a brother who was a Notre Dame priest, and Fritz became sort of a bird dog for Notre Dame in the Pittsburgh area.

Wilson took an immediate interest and arranged for a visit to Notre Dame, and when I met coach Frank Leahy for the first time, he offered me a scholarship. That was a big moment for me, but I wondered a little about coach Leahy and why he would offer me a scholarship.

I had been a single-wing halfback at Connellsville, and in 1942 coach Leahy had decided to switch Notre Dame to the Chicago Bears' T formation. I guess he envisioned me as a quarterback and passer.

14

The Bears sent their quarterbacks, Sid Luckman and Bob Snyder, to help us. Sid was there mostly for show, but Snyder stayed on as an assistant coach to help Angelo Bertelli and me make the switch to T quarterback. Angelo had been there for spring practice, and he was really getting the T down pat.

Freshmen were not eligible, so I had to learn the job on the practice field. We scrimmaged almost daily against the varsity. It wasn't a great season. There was a [7–7] tie at Wisconsin and then a [13–6] loss to Georgia Tech. And not only that, but coach Leahy came down with a back ailment that sent him to the Mayo Clinic for treatment. We lost to Michigan [32–20] and also tied Great Lakes [13–13] for a 7-2-2 record. Notre Dame had several navy programs on campus, and we were enrolled as future officers.

Our opening game in 1943 was in Pittsburgh, and coach Leahy decided to start me at quarterback ahead of Bertelli. When Leahy explained to Bertelli that I would be playing before my folks from Connellsville, Angelo agreed. To hear him explain it later, he said he told Leahy that if he didn't want to win the game, he should go ahead and start Lujack. I don't think he was too happy about it.

I did start, but Bertelli came in and played most of the game and we won easily [41–0]. Halfback Creighton Miller, who became my best friend and was a great running back, liked to tell a story of how I turned the wrong way and missed the handoff to him. It actually happened twice.

15

We were having a good season in 1943. We won the first two games and then went to Michigan for the big game of the season. Creighton had just a fantastic game and we won easily [35–12]. After that loss, Michigan wouldn't play us for 35 seasons.

We had won six straight and were ranked No. 1 in the nation. But after we beat Navy [33–6], the marines called Bertelli to active duty, and I was going to get my first real action against Army. I had a pretty good day, passing for two touchdowns and running for another, and we won [26–0]. Two games later, we nipped No. 2 Iowa Preflight, 14–13, on Fred Earley's extra points. But the next week at Great Lakes, the Sailors came from behind on a long pass play to beat us [19–14]. Despite that loss, we were still picked as national champs.

That would be my last Notre Dame game for a long while. The navy sent me to Asbury Park, New Jersey, and then Columbia, where I graduated from midshipman's school and became an ensign. They sent me to the Pacific where I was aboard a 110-foot, wooden subchaser.

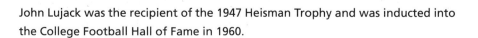

John Lujack was the recipient of the 1947 Heisman Trophy and was inducted into the College Football Hall of Fame in 1960.

Fortunately, we didn't run into any fierce action because I think you could have wrecked that subchaser with handguns.

[Notre Dame] had assembled a great squad in the spring of 1946. We had former Irish players from as far back as 1941, and Leahy had persuaded some veterans to transfer to Notre Dame. That meant we had players like George Connor, who had been an All-American at Holy Cross, and George Strohmeyer from Texas A&M.

After defeating a good Illinois team in the opener [26–6], we had an easy time of it getting ready for Army. The Cadets had beaten wartime Notre Dame teams 59–0 and 48–0, and all the Irish cried out for revenge.

Army had Doc Blanchard and Glenn Davis and again was undefeated. There was a huge buildup in the press and on radio, and tickets for the Yankee Stadium game were selling for ridiculous prices.

The way we former players remember it, both coach Leahy and his Army counterpart, Earl Blaik, played very conservatively. We had one good chance, but we were stopped on the 2-yard line. Why coach Leahy didn't call for a field goal, I will never understand, but in those days, there wasn't much emphasis on kicking.

17

My big play supposedly came on defense when I tackled Blanchard in the open field to prevent a touchdown. It really wasn't a great tackle, and years later I was on a program with Blanchard and he joked that he thought he had killed me on the play.

After that 0–0 tie, we went undefeated and were No. 1 ahead of the Cadets and Michigan. With most of our players coming back, we were favored to repeat as national champions in 1947.

Purdue had a new coach, Stu Holcomb, who had been an Army assistant, and he had a good team ready for our second game after we opened with a [40–6] victory over Pittsburgh. I had one of my best games that day, running for a touchdown and passing for another, and we won [22–7].

Our big game was to be at home against Army. The Cadets decided to end the long series with Notre Dame and would play the final game at Notre Dame. There was almost as much hype for the game as [there had been] a year earlier, but after Terry Brennan ran the opening kickoff back, there wasn't as much fight in the Cadets. We won, 27–7, and it could have been a bigger score.

We ended the season with a 9–0 record by walloping Southern California in Los Angeles [38–7], and we were again national champs.

I went to New York for the Heisman Trophy, but it wasn't such a big televised deal as it is today. There was the dinner and the presentation, that's all.

The Chicago Bears had selected me in the 1946 draft, and in 1948 I signed a four-year contract with George Halas. He must have been looking for a kicker because he asked me if I had kicked extra points. I told him I had tried one and missed, but he made me the extra-point kicker anyway.

Luckman was still the Bears' number one quarterback, so I played mostly defense, and when I did take over at quarterback, I played both ways and had good seasons. After four years, I had some injuries and decided to give up football. And wouldn't you know, coach Leahy asked me to come back as quarterback coach.

It was a good move for me. I got to be around coach Leahy more and I was able to help quarterbacks Ralph Guglielmi and Tommy Carey for the coach's final undefeated season [9–0–1] in 1953.

What a remarkable man and coach he was! I enjoyed every moment of playing for him and coaching with him. I really admired him.

What has been so rewarding for me is the great associations that I have had at Notre Dame. At first we had "Ziggy reunions" with Zygmont Czarobski, our fun-loving and talented tackle, and now it's an annual gathering of Leahy's Lads. We raised a scholarship for our coach and had a larger-than-life sculpture erected alongside the stadium. It was our tribute to him.

I get back to Notre Dame as often as I can, usually for early season games. When I went into the automobile business in Davenport, Iowa, it was only about 250 miles from campus. My buddy Creighton Miller was an attorney in Cleveland, also about 250 miles away, and we would get together for golf games before Notre Dame home games.

Every time I get back there, it's like a spiritual retreat. It's such a great place and brings back so many memories. Creighton Miller died a few years ago, and I was able to put together a scholarship fund in his name. My wife, Pat, and I have other scholarship funds that total about $1 million.

I have been fortunate in life, but I owe much of that to Notre Dame. Any time I get a chance to help the university and its people, I do. What a great place! It helped shape me into the person I am today.

John Lujack quarterbacked three national championship teams (1943, 1946, and 1947) at Notre Dame and played in only one losing game. He was an All-American for two years, became Notre Dame's second Heisman Trophy winner in 1947, and was elected to the College Football Hall of Fame in 1960.

The 6'0", 180-pound standout from Connellsville, Pennsylvania, passed for 778 yards and six touchdowns in 1946 and another 777 yards and nine touchdowns in 1947. He went on to play quarterback and defensive back for the Chicago Bears from 1948 to 1951. He remains one of Notre Dame's most beloved stars and enduring personalities, as well as one of the school's most generous benefactors.

BILL FISCHER

1945–1948

Iᴀ I ʜᴀᴅ ᴜꜱᴇᴅ ᴛʜᴀᴛ Iʟʟɪɴᴏɪꜱ Cᴇɴᴛʀᴀʟ train ticket I had in my hand in 1945, I would have been called a Fighting Illini from Illinois instead of a Fighting Irish from Notre Dame. Fate and Notre Dame assistant coach Gene Ronzani intervened.

That South Shore train to South Bend left from the same 12ᵗʰ Street Station, but Ronzani, who was working for Irish interim head coach Hugh Devore, persuaded me to come to Notre Dame instead of going to Illinois.

Ronzani and Devore had visited me at Chicago Lane Tech High, but Ray Eliot, the Illinois coach, was more persuasive. He sent me the one-way ticket to Champaign-Urbana.

I liked both schools. But I thank my lucky stars that Ronzani showed up at the station. I rode with him to the [Notre Dame] campus and have never regretted it one bit.

About a month after I made that decision in the train station, Notre Dame played Illinois in South Bend. I kicked off that day and we won [7–0], as we did the next year in Champaign [26–6]. I started both of those games.

Other than that game my first year, most of my memories come from 1946 to 1948, when we never lost a game and tied twice and won a couple of national titles.

In 1946, the veterans were back at Notre Dame and I got a chance to play for coach Leahy. He was tough and he was demanding, and I'm sure some wondered whether all those freshmen that played in 1945 would be able to compete with those guys coming back from the war. But several of us were able to make a contribution.

I lined up at left guard next to the great George Connor, a fellow Chicagoan [who had transferred from Holy Cross]. We also had Terry Brennan and John Mastrangelo from the 1945 team, and some veterans who were freshmen, like Jim Martin and Emil Sitko.

Of course during those years, Navy and Army were powerhouses. In 1945, with all those freshmen playing, we tied Navy [6–6] and were a foot away from the winning touchdown when the game ended. I remember Rip Miller, a Navy assistant athletic director and former Notre Dame player, saying, "Those little freshies from Notre Dame were tough!"

The next week we played Army, and they walloped us [48–0] in Yankee Stadium. They were pushing us all over the place, so our other tackle, Jack Fallon, told me I should take a pop at my opponent.

Well, I took a swing at my opponent and he grabbed me after the play and said, "Look, fat boy, if you try that again, you're apt to get killed!" Little did I realize that I had taken a swing at big Tex Coulter, who was not only an All-American tackle, but also the academy's heavyweight boxing champion.

So we were looking for a little revenge against Army in 1946. Not only had they beaten us 48–0 the previous year, but they had walloped us pretty good [59–0] the year before I got there. The hype for that game in New York City was tremendous.

Even though the game ended in a 0–0 tie, that was a great game. Do you realize that there were three Heisman Trophy winners—Glenn Davis and Doc Blanchard for Army and John Lujack for us—in that game? [Editor's note: there also were three Outland Trophy–winning linemen in that game: Notre Dame's George Connor and Fischer and Army's Joe Steffey.]

One of my proudest achievements was being named captain of the 1948 team, and only a [14–14] tie against Southern California in the last game of the season prevented us from winning our third straight national title.

Playing for coach Leahy was a privilege, but it wasn't easy. He was demanding and he believed in scrimmaging every day. The games were easy after we did so much work Monday through Friday.

How tough was coach Leahy? I suffered a broken nose in a game against Purdue one year. I came to the sideline and the team doctor stopped the bleeding and then twisted my nose back into its normal position.

Bill "Moose" Fischer (left), winner of the Outland Trophy as the nation's top lineman, anchored the line of the Notre Dame team that never lost a game from 1946 to 1948.

A couple of plays later, coach Leahy called for me to go back into the game. Bill Earley, an assistant coach, said, "Coach, he has a broken nose!" And coach Leahy said, "Nothing else can possibly happen to it now!"

There never was anyone like coach Leahy. He was tough, he worked the players extremely hard in practice, and he insisted on their loyalty to the team and the university.

Going to Notre Dame gave me a chance to play with a great team and a great coach like Frank Leahy as well as great assistant coaches such as Joe McArdle [guards] and Ed "Moose" Krause [line]. Had I not gone to Notre Dame, I wouldn't have been an All-American, nor would I have been a Hall of Fame player. It all came about because of Notre Dame.

I remember once in the Pro Bowl, the head coach, Blanton Collier, was detailing how to handle certain situations on the field. And he said, "You Notre Dame guys don't have to pay attention. You were so well trained that you do things automatically." That was because Collier knew the way that Leahy and his coaches worked. There was nothing like it and never will be again.

Chicagoan Bill "Moose" Fischer was a consensus All-American left guard for the Irish in 1947 and 1948. After being named captain in 1948, Fischer was awarded the Outland Trophy as the top lineman in the country. Notre Dame never lost a game during his final three years anchoring the Irish line with such standouts as Jim Martin, Leon Hart, Bill Walsh, and Marty Wendell (1948); George Connor and Ziggy Czarobski (1947); and John Mastrangelo and George Strohmeyer (1946).

After being named the Most Valuable Player of the 1949 All-Star Game, the 6'2", 226-pound Fischer was the first-round selection of the Chicago Cardinals, with whom he played from 1949 to 1953. Fischer returned to Notre Dame as an assistant coach under Terry Brennan from 1954 to 1958 and eventually became the president of the Notre Dame National Monogram Club.

JOHN PANELLI

1945–1948

IN 1945, I HAD COMPLETED A YEAR of intense study at Cheshire Prep School near New Haven, Connecticut, and I was ready for college. My coach at Cheshire, Arthur Sheriff, wanted me to attend his school, Yale, but I wasn't sure it was the place for me. Ed McKeever, then the interim coach at Notre Dame, had seen me play and indicated an interest in me.

When I was back home in [Morristown] New Jersey that summer, Hugh Devore, who had become the Notre Dame coach, stopped in to see me, and he definitely wanted another Jersey boy on his team. I had been an all-state player, and Amelio Gervasio, the mayor of Morristown, had been Devore's classmate.

There was a Fourth of July celebration in Morristown, and I was there, along with Hughie and Amelio, and everything was all set for me to leave for Notre Dame on the train the next day.

At Grand Central Station in New York City, I first met two other Notre Dame recruits from New Jersey, Frank Tripucka from Bloomfield and Bill Walsh from Phillipsburg. And there was another Notre Dame player, Pete Berezney from Northvale, New Jersey, also catching the same train. I had played against Walsh in high school and knew about him, and Tripucka was an all-state player.

We arrived at Zahm Hall on campus. There weren't many civilian students around. Most everyone was in the naval V-12 or V-5 programs. Notre Dame was on a three-semester schedule, so we went right to classes in July.

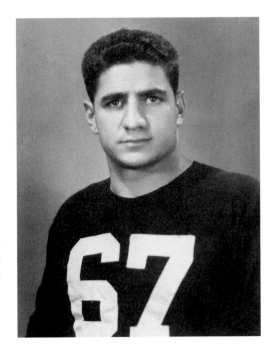

John Panelli's 70-yard fumble return for a score against Purdue in 1948 helped lead Notre Dame to a 28–27 victory over the Boilermakers.

It's a good thing I had been to Cheshire because I had taken some courses there that I had skipped in high school. At Cheshire, we had to work for our tuition and board. But I was captain of both the football and basketball teams. For good measure, I also played golf and baseball.

At Notre Dame, the football squad wasn't very big—no more than 30 to 35 players. But there were some good ones there. Phil Colella was a good running back who later transferred to St. Bonaventure when Devore became the head coach there. One of our quarterbacks was Joe Gasparella, another Italian boy.

Devore used to tell the story of the time he asked assistant coach Gene Ronzani who would make up the starting backfield. When Ronzani told him, "Gasparella, Colella, Frank Ruggerio, and Panelli," Devore quipped, "Gene, we're not selling bananas, we're playing football!" All of us started at one time or another, although our best quarterback was Frank Dancewicz, and he was Polish.

Freshmen were able to play in 1945, and we had some good ones. Terry Brennan from Milwaukee played a lot at halfback. Walsh became our center, and Bill Fischer, another freshman, was at tackle. There were some veterans, too, such as Berezney, halfback Elmer Angsman, and our dropkicker, Stan Krivik.

We had a pretty good season in 1945 [7–2–1]. We tied Navy [6–6] in Cleveland. We should have won but they ruled Colella out of bounds at the goal line. Army really pounded us the next week [48–0], and then in the last game at Great Lakes, the Sailors also beat us easily [39–7].

We found out what hard work was when Frank Leahy came back from the service in 1946. He put us through a long spring practice and then a tough fall. He did the right thing, of course. It got us ready for a tough season and beyond.

Only the 0–0 tie with Army marred our season. I still tell Johnny Lujack that if he had given me the ball on the 2-yard line, I'd have carried it halfway to Morristown. But we finished undefeated with that one tie.

On good college teams there always is a lot of camaraderie and kidding. We were playing Iowa [in 1946] and the line opened a hole big enough for an elephant to run through. When Lujack went to give me the handoff, he dropped the ball but picked it up and ran behind me for an easy touchdown. I used to razz him about taking a touchdown away from me.

One of my best games was against Purdue as a senior in 1948. We were in a tough battle, but late in the third period we were behind by a point, and Jim Martin blocked a Purdue punt. The ball bounced around off of several helmets and finally popped out to the side. I grabbed it and took off for the end zone, 70 yards away.

A bit later, Steve Oracko, who had missed two extra points, came through with a 33-yard field goal, and Al Zmijewski intercepted a Purdue pass in the end zone for a one-point win [28–27].

I also got to play a little bit of golf for Notre Dame. The golf coach was Reverend George Holderith, and he let me play in one college match. Then spring football intervened.

After Notre Dame, I signed with the Lions, who made me their No. 1 pick. Curly Lambeau, who had coached me in the All-Star Game, arranged for a trade to the Chicago Cardinals. In three years with Chicago, I played for four or five different coaches, including Lambeau and Joe Kuharich, who would go on to coach at Notre Dame.

As an alumnus in the Detroit area, I became quite active with Notre Dame. In the days when you could talk to prospective players, I lined up some good ones for Notre Dame. One was Greg Marx, a very good defensive tackle who played for Ara Parseghian.

Any time I can help Notre Dame, whether it's an alumni dinner or fundraiser, they can count on me. I enjoyed my years on campus and look forward to every opportunity to get back. Like everyone else, I grouse a bit when the team doesn't win. But I'm still a Notre Dame man, through and through.

> John "Pep" Panelli came to Notre Dame from Morristown, New Jersey, in 1945 and played four seasons at fullback, two of them for national championship teams (1946 and 1947). In those last two years, Panelli was part of a starting backfield that included right halfback Emil Sitko, who paced the Irish in rushing four straight seasons from 1946 to 1949, and left halfback Terry Brennan, who would go on to become the head coach of the Fighting Irish from 1954 to 1958.
>
> Panelli played five seasons in the National Football League, two with the Detroit Lions and another three with the Chicago Cardinals.

FRANK TRIPUCKA

1945–1948

THE FIRST TIME I WENT TO NOTRE DAME, I figured there was no reason to waste any time. I knew what I wanted. So I went from the athletic offices to the admissions office so I could enroll as a freshman in 1945.

I had always wanted to go to Notre Dame. I had lived and breathed stories of the Fighting Irish from my days in grade school. So when I was asked to visit the campus, I thought, "Why go for a visit? I have a chance to go there, so I'll just go and enroll!"

Hugh Devore was the interim coach for the 1945 team, and like me, he was from New Jersey. He knew about me from Bloomfield, center Bill Walsh from Phillipsburg, and fullback John Panelli from Morristown. He wanted all of us to come to Notre Dame. None of us knew each other, although we talked on the phone once we found out we were all going to Notre Dame. We met under the big clock in Grand Central Station in New York City and rode the train together to South Bend. When we arrived we took a taxi to the campus and met assistant coach Wally Ziemba. An hour or two later we were enrolled in classes and preparing for our first football practice on Cartier Field.

I was 17 years old and away from home for the first time. I was lucky to at least have two Jersey boys, Pep [Panelli] and Bill Walsh, as my new friends and teammates. For Devore and his new freshman-dominated team, it was hard work but still a lot of fun. I didn't get to play much at first, but I was a good punter.

I'll always remember my first touchdown pass as a quarterback. It was in the Tulane game in New Orleans [in 1945]. I threw it to Johnny Agnone and it helped us win, 32–6.

What I remembered most about that game was that Frank Leahy (dressed in his navy lieutenant commander uniform) came into the locker room after the game and came up to me and said, "Francis, that was a good pass you threw." He called me by name, formally too, and I didn't even know how he knew who I was. Then he said, "Please sit with me on the bus back to the hotel." Boy, did I ever shower quickly and get to that bus! And sure enough we rode together. That was the first time I ever saw him. But it wouldn't be the last.

We started getting ready for 1946 right after our final game. Leahy was back on campus from the navy and said, "We will work out in the old upstairs gym in the field house." I didn't even know where it was. We were so busy with studies and football, we didn't even know the campus.

Well, I found it all right, and we worked and worked inside until spring practice started in March. And then all the veterans came back from the war and we had a long and tough spring practice. We scrimmaged every day, or at least it seemed like it.

The one thing I remember about the spring of 1946 was that [quarterback] George Ratterman was on the tennis team and Leahy didn't like it one bit. He would say, "George Ratterman, oh George Ratterman, when are you going to get out of those short pants and play a really tough sport like football?" Leahy knew, and we all knew, that Ratterman was a great athlete. He was tough and smart, as he later proved in pro football. But Leahy demanded unquestioned loyalty.

Even though Frank Dancewicz and George were ahead of me on the depth chart in 1945, I played enough to win a letter and put myself in position for more playing time the next three seasons. I played quite a bit in 1946 with John Lujack and Ratterman ahead of me. And it was a great season, except for that 0–0 tie against Army in Yankee Stadium. I sat on the bench alongside Ratterman as Lujack played the entire game. The two coaches, Leahy and Red Blaik for Army, elected to play a defensive struggle. Instead of playing to win, they played not to lose.

Practices at Notre Dame were rough, but occasionally Leahy would have surprises for us. Sid Luckman of the Bears, the T formation master

Caught in a logjam of talent at quarterback, Frank Tripucka made the most of his one year as starter in 1948 by helping lead the Irish to an undefeated season and a No. 2 ranking.

quarterback for George Halas, came down one time to work with us. Luckman confided in us one time, "I don't know why coach Leahy wants me here. That Lujack knows the T formation better than I do. And he can pass better, do the mechanics better, and he surely can outrun me."

Leahy's quarterbacks always called their own plays. Oh, sometimes he would send in a message with a player or the trainer, but we had regular sessions on calling the plays.

I was the punter, and in one game it was fourth-and-short, and I called a short pass play. It worked for the first down, only the player—Panelli, I think—fumbled, and we lost the ball. It was only a minute or so until half-time, and it didn't hurt us a bit. But Leahy came up to me and said, "Francis, you don't like me! You don't like Notre Dame! You don't like our Blessed Mother on top of the dome! Why would you call such a play?"

Boy, he was tough to play for, but everyone respected him and knew that he and his coaches were the very best. And we won and won and won.

In 1946, I got a chance to meet the man who would become such an important part of my life—[1943 Heisman Trophy winner] Angelo Bertelli. He came back to campus from the marines and joined Lujack and me in a little passing session on the practice field. He actually could have come back and played in 1946, but he finally decided against it.

31

Lujack told me that there never was a passer as accurate as Angelo. He was just the best and had won the Heisman Trophy in 1943 after playing in only six games.

The Boston Yanks had drafted Bertelli in 1944, but he ended up playing in the new All-American Conference with the Los Angeles Dons and then the Chicago Rockets. He eventually gave up because of injuries, but back home in Jersey, I discovered he was going to coach Paterson in one of the minor leagues. That was right near my home, and I got to know him well. Eventually we became partners in business [Bert-Trip Liquors]. Angelo was like a brother to me. We were the only boys in our families, and Bert was like the brother I never had. It was the same for him.

Pro football eventually became a major part of my life. I recovered from a severe spinal injury from my final game at Notre Dame and was able to play for Philadelphia the next season. Then it was on to Detroit, the Chicago Cardinals, and Dallas until 1952. Then I played football in Canada before joining Denver in the new American Football League. I played through 1963, and

I'm proud to say my name is inscribed on the Ring of Fame in [Invesco Field at Mile High] Stadium, right up there with John Elway. I even had my jersey number retired, and that has happened for only three Broncos.

That decision I made as a kid in 1945 to go to Notre Dame was the greatest thing that ever happened to me. The coaching that we got was absolutely the best, as I learned when I was exposed to others in pro football. And the education was the best. Anywhere I go, I am proud to be a Notre Dame man, and it has helped in business. I enjoy doing things for Notre Dame and for old teammates. It is simply great to be known as a Notre Damer. Playing for the Irish was simply the best.

There was a time when Frank Tripucka was known more for his exploits on the football field than for being the father of Irish basketball star and long-time NBA player Kelly Tripucka.

Frank Tripucka, from Bloomfield, New Jersey, was a bona fide football star in his own right. At Notre Dame, the 6'2", 172-pounder ended up getting caught in a quarterback logjam with 1947 Heisman Trophy winner John Lujack, 1945 captain Frank Dancewicz, and George Ratterman.

Tripucka played professional football from 1949 to 1963, with stops in the NFL, the CFL, and the AFL.

BILL WALSH

1945–1948

As a longtime line coach in the NFL, I took my share of needling about my Notre Dame days. I would tell them they were all jealous because they never had the thrill of running out the tunnel and into Notre Dame Stadium. I used to say to them, "That's where we played real football!"

I was only three months out of high school in New Jersey and an 18-year-old freshman when I started at center for Notre Dame. My first game was against Illinois, and they had a speedster, Buddy Young, playing for them. We held him in check and Phil Colella broke open the game with a long scoring run in the fourth quarter to win, 7–0. That was a long time ago.

We were 7–2–1 that year with losses to national champion Army and to a pro football–stacked Great Lakes team. The tie was a memorable 6–6 clash with Navy. We were stopped on the goal line as the game ended, and the referee flipped a coin to decide who got the game ball. I think one of the radio announcers said, "They're flipping a coin to decide if Notre Dame scored."

One of the most memorable games I played in was a loss because we lost so infrequently. It was 1945 and Army beat us 48–0. I remember trying to tackle [Heisman Trophy winner] Doc Blanchard. I hit him as hard as I could, but he shook off that tackle and left me grasping for air. He was some back that day.

Back in 1944, Ed McKeever was the interim head coach at Notre Dame before leaving for San Francisco. McKeever recruited me, but it was another interim head coach, Hugh Devore, who awarded me the scholarship.

34

Center Bill Walsh was never on the losing end of a game at Notre Dame while snapping to quarterbacks John Lujack, George Ratterman, and Frank Tripucka.

The regular center at Notre Dame was Frank Szymanski from Detroit, but he was suddenly declared ineligible because he had played and talked to pro football people in an All-Star Game. The talent was pretty thin in that last year of the war, and I was called on as the starter. It was a great experience, but the next year when the war veterans came back to school, I was dropped to No. 3 behind transfer George Strohmeyer and Marty Wendell. I worked my way back up the next year and ended up playing in all 38 games while I was at Notre Dame.

The Pittsburgh Steelers drafted me in the third round, and I started every game for six years. After that, I came back to Notre Dame to coach for my former teammate, Terry Brennan.

Those were good years, even though they ended after four seasons. Terry and my other teammate, Bill Fischer, remain close friends, even though I see them only occasionally when we get back to Notre Dame.

We were fired after the 1958 season, and if firing is good for you, I have had plenty of experience. In 37 years of coaching, I've been through a few of them. I coached at Kansas State and joined Hank Stram—who was on the Notre Dame staff with me—with the Dallas Texans [who eventually became the Kansas City Chiefs] of the American Football League. Then I went to the Atlanta Falcons, Houston Oilers, and Philadelphia Eagles.

The really solid coaching I got at Notre Dame came from Frank Leahy, Hugh Devore, and Wally Ziemba, but especially Frank Leahy. Those guys gave me a great background in coaching. That's why I was able to serve for 37 years: 32 years in the pros and 5 in college.

35

It was an honor to play for Notre Dame and then a great thrill to come back and serve as an assistant coach. Not many people can say they played and coached for Notre Dame. I got the chance to do both. There's no place quite like Notre Dame.

Bill Walsh, originally from Shawnee Mission, Kansas, was a force for Notre Dame at center and in the middle of Notre Dame's defensive line during an incredible 33–2–3 run from 1945 to 1948. Fellow line stars Jim Martin, George Connor, and Bill Fischer often overshadowed the 6'3", 205-pounder. Yet Notre Dame never lost a game with Walsh snapping the ball to quarterbacks John Lujack, George Ratterman, and Frank Tripucka.

After a stint with Pittsburgh in the NFL (1949–1954), he returned to Notre Dame to serve as an assistant coach for head coach Terry Brennan. His coaching career spanned 37 years, most of which came in the NFL.

C

The
FIFTIES

JERRY GROOM

1948–1950

I LOVED NOTRE DAME FROM THE START, but the football was pretty tough when you had to live up to the expectations of Frank Leahy. Leahy and his coaches meant business, and the freshmen of 1947 scrimmaged almost daily against the varsity teams that were headed for another national championship.

We even scrimmaged against the number one team on Friday afternoon before the climactic Army game [a 27–7 victory] in 1947. I guess Leahy thought his top team wasn't ready for Army the next day. Believe me, they were ready, and I had the bruises to prove it. They ran all over us in the scrimmage.

As for how I ended up at Notre Dame, Bishop Jerry Bergin from Des Moines had called coach Leahy to see if he would come and give a speech for the Dowling High School football banquet, and coach Leahy agreed.

Army, Navy, Southern California, and Iowa had expressed an interest in me, and coincidentally all four schools were on the Notre Dame schedule. Coach Leahy offered me a scholarship. But an old Notre Damer, Dr. Eddie Anderson, was the Iowa coach, and he went all out to get me to go to Iowa. Iowa created the Nile Kinnick scholarship, named after the deceased World War II flyer and Iowa great, and I was awarded the honor. But I told Dr. Anderson that I had promised coach Leahy that I would visit.

What a visit it was! Johnny Lujack was Notre Dame's star player, but he was away from the campus making a speech somewhere. In his absence, his room was turned over to me and I hit it off with the coaching staff and the players. The school just fit.

Jerry Groom captained the 1950 squad and went on to a successful professional career that led to his selection to the NFL Hall of Fame.

When the 1948 season began, I was in the battle for the number one center job with Bill Walsh, who was the incumbent, and Walt Grothaus. I held my own at number two but played more as a middle linebacker. A year later, Leahy switched mostly to platoon football and I was the number one middle linebacker and again the number two center.

We continued to win, although a 14–14 tie with Southern California in the Coliseum at the end of the 1948 season cost us a third straight national title. In 1949, coach Leahy fielded one of his best-ever offensive teams, and we were again No. 1.

I was elected captain in 1950, but I knew it was going to be a tough season. When I came in for the 1947 school year, there were only about 15 other scholarship freshmen, and it was pretty much the same in 1948.

On the practice field, you could see the lack of numbers. We had good, solid number one units, but the backups were not nearly as good. When injuries hit, and they always do, the reserves just didn't match up.

We struggled in the opener against North Carolina and won [14–7] to increase our undefeated streak to 39 games. But then we played Purdue in the rain at home. Purdue's quarterback, Dale Samuels, had a good day and we lost, 28–14. We suffered some injuries in that game and a few more the next week [a 13–9 victory over Tulane]. The rest of the season was a struggle. We lost to Indiana [20–7] and Michigan State [36–33], we tied Iowa [14–14], and then we lost a low-scoring game to Southern California [9–7] in Los Angeles.

It was tough being regarded as the captain of the worst team that coach Leahy ever fielded. He didn't blame me or the team—just the fortunes that came from the recruiting cutbacks a few years earlier. And he vowed to come back.

My feelings toward Notre Dame have never changed. I just love that place. It was very good to me and to my family. Without it, I wouldn't have been an All-American, been in the College Hall of Fame, or had the all-pro experience in the National Football League.

Jerry Groom, a center/linebacker from Des Moines, Iowa, was captain of the 1950 Notre Dame squad and a consensus All-American. He started at linebacker for the Irish in 1949 and 1950, helping lead the team to the national championship.

Groom played 465 career minutes—86 percent of the total time played by Notre Dame—which means he seldom left the field during his career for the Irish.

The 6'3", 210-pounder played in the 1951 East-West Shrine Game and the College All-Star Game before being selected by the Chicago Cardinals in the first round. He played with the Cardinals from 1951 to 1955 and was selected to the College Football Hall of Fame in 1994.

BOB WILLIAMS

1948–1950

I T WAS JUST AFTER MY JUNIOR YEAR IN HIGH SCHOOL, and when I was visiting an aunt in Chicago, I persuaded her to drive me to see Notre Dame for the first time. I was a very good high school player, but I didn't think I was good enough to play at Notre Dame. But I went over to the athletic department anyway.

Most of the coaches were on vacation, but line coach Joe McArdle was there. I'm sure he thought I was too small and too slight of build to play for the Irish.

He was pleasant—later I got to know other sides of him—and he told me to work hard at my game that fall and to send him some newspaper clippings of our games. There weren't any high school game films in those days.

I did send along some clippings during the year, but I didn't hear a thing from the school. Finally, in the late spring, I received a letter from Ed "Moose" Krause encouraging me to apply for admission.

At the time, I think they were trying to recruit some hotshot quarterback from somewhere else, but I heard that he went elsewhere. And thus, I got my chance.

I knew a little bit about Notre Dame because my older brother, Hal, was a 1938 graduate and was a newspaperman in Baltimore. Hal didn't know anyone in the athletic department except for Charlie Callahan, the sports information director. So Charlie at least knew my name and maybe he put in a good word for me, but I arrived on campus and reported for the freshman team.

41

The surly old equipment manager, Jack MacAllister, gave me some ratty equipment, including a pair of shoes, one size about 6 or 7 and the other one 10 or 12. When I complained, Mac snarled, "What's the difference? You'll be gone in a week anyway!"

The freshman coaches in 1947 were some varsity seniors who wouldn't make the team that were coming back from the 1946 national championship. They put the green-shirted frosh through their drills.

I had met some of the assistant coaches, but not coach Leahy himself. One day he came over and watched the freshmen for a while, and he came up to me and said, "Robert Williams from Baltimore!" For me it was like meeting God, and he even knew my name!

After a while, we had practiced enough to work against the varsity. Before the scrimmage, they would line up the freshman backs and send them down a line to be tackled by varsity players. Here I was, skinny little me, trying to run the gauntlet against big veterans like Leon Hart, Jim Martin, Marty Wendell, some of the real hitters. I tried to protest that I was a quarterback and not a running back, but they said, "Get in the line!"

Football practice under Leahy was really something. He scrimmaged every day, and when the varsity wasn't beating up on us little freshies, they were going head-to-head, first team against second team.

The craziest thing I was ever involved in was the day before Army arrived on campus that fall in 1947. It was the biggest game of the year after that 0–0 tie in 1946. On Fridays, most teams just have a light workout, brushing up on assignments or maybe a little kicking practice. But coach Leahy was so intense. He must have thought the team wasn't ready. They scrimmaged against us. And brother, they were really ready. They stuffed every play we ran, and they ran all over us on offense. It was some show.

After that freshman season of getting battered around, I moved into the number two spot at quarterback. John Lujack had graduated, and Frank Tripucka was the quarterback. I actually got to play in the opener against Purdue because coach Leahy liked to dabble in a little trickery. He came up with the idea of two quarterbacks behind the center. One would pivot left and the other right, trying to confuse the defense. After a few plays the strategy didn't work and coach Leahy went back to the regular formation.

I was the punter too, and I remember on my first punt, the ball popped off my foot almost straight up in the air. It didn't travel 15 yards. I came back to the bench and figured the coaches would be all over me. But little was said,

Bob Williams (No. 9) passed for 1,374 yards in 1949 to set an Irish single-season record that would last for 15 years.

and when the next punt was called for, Leahy just said, "Robert, get in there and kick!" I boomed a good one and the job was mine the rest of the year.

Coach Leahy wanted his quarterbacks to call the plays. Occasionally, someone would come in and mention a particular play, but generally, we called everything. The most unusual play I ever called was in the North Carolina game in Yankee Stadium in 1949.

We were leading 6–0, but we were pinned back at our own 6 and we were going to punt. I called a screen pass from the punt formation and it worked, despite the fact the receiver, Larry Coutre, had terrible vision. Throwing a fourth-down pass to a nearly blind man was not very sound judgment, but it worked out OK.

We won all 10 games that year and were threatened only once, in the final game at Southern Methodist. They had Kyle Rote at halfback, who was playing for injured Heisman Trophy winner Doak Walker, and they played a great game. Jerry Groom and Bob Lally saved us and we won, 27–20. [It was Notre Dame's 38th straight game without a loss.]

The key game of that 1949 season was at home against Tulane. They were ranked No. 4 and we were No. 1. Our scouts, particularly end coach John Druze, did a fantastic job on that game. We were able to key on their defensive alignment. When they went left, we went right, and as a result, we rolled up a 28–0 first-period lead and won easily, 46–7.

Our undefeated streak came to an end at 39 against Purdue in the second game of the 1950 season. We were outmanned and finished 4–4–1, which was Leahy's worst season. It was kind of sad the way that season went. But in truth, a cutback in scholarships in 1948 and 1949 left us with no reserve strength. But we knew that the freshmen of 1950—John Lattner, Neil Worden, and some good linemen—would be able to bring the team back.

I was selected to the College Football Hall of Fame in 1988, but without the background of Notre Dame and the great coaching that I had from Leahy and his staff, I never would have made All-American or the Hall of Fame. Those honors were like the icing on the cake compared to the ultimate value of having a Notre Dame degree.

Anywhere I went, any business deal I was involved in was so much better because of that degree. It really opened a lot of doors for me. And it continues to do that even in retirement.

Notre Dame was the best thing that happened to me in my life at that time, and it remains that way today.

Unlike many other Hall of Fame quarterbacks, Bob Williams more or less recruited himself to Notre Dame. Notre Dame will be forever thankful.

Williams went on to become just the second quarterback in Irish history (Angelo Bertelli was the first) to throw for more than 1,000 yards in a season. Williams' 1,374 yards passing in 1949 set a Notre Dame record that lasted until John Huarte's Heisman Trophy season in 1964. He threw an incredible 26 touchdown passes in two seasons at a time when the running game still dominated.

In 1949 as a junior, the 6'1", 180-pound Williams helped lead Notre Dame to a perfect 10–0 record and the national championship. Notre Dame's 360 points in 1949 were the most since Knute Rockne's 1921 team scored 375.

JOHN LATTNER

1951–1953

WHEN I WAS PLAYING HALFBACK at Fenwick High in the tough Chicago Catholic League, I knew I wanted to play college football, but I didn't know where it would be. I certainly wasn't convinced that it would be Notre Dame.

Notre Dame had just completed four years of football without a loss, and as much as people tried to sell me on Notre Dame, I wondered if I'd be good enough.

My coach at Fenwick, Tony Lawless, said to me, "Notre Dame? If you go down there to look the place over, make sure of one thing: don't let them time you!"

At a time when the great emphasis in college football was on speed, I really wasn't fast. I could run pretty well and I could pass a little. I punted, too. But make no mistake about it, I was not a burner. When I visited Notre Dame, they offered me a scholarship and I quickly accepted. I didn't want them to change their minds.

I was a freshman in 1950. The varsity wasn't having a good year and coach Frank Leahy believed in lots of scrimmages. We went up against the varsity almost every day. Neil Worden was from Milwaukee and was a small fullback. We were the workhorses among the freshmen, and we were called on regularly to scrimmage against the varsity, a team that would end the season 4–4–1.

My coaches thought I could play, maybe not as a runner but probably as a defensive back. Leahy was a slow convert to two-platoon play, and the defensive coaches wanted me with them despite my lack of speed.

Assistant coach Bill Earley was my primary offensive position coach, and that's why I ended up with No. 14. For four years, Emil "Six Yard" Sitko had worn that number, and Earley assigned that number to me, hoping I could replace that All-American back.

Those would be pretty big shoes for me to fill, but when you're young, you think nothing is impossible. I wanted to play and I wanted to be another Sitko.

When Sitko finished playing for the Irish in 1949, only the famous George Gipp had gained more yardage. Years later, Sitko was picked for the College Hall of Fame.

All I wanted was a chance to play as a sophomore in 1951. Starting was just something to dream about. Leahy had converted to platoon football, but he liked players who could go both ways. I quickly became one of the three defensive backs. In those days, the Irish were playing sort of a 5-3-3 defense, and I was one of the halfbacks.

47

On offense, the right halfback ahead of me was John Petitbon, a real speedster from New Orleans. He was the fastest player on the team, and he also could play defense. He once had been timed at 9.6 in the 100-yard dash. On my best day, I was no better than 10.2, 10.3, maybe worse.

Notre Dame was coming back from its worst season and everyone was working hard. Because of the Korean War, freshmen were eligible again in 1951, so there were a lot of sophomores and freshmen trying to make the team. I got to play a lot, most of the time on defense, but I also became the punter and had plenty of action at halfback. My buddy Worden was the regular fullback, and in our first game, he scored four touchdowns and we won handily over Indiana [48–6], and then we went to Detroit to play in a night game against the University of Detroit [a 40–6 victory].

Those first two games were easy, but we found out about our defense in the third game. Southern Methodist came to Notre Dame, and Fred Benners threw on every down. We tried to match them pass for pass, but our quarterback, John Mazur, was no match. Our freshman quarterbacks, Tommy Carey and Ralph Guglielmi, got to play in that game.

Winner of the 1953 Heisman Trophy, John Lattner was also awarded the Maxwell Award as the nation's top back two years in a row.

We lost only 27–20, but we knew we had to play much better in order to win. We ended up 7–2–1 that year, which was an improvement over the previous season.

The game I remember from 1951 was the Iowa game, which ended in a 20–20 tie. I will always remember that game because two seniors on our team, captain Jim Mutscheller and tackle Bob Toneff, defied the coaching staff late in the game.

We were behind and on fourth down, and we were supposed to punt. There wasn't much time left, and the seniors said, "We are not going to give them the ball and lose the game! Lattner, go back to punt and throw the ball!"

I was shaking in my boots, but I threw a wobbly pass that Mutscheller caught for a first down, and we went down the field to tie the score on Bobby Joseph's extra point. Coach Leahy never said a word to me afterward, but he probably talked to Mutscheller. That's the only time I ever remember actually defying him.

The 1952 season was a memorable one. I'll never forget our trip to Texas for the second game of the season [a 14–3 victory]. To prepare for the heat, coach Leahy got Texas to agree to let us sit on the same side of the field, so we wouldn't be facing that blazing sun. [Guards coach] Joe McArdle went out that morning and bought every Frank Buck–type hat in Austin, and we sat on the bench with our heads shaded by those big hats.

49

Then there was the Purdue game in 1952. Fumbles were the big story of the game. There were 22 in all, 13 by Purdue. We had nine and lost six. I was charged with five lost fumbles. We won the game, 26–14, but at our Monday meeting, I caught the wrath of coach Leahy.

"Oh, John Lattner!" he said to me. "How could you commit those five mortal sins for Our Lady's school? Do you hate her? Don't you like your teammates?" My punishment was to carry a football with me to my classes all that week.

After that season and despite a 7–2–1 record, we were voted No. 3 in the nation. In voting for the Heisman that year, I was placed fifth, mostly because I had played both ways. A year later, after an undefeated season, I beat out Paul Giel of Minnesota for the 1953 Heisman Trophy. I had won the Maxwell Award in 1952 and again in 1953.

Our 1953 season was remarkable. We defeated Oklahoma in Norman [28–21] in the opening game, which was another time that we had to play in searing heat. We won the first seven games against some top teams.

The Georgia Tech game was played on my birthday that year. We were ranked No. 1 and Tech was No. 4. They had a 31-game undefeated streak. But we grabbed an early lead and were ahead at halftime, 14–7, when coach Leahy suffered a fainting spell. We didn't know much about it, but coach McArdle handled the team in the second half. They came back to tie, but I remember scoring the final touchdown while the student body was saluting me with their rendition of "Happy Birthday."

Coach Leahy was gone the next couple of games, but we kept on winning and were 7–0 when Iowa came to town. Coach was back, but not looking very good. We played our worst game of the season and tied them [14–14].

We managed to tie 7–7 at halftime when Guglielmi threw a short pass to Dan Shannon. They repeated it late in the game for a 14–14 tie. That knocked us out of No. 1, but we romped over Southern California [48–14] and Southern Methodist [40–14] for Notre Dame's first undefeated season in four years. It turned out that it was coach Leahy's final game when he retired in late January.

It was a great off-season for me. When I went to New York for the Heisman Trophy dinner, I took my mother along. She had never been on an airplane and it was her first visit to New York. She had a ball. Having my mother along really made it a memorable trip. She had more fun than I did.

I did receive the Heisman in December of 1953, but not everyone knows that I have had three of them. When I opened a restaurant in the Chicago Loop, we had been there only a few years when we had a devastating fire. I had put the Heisman Trophy on display in the foyer, and it was destroyed in the fire. They were able to cast another one, and I had that on display for a few years in another restaurant. Some time later, Notre Dame wanted to put all seven Heismans on display at the university. So I, along with Angelo Bertelli, John Lujack, Leon Hart, Paul Hornung, John Huarte, and Tim Brown, took our trophies "home" to Notre Dame for this display.

Shortly after that, the Heisman committee decided to cast two trophies each year, one for the player and the other for his school. So that made it my third Heisman Trophy.

When I was a senior, I was featured on the cover story of *Time* magazine. I use the reproduction of that cover for autograph sessions. That green uniform and that leather helmet look a little funny, but that's what we wore in those days.

After graduation in 1954, I played a little with an Air Force team [Bolling Field] and part of a season with the Pittsburgh Steelers, but a knee injury ended my career. I was in the restaurant business in my home city of Chicago and later was involved in a company dealing in office and other paper products.

One thing I learned through the years: those names Notre Dame and Lattner really sell.

John Lattner came to Notre Dame from Fenwick High in Chicago and quickly became a starter for the Irish as a sophomore. He played defense at first and then gradually became the premier running back in a backfield boasting other stars such as quarterback Ralph Guglielmi, left halfback Joe Heap, and fullback Neil Worden.

As a junior, Lattner won the Maxwell Award as the top back of the year while finishing fifth in the Heisman Trophy balloting. He led the Irish in rushing in 1952 with 732 yards.

As a senior, Lattner became the fourth Notre Dame player in 11 years to win the Heisman Trophy. A two-time consensus All-American, Lattner won the Maxwell Award for the second straight year while establishing a school record for all-purpose yardage that wasn't broken until Vagas Ferguson surpassed Lattner's total in 1979.

Lattner was inducted into the College Football Hall of Fame in 1979.

RALPH GUGLIELMI

1951–1954

WHEN I WAS A SENIOR QUARTERBACK and baseball player at Grandview High in Columbus, Ohio, I visited some 12 to 15 schools. I got to meet such famed coaches as Paul "Bear" Bryant at Kentucky, General Bob Neyland at Tennessee, Biggie Munn at Michigan State, and a rookie coach who had yet to field a team at Ohio State—Woody Hayes.

My mother had been a fraternity house mother at Ohio State, and she was determined that her son would attend a no-fraternities college. She said, "I saw how they acted at Ohio State and Ralph won't be going there!"

When she found out that Notre Dame was a nonfraternity school, she quickly decided that Notre Dame was the best place for her son. There was one small problem: Notre Dame wasn't showing much interest in me. That all changed one day in May.

We lived in a house that was attached to the house my grandmother lived in. When I got home that day, Ohio State graduate John Igel was on my front porch talking to my mother. On the adjoining porch was my grandma with Notre Dame coach Frank Leahy. It couldn't have been much of a conversation. Grandma couldn't speak a word of English and I'm sure coach Leahy didn't know Italian.

I remember coach Leahy telling me, "I think you will be able to play for us this year." This was during the time of the Korean War, and freshmen were eligible to play in 1951. My mother was happy that I was going to be

Ralph Guglielmi finished fourth in the 1954 Heisman Trophy balloting and helped lead the Irish to a 9–1 record.

taken care of at Notre Dame. But what really clinched things was that after coach Leahy left, grandma came over and in Italian told me, "You go with that man. I liked him and I just feel that it will be best for you."

So I joined other freshmen such as Joe Heap, Dan Shannon, Jack Lee, Frank Varrichione, Tommy Carey, and two other Ohio players, Sam Palumbo and Dick Szymanski, at Notre Dame that fall. Coming up as sophomores were Johnny Lattner, Neil Worden, Art Hunter, and Jim Schrader, all highly regarded players.

Notre Dame had been 4–4–1 in 1950, and nobody was satisfied with that. John Mazur was the quarterback, and we had some solid veterans like Jim Mutscheller, our captain; big Bob Toneff at tackle; and John Petitbon at halfback.

Carey, Don Bucci, and myself battled for the backup role behind Mazur. We beat Indiana in the opener [48–6] and then Detroit in a night game [40–6]. Then came my baptism by fire. Southern Methodist came to town and their quarterback, Fred Benners, passed on the first 26 plays. I came in for Mazur and played like the inexperienced freshman that I was, and we lost [27–20].

54

We were 5–1 going against No. 5 Michigan State. They scored on their first play and beat us 35–0. I don't think I ever got into that game. It was awful. But a week later I started and we won at North Carolina [12–7 for Notre Dame's 400th career victory] with Carey alternating with me. After we tied Iowa [20–20], Mazur started at Southern California. I came into the game early and we won in the Coliseum [19–12].

That's when Woody Hayes at Ohio State learned that my girlfriend was at Ohio State, and he asked me if I'd transfer. I really never considered it seriously. I had some thoughts about going to medical school, but I really liked Notre Dame. Plus, [1947 Heisman Trophy–winner] John Lujack had retired from the Chicago Bears and was now Notre Dame's quarterback coach. He taught us how to read defenses and to call plays.

We started slowly in 1952 with a tie, a win, and a loss. We worked our way up to 4–1–1 and played No. 4 Oklahoma at home and won [27–21]. Tommy Carey played a great game. I don't think we would have won without him.

We lost to Michigan State [21–3] but beat Iowa [27–0] and Southern Cal [9–0] to finish 7–2–1. We were voted No. 3 in the country because we had beaten the champs of the Southwest, Big Seven, Big Ten, and Pacific Coast conferences.

In 1953, the rules makers limited substitutions, which meant that I had to play defense, too. I liked it and led the team in interceptions the next two years. We won every game but one that year, and that was a [14–14] tie with Iowa.

That was the final season for coach Leahy, and no one admired the coach more than I did. No one worked harder with us to make us better. He was very disciplined and he expected you to be the same. The practices were so tough that the games on Saturday seemed to be easier.

I went on to play professional football for eight years, and that's when you could see the difference. No one was like Leahy, and it really showed by comparison. But I enjoyed my last year under Terry Brennan. We went 9–1, with our only loss to Purdue [27-14].

What a great experience it was for me to have gone to Notre Dame. When you are known as a Notre Dame graduate, and particularly a football player, you are looked up to by just about everybody you come in contact with. You can't say that about too many places. It's just a special place.

55

Ralph Guglielmi, a Columbus, Ohio, native, began his Notre Dame football career as a freshman in 1951. He started in the 8th game of the season and starred in the 10th, a 19–12 victory in the rain against Southern California.

Guglielmi alternated at quarterback with Tommy Carey in 1952 but was number one during his junior and senior seasons when the Irish recorded an 18–1–1 record. Notre Dame didn't add to its national title total during the 1953 and 1954 seasons, but the Irish finished second and fourth in the Associated Press polls, led by Guglielmi.

In 1954, Guglielmi became just the third Irish quarterback (after Angelo Bertelli and Bob Williams) to pass for more than 1,000 yards in a season, and he finished fourth in the Heisman Trophy balloting.

During Guglielmi's four years at Notre Dame, the Irish recorded a 32–5–3 record while he passed for 3,073 yards in his career. The 6'0", 180-pounder earned unanimous All-American honors in 1954 and was elected to the College Football Hall of Fame in 2001.

JACK LEE

1951–1954

I GREW UP IN HIGH SCHOOL LISTENING to the feats of Johnny Lujack, Leon Hart, and the Irish winning game after game in the late forties. My father was a supervisor at the Boston Garden and as a result, I met all the famous people in sports. I was determined that someday, somehow, I would play for the Irish.

But it wasn't a straight path to Notre Dame. First there was a stint at Aquinas Institute, a preparatory school in Rochester, New York. My football coach was Mickey Connelly, and that was my first link to coach Frank Leahy of Notre Dame.

Coach Connelly was a Boston College grad who had played for Leahy's Eagles in 1939 and 1940. In fact, he was the star of Boston College's Sugar Bowl victory over powerful Tennessee.

Coach Leahy was the speaker at the Aquinas football banquet in 1949. He told me, [right tackle] Frank Varrichione, [left guard] Bob Ready, [left guard] Tom Seaman, and a couple of others to "stay on at Aquinas until we need you at Notre Dame."

In 1950, Notre Dame had its worst record [4–4–1] under coach Leahy. So when the February 1951 semester began at Notre Dame, we were there for school and spring practice.

Because of the Korean War, the NCAA allowed freshman eligibility, which meant we would be eligible for the 1951 season. We had about a half-dozen freshmen in the lineup in 1951 and went 7–2–1.

I remember my first road game at Notre Dame. It was a night game at Detroit, a game that was added to the schedule in midsummer because it was the 250th anniversary of the founding of the city.

We had easily defeated Indiana, 48–6, in the opening game at home with sophomore fullback Neil Worden scoring four touchdowns. And we won at Detroit, 40–6. Maybe we were confident, maybe too confident the next week at home. Fred Benners of Southern Methodist kept throwing pass after pass; we got behind and never caught up.

The only other loss that year was a nationally televised game at Michigan State. Dick Panin scored on an 88-yard run on the first play, and they beat us badly [35–0]. Several accounts blamed me, a 190-pound middle guard, for the big hole. But I still have a picture of the play that shows me standing and [freshman middle linebacker] Dick Szymanski flat on his back. Regardless, we were no match for Michigan State that year and they would win a national championship a year later.

Despite being just 5′11″, 190 pounds, I had professional football aspirations until a knee injury in the Navy game in 1954 changed my mind. That knee injury also delayed my air force career.

I had always wanted to be a pilot. I was in the ROTC program at Notre Dame, and I was one of the cadet leaders in the air force program. But when I applied for flight training after graduation, the knee problem kept me out of the flying programs. After two years of strictly ground duty, I was cleared for flight training.

I had the opportunity to fly several different types of aircraft, including a B-56 bomber called the *Hustler*. Ironically, that brought me back closer to Notre Dame when I was stationed at Grissom [then Bunker Hill] Air Force Base in Indiana, about 70 miles south of the Notre Dame campus.

I served on the board of directors of the Notre Dame Monogram Club and also ended up on the board of the Independence Bowl in Shreveport, Louisiana. I considered it a real coup as a director to help arrange Notre Dame's trip to the Independence Bowl in 1997.

Playing football at Notre Dame, particularly for coach Frank Leahy, was a great experience for me. But graduating and earning that Notre Dame degree was something special.

When you top that off with a 29-year career as an air force officer, my life has been a very fulfilling experience. I thank my lucky stars—really, my

Guard Jack Lee blocked for Notre Dame's No. 2–rated total offense in 1953 and No. 6–ranked unit in 1954.

creator—for all these great things in my life, especially the opportunity to attend and play football for Notre Dame.

Jack Lee, from Medford, Massachusetts, was a regular starter on defense for Notre Dame in 1951 and 1952 and then a two-way performer at guard for the next two seasons. The 5'11", 190-pounder helped block for the No. 2–rated total offense in the country in 1953 and No. 6–ranked unit in 1954. In his four years, Notre Dame won 32 games, lost 5, and tied 3.

DAN SHANNON

1951–1954

WHEN I WAS A SENIOR FULLBACK and linebacker at Chicago's Mount Carmel High, I had visions of getting away from the area and playing college football at some place such as Stanford or another West Coast school. I had never been any farther north than Evanston, and I really wanted to see other places.

There was one problem with my idea. My father, Peter, was a Notre Dame fan, and he always wanted a son to attend [Notre Dame] and play for the Irish. My two older brothers went into the seminary, and one is now a Catholic priest. So Dad knew it had to be me at Notre Dame.

When I broached the subject with my father about looking out west, he was adamant. He said, "You'll go to Notre Dame!" and that was that.

Not that I was reluctant to go to Notre Dame. My coaches at Mount Carmel, Terry Brennan and Bob McBride, both had played for Frank Leahy at Notre Dame. I knew what the place was all about.

What I liked best about my career at Notre Dame was that my dad and mom were able to attend every game, home and away. That's a real boost for a player, especially one from a close-knit family.

My dad thought I would be a powerful fullback for Notre Dame. But when the Notre Dame coaching staff sized up my talent, they thought I could be a pretty good linebacker. Notre Dame already had a couple of pretty good fullbacks in Neil Worden and Tom McHugh. I was confident, but not *that* confident. They had the advantage of fall and spring practice in 1950–1951. I was coming in as a freshman and eligible to play because of the Korean War.

A cocaptain of the 1954 Notre Dame squad, Dan Shannon is best known for his devastating hit on Oklahoma's Larry Grigg in Notre Dame's 27–21 victory over the Sooners.

As a freshman I stepped in at left outside linebacker alongside another freshman, Dick Szymanski, and junior Jack Alessandrini. We were coming off coach Leahy's worst season [4–4–1], and the new sophomores and the freshmen added a spirit to the season.

We went 7–2–1 in 1951; avenged losses to Purdue, Indiana, and Southern California; and came close [36–33] against a powerful Michigan State team. I was able to use my quickness to make up for my lack of experience.

Two games in particular stand out in my mind. In my sophomore year [1952], we had a pretty fearsome defense. We beat four or five conference champions and finished third in the nation, despite another 7–2–1 record. We had already defeated Southwest Conference leader Texas and Big 10 coleader Purdue, when a powerful Oklahoma team came to play us for the first time.

Coach Bud Wilkinson had a bunch of great players, such as halfback Billy Vessels and fullback Buck MacPhail. Vessels played very well against us [195 yards rushing], but it was a 21–21 tie in the fourth quarter.

We kicked off after tying the game and I came downfield and had my sights on their return man, Larry Grigg. We collided at about the 20-yard line. It was a massive collision and the ball popped loose. Both of us had to be helped from the field. I had no idea where I was. I had one helluva headache, and I didn't even know we had the ball. Tommy Carey eventually scored for us, the defense held them the final 12 minutes or so, and we won, 27–21.

I actually got back in the game. I don't know what I would have done if they had come at me, but I do remember this. McHugh came up after the game and congratulated me and I asked, "Who won?"

The next year [1953] we were battling Iowa in a home game and I was playing both ways, at end on offense and linebacker on defense. Late in the first half, Iowa was leading 7–0, but we were driving. The clock was winding down and tackle Frank Varrichione suddenly collapsed. Naturally, the officials called timeout. One second remained on the clock, and Ralph Guglielmi threw me the game-tying touchdown pass. We did it again in the fourth quarter, and Don Schaefer kicked the extra point for a 14–14 tie. We dropped in the polls to No. 2 because of that tie and that's where we finished, No. 2 behind Maryland with a 9–0–1 record.

We were 9–1 in 1954 for Terry Brennan in his first year as head coach, and that was the end of my football-playing career. But I came back to Notre Dame often. One of my sons, Gerard, went to Notre Dame and played football until a leg injury prevented him from playing.

My career after football kind of followed the same path as my football career at Notre Dame. It was almost like my start at Notre Dame. I wanted to play in the Chicago All-Star Game, but my dad said, "That's the time you will be taking the Illinois CPA exam." So that was my route—the exam and then joining my father's business.

I've been back for many games at Notre Dame. I would look fondly on the spot on the field where I hit Grigg that day, but I don't know where that spot was. I don't remember a thing about it.

Chicagoan Dan Shannon's speed and quickness as a linebacker/left end for the Irish in the early fifties is legendary among his peers. The 6'0", 190-pound cocaptain of the 1954 squad is best known for his hit on Oklahoma's Larry Grigg in the 1952 battle between No. 10 Notre Dame and No. 4 Oklahoma. The hit caused a fumble and led to Notre Dame's 27–21 victory.

PAUL HORNUNG

1954–1956

I CHOSE NOTRE DAME BECAUSE OF MY MOTHER, plain and simple. Back in the fifties, even before that, the majority of kids went to colleges because of where their parents wanted them to go. I don't think it's like that today. But I really wanted to go to Kentucky.

Bear Bryant was the head coach at Kentucky and I was going to play my first year, so I was excited about playing for the Wildcats. At Notre Dame, freshmen were ineligible then, so that was the main reason I wanted to go to Kentucky. I had been with Bear Bryant maybe 30 or 40 times during the recruiting season.

He offered every senior on my football team in high school a scholarship if I would go to Kentucky, and we had 19 seniors. So he really put the pressure on me. Of course, back then, you could run [players] off. If you saw *The Junction Boys*, you knew he was going to run them off anyway.

But he did want five kids from my high school football team and Notre Dame wanted five of them. I went [to Notre Dame] along with another teammate who had a scholarship. We went together, and we've been like brothers ever since. The way it turned out, I was glad. I made the right decision.

People always talk about the social life at Notre Dame. Of course there was no social life! But you make your own social life. You had to find a girl who had a car. That was your main objective when school started. Find a girl who had a car because you get a little tired of riding a bus to downtown. And

I did that, so I was fortunate. I had a girl who had an automobile who was a little bit older, a little bit more mature. I learned a lot of things from her.

The 1956 season was a very unusual year. The top 10 guys in the Heisman balloting that year were, in my opinion, the best 10 guys who have ever come out of college football in one year. All 10 of those guys went into the College Football Hall of Fame. Six went into the Pro Football Hall of Fame. So we're really talking about an excellent group. I was very fortunate to win the award.

I had gathered more votes as a junior than any other junior in 1955, so theoretically, I was kind of like the favorite entering the 1956 season. But the Heisman Trophy wasn't promoted the way it is today. You never saw an article until November about the Heisman Trophy back then. Today, sports information directors all over the country start propping their kids up in January.

Like most things that occur during your life, at the time, I really didn't have a full appreciation for the opportunity that was presented to me at Notre Dame. I knew I was at a school with a great amount of tradition.

I loved Frank Leahy. He recruited me and he said some awfully strong things about me when I was a freshman and a sophomore-to-be. I was hoping I would have an opportunity to play for coach Leahy, and it was very disappointing when I didn't have that chance.

63

He was one of the great recruiters in America and one of the greatest coaches that ever lived.

When [Leahy retired], the guy they gave the opportunity to was Terry Brennan, and I loved Terry. I thought Terry did a great job and should never have been fired from the university. He really got a raw deal.

Terry was 27, 28 years old, but he was a very mature man. He had been a successful coach in high school in Chicago, and he was a Notre Dame player for four years under Frank Leahy and had a wonderful career at Notre Dame. He was the right choice. He had been the freshman coach when I was a freshman.

You had to play both ways back then, and I loved playing defense. My junior year they carried me off the field in the Iowa game after I kicked a field goal in the last seconds.

The next week Terry brought me into his office and he said, "No Notre Dame player has ever been carried off the field and we don't want to start that here."

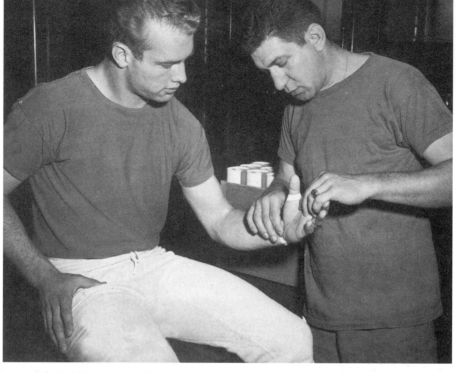

How did Paul Hornung (left), pictured with head trainer Gene Paszkiet (right), win the 1956 Heisman Trophy on a 2–8 team? By being the most dominant football player on the field at a variety of positions.

I said, "Well, Coach, I didn't carry myself off the field. It wasn't me." And he said, "I just want you to know that that's not going to happen again, no matter what happens."

He never said anything to the team about it, at least not that I was aware of, but by the end of the week, the word had spread that there would be no more of that.

I had dinner with Mike Ditka a few years ago, and he said, "I was in high school and I watched you play against Pitt and you played seven positions." I said, "What?" He said, "Yeah, you played defensive line, you played defensive end on some plays, you played linebacker, you punted, you kicked off, you returned kicks, you returned punts, you played quarterback. . . ." I said, "Well, back then it was one platoon and your best players had to play both ways." We just got caught short playing a very tough schedule, like they do today.

I hear people talk about Notre Dame's schedule today and how difficult it is. They say Notre Dame should lighten up its schedule to make it easier to win. But you know, Notre Dame has always prided itself on playing a tough schedule. That shouldn't change.

If Joe Montana and Joe Theismann are two of the more beloved players of the "modern era" of Notre Dame football, 1956 Heisman Trophy winner Paul Hornung—the original Golden Boy—was the hero of Irish fans waiting for the "television era" of Notre Dame football to arrive.

A true multithreat who seldom came off the field, the 6'2", 205-pound Hornung claimed college football's most coveted individual prize despite playing for a team that managed just two victories in 1956. Hornung led the Irish in rushing, scoring, and kickoff return yardage that year, and he even finished second on the squad in tackles.

After a brilliant career in the NFL with the Green Bay Packers, the Louisville, Kentucky, native remains involved with Notre Dame football today as a member of the broadcast team for the Mutual Radio Network.

JIM MORSE

1954–1956

I GUESS YOU COULD SAY THAT I AM a Fighting Irishman to the core. Three of my children were born at Notre Dame while my wife [Leah] and I were staying in the military barracks housing complex used by returning World War II veterans. It wasn't much of a place, and it was pretty worn down after the veterans and their families had lived there for five or six years. But it was a home for a growing family.

I debated between Notre Dame and Michigan State. They were the only schools I was interested in. Michigan State was closer to my home in Muskegon [Michigan], but Notre Dame was only a little bit farther away.

At my small high school [St. Mary's], I played halfback and was a good pass catcher, too. During my senior season in 1952, we played a game in South Bend. I don't remember whether it was against Central Catholic or South Bend Catholic. A year later, they merged into St. Joseph's High School, which was just across the highway from Notre Dame.

One of the Notre Dame assistants, backfield coach Bill Earley, scouted me in that game. I guess I impressed him because eventually Notre Dame offered me a scholarship and I finally made up my mind to play under the great Frank Leahy. It was a good choice even though it was much tougher football than I was used to. I remember being impressed at how serious everyone was about the team.

On the field that year [1953], when freshmen were ineligible, it was a great season, undefeated with a late tie against Iowa. I don't believe I ever saw a better team, and coach Leahy called it the best college-aged team he had ever coached.

Leahy collapsed at halftime in a game at midseason, and in late January he made the decision to retire. It was mostly because of his illness. He put such a demand on himself to develop a team that he was burnt out, and yet he was only 45.

Terry Brennan, who had been our freshman coach, was named to succeed him in 1954, so at least he knew who I was. My teammate and longtime friend, Paul Hornung, was the freshman star, and even though Ralph Guglielmi was back at quarterback, everyone was counting on Hornung to someday be the team leader.

Fortunately for me, John Lattner and Neil Worden had graduated and there was going to be room in the backfield. There was plenty of competition. Joe Heap was back for his senior season at left half, and Paul Reynolds, Sherrill Sipes, and Dick Fitzgerald were all back.

I was able to move in at right half with Heap at left half and Don Schaefer, a great player, at fullback. Hornung had to be content as the number two fullback and a reserve quarterback behind Guglielmi and Tommy Carey.

The lone captain of Notre Dame's 1956 squad, Jim Morse (right), pictured with head coach Terry Brennan, joined forces with Paul Hornung, Joe Heap, and Don Schaefer to form one of Notre Dame's all-time best backfields.

We started out by shutting out a good Texas team [21–0] in my first game, but a week later, Purdue arrived with new quarterback Len Dawson, a really good passer. He threw four touchdown passes, one of them to a big end, Lamar Lundy, who ran through the rain for a touchdown in a 27–14 Purdue victory.

We bounced back against Pittsburgh on the road [33–0] and again at home in the rain against Michigan State for a come-from-behind win [20–19]. My choice of schools seemed vindicated because that was the first time the Irish had beaten the Spartans in four games.

We stayed undefeated but had a close call against Navy in the rain at Baltimore. The field was almost totally covered by water. There were a few dry spots, and in the second half, Ralph found one and I found another one. He threw me a perfect pass and the Middie defenders fell down. I ran for a touchdown for the only score in a 6–0 game.

We had climbed up to No. 4 in the polls, but Southern California also was rated [No. 17]. In the best game I ever had running the ball, we beat USC, 23–17. I carried the ball 19 times for 179 yards. We ended the 1954 season with a 9–1 mark, good for No. 4 behind Ohio State, UCLA, and Oklahoma.

In our junior season, Guglielmi and a half dozen other regulars had graduated, and Hornung had no problem moving in at quarterback. I was still the right halfback with Dick Lynch my backup. My classmate, Dean Studer, was the left half with speedy Aubrey Lewis his backup.

68

We won the first three games, including the first-ever game against Miami in a night game at the Orange Bowl. But then Michigan State beat us at East Lansing [21–7]. We dropped off from No. 4 to No. 11 in the polls, but then won five straight to climb back to No. 4.

In our final home game against Iowa, the Hawkeyes went ahead 14–7 late in the game, only to have Hornung take over. He directed a long drive to tie the score and then another shorter one to put us in position for a field goal. Even though we were penalized 15 yards for coaching from the sidelines when a manager threw the kicking tee on the field, Hornung still boomed the winning field goal, 17–14, with 2:15 to play.

The students rushed the field and carried Hornung off on their shoulders, and fans tore down the wooden goal posts for the first time in stadium history.

The momentum didn't carry over to Los Angeles, and in a great battle of Hornung vs. Jon Arnett, we rallied to trail 21–20 as the fourth period started. But then the Trojans scored three touchdowns in the fourth quarter to win [42–20].

I had an unbelievable game catching the ball, something like five receptions for 208 yards [41.6 yards per catch]. It was an NCAA record for a long time, but the loss dropped us to No. 9 in the polls.

For the 1956 season, I was elected captain, the first time for a back in a dozen years. But it wouldn't be a memorable season. We lost the opener at Southern Methodist [19–13], but beat Indiana at home for a 1–1 mark. Then Purdue, Michigan State, Oklahoma, Navy, and Pitt beat us before we managed to win over North Carolina. Iowa and USC then dropped us to a 2–8 record, the worst in school history—not a very good year to have been captain.

I had made it for three years on the field along with my close friend, Hornung. He was the bonus pick of Green Bay, and I went to the Calgary Stampeders in Canada where our 1956 backfield coach, Jim Finks, was an assistant coach and general manager.

It was great being with Finks for those two years. He was a classy guy and after Calgary he went to the Minnesota Vikings, the Chicago Bears, [and even the Chicago Cubs for a while], and the New Orleans Saints. We were close friends until he died at a young age. I had a good time in Canada. Finks was absolutely one of the greatest people I have ever been associated with.

I eventually became a radio and television announcer, and I really think the Notre Dame connection and the football connection helped get me that job.

Notre Dame was good to me and for me, and as long as we can afford it, we believe in giving back. The Morse Center for Academic Services is located in the center of the old campus. I hope they remember me for something other than football.

69

Jim Morse was a 5'11", 175-pound running back out of a small Catholic high school in Muskegon, Michigan. He was first spotted by Notre Dame assistant coach Bill Earley, who observed one of his prep games and came away convinced Morse could help the Fighting Irish.

Morse moved into the starting lineup as a sophomore in 1954 at right halfback, a spot that he occupied for three seasons. He never led the Irish in rushing, due in large part to the fact that the Irish backfield boasted such standouts as Paul Hornung at quarterback, Joe Heap at left halfback, and Don Schaefer, who paced the Irish ground game in 1954 and 1955, at fullback. Yet Morse was named the lone captain of the 1956 squad.

ED SULLIVAN

1955–1957

ICAME FROM MCKEESPORT, PENNSYLVANIA, and was fortunate to have a magnificent coach by the name of Duke Weigle. He was known all over the country by people in college football. He was a great coach and a great person. We had guys at my high school that were second-teamers but got scholarships because coaches knew if the guys had played for Duke, they knew what they were doing.

Duke was the kind of guy who would not let your head swell. Bob McBride was the Notre Dame line coach, and he came to scout me in high school. After the game, Duke introduced me to Bob McBride, but he never let on that McBride was there to look at me. When the season was over, then it was OK. But up to that point, the focus was on the team.

My earliest recollection, as a very young boy, was that Notre Dame was an actual player. I pretended like I was Notre Dame. It's funny how those memories stick with you for a lifetime.

So attending Notre Dame was a dream of mine, but just a dream. In my mind, Notre Dame was college football. I did not believe that I was good enough to go to Notre Dame.

But there was a local guy who was recruiting me. He ran a switch engine in a steel mill. They had those unpaid scouts all over the place, and those guys built a reputation for recommending good players.

He loaded about four of us guys from my area who were being recruited by Notre Dame into an old DeSoto, and we drove to Notre Dame and saw them play Southern Cal. We stayed in the dorms and met the coaches.

I remember they got us in a game of basketball down at the Rock: shirts and skins. Every now and then they would say, "You guys be shirts now and you guys are skins." In other words, they wanted to see who they were recruiting. They wanted to see us in just shorts.

Later, in fact after I was out of Notre Dame, Bob McBride told me that Leahy said to him, "Stop recruiting Sullivan. He doesn't meet our physical standards." And McBride responded to him, "Yeah, but he's always where the ball is!"

After we got home, I didn't hear much from Notre Dame. I think they were kind of backing away from me because of my size. But whether they pursued me or not, I just felt like I wasn't the caliber to come here. I decided Notre Dame was not for me. It was for the All-Americans and guys like that. The best in the country, and that wasn't me.

We had a high school coach who had left the coaching staff a few years before and had gone to William & Mary, so he was recruiting me. I was recruited by Penn State, Kansas, Miami, and a couple of others. My mother wouldn't let me go to Miami. She said, "No, they don't have good academics!"

So I was all signed up to go to William & Mary. I had my books; I had my room number; I had the name of my roommate. But then I went to the Pennsylvania All-Star Game, which was the Western Pennsylvania guys against the guys from Allegheny County. McBride was there, and the guy I was playing against, who went on to play at Pitt, had fingers the size of my wrist. I thought I had a pretty good game against him. I met him later and he said, "I think I had a good night against you."

I must have done something right because McBride started back on me again. But I was still going to go to William & Mary. I thought, "If I go to Notre Dame, some All-American is going to beat me out and I'm going to sit on the bench at Notre Dame."

And then I thought to myself, "What if that All-American goes to William & Mary? Then I'm going to sit on the bench at William & Mary!" So on that kind of reasoning I thought I might as well go to the place I had dreamed of and loved.

We were not eligible to play as freshmen, and we did not have games. We practiced against the varsity every day. Frank Leahy was still the head coach in 1953. We were up against the likes of John Lattner and Dan Shannon and Ralph Guglielmi. These were guys who just a few months ago, I was listening about them on the radio. They were my heroes!

Frank Leahy was one of a kind. As a player, you didn't get too close to him. Even the varsity people who played four years for him had very little one-on-one contact with him. He was the kind of guy who would say, "Coach Earley, coach Earley, ask that lad not to do that again!" He wouldn't talk directly to you.

But he was such a great coach, such a great organizer. He also had such a great staff and was so organized that Frank Leahy could have been ignorant of football and still been successful.

My sophomore year I was ineligible. The rule at Notre Dame was that if you did not have a *C* average in this semester, you were not eligible the next semester. The rule also said that if you failed to get a *C* average in two straight semesters, you lost your scholarship. My freshman year I did not have a *C* average for two consecutive semesters, so I lost my scholarship. I was devastated.

But I had somebody looking down on me, and I was told that if I wanted to come back and pay my way as a regular student and get my average up, I could get my scholarship back. So my parents agreed, I came back my sophomore year, and I played interhall football. I was a halfback. I wasn't going to play the line.

By 1955, I was probably 170 pounds and they immediately moved me from center to tackle. We were playing the split-T then, and at 170 pounds, I was pretty quick. I became the backup to Ray Lemek, the captain of that team. But he had a bum knee. He started every game but one, and within five minutes after the game started, I was in the lineup. I almost had more minutes than anyone else because when the second team came in, I was already in there. I used to tell Lemek, "Don't walk down the stairs in front of me because I might push you!"

The cutbacks affected us in 1956, and not having a coach like Frank Leahy around anymore played a role as well. That was more of a factor than Terry Brennan's age, which was 25 when he took over as head coach. In fact, when my youngest son, Michael, turned 25, I joked, "Terry Brennan was the head coach at Notre Dame when he was 25. What are you doing with your life?"

Terry had been a successful high school coach in Chicago. I don't think there was a lack of respect from the players. He did a fine job with us. It's just not easy following a coach like Frank Leahy.

They had a testimonial for Paul Hornung a while back, and the things they said about him were just over the top. He was heaped with praise that night,

Once considered too small by Frank Leahy's standards, center Ed Sullivan went on to captain Notre Dame's 1957 squad.

and you know what? Everything they said about him that night was true! He was a phenomenal football player. He was a great player on both sides of the ball. I led the team in tackles in 1956, but Paul was second. He was just a great football player.

I don't think he was affected by winning the Heisman. In fact, he may have been affected by it more if he *hadn't* won it because he had great confidence in himself. People said he was cocky and had a big head. He was cocky, but he didn't have a big head. He knew what he would do and he produced.

The best play we had in 1956 was when Paul would go back to pass and everybody would be covered. In other words, we couldn't run a play that was better than keeping it in Hornung's hands.

Going through the 2–8 season in 1956 was a devastating year. I'm thankful that we had the following year when we were 7–3, the year I was captain. I have to say, 2–8 hurt like hell, but I wouldn't have wanted to be anyplace else and be 10–0. This is a place like no other.

To be named the captain of the 1957 team was truly an incredible honor. I was a confident football player because I knew I could work harder than anybody else. Somebody might be a better football player, but I knew I could outwork anybody. So when I was able to come here and play—and play on a regular basis—and then to be named captain . . . I'm 68 years old and I still can't believe it!

So many people from Notre Dame had such a positive influence on me as a person. I think of people like our class secretary, John Slevin, who has been writing a column in the alumni magazine since we graduated.

John has a polio leg. He's been in a brace since he was in school. He's never let it be a burden to him. We'd go to pep rallies, and during the pep rallies, the guys would take the screws out of it and then John would take a step and collapse. It wasn't done maliciously. We were just having fun with him and he took it well, and he's a dear friend today. John is one of my heroes. He plays golf and we don't drive the cart into the fairway for him. He walks out there. That's the kind of guy John is. He doesn't want any quarter.

The fellowship at Notre Dame has been one of the great impacts and influences on my life. Just about every practice they'd come off the field with blood on their shirts and none of it was theirs. Two of my coaches, Bob McBride and Joe McArdle, had a great influence on my life. They were great men and great teachers, and to this day, they're old buddies.

That's Notre Dame. Once you establish that relationship, it's a relationship you have for the rest of your life. And it means as much to me today as it did when I was playing for Notre Dame.

By his own admission, McKeesport, Pennsylvania, native Ed Sullivan was a bit of a long shot getting into Notre Dame. Weighing just 155 pounds out of high school, Sullivan bypassed an opportunity to play football at William & Mary to take the ultimate challenge at Notre Dame.

After arriving as a freshman in 1953, he overcame academic difficulties, bulked up to 6'0", 190 pounds, and not only worked his way into the lineup at tackle, center, and linebacker, but became captain of the 1957 Fighting Irish.

AL ECUYER

1956–1958

JESUIT HIGH IN NEW ORLEANS had sent many graduates to Notre Dame, including star football players John Petitbon and Joe Heap, and I wanted to follow them. But I wasn't very big [5′10″, 190 pounds], and I wasn't sure if I would get a chance.

Since I was from New Orleans, Tulane was an option, or I could give it a try at Louisiana State. I eventually signed with Tulane, which was a member of the Southeastern Conference at that time.

Then a Notre Dame booster named Hal Sporl got involved, and on his recommendation, I was asked to visit. Terry Brennan was the head coach, and he expressed an interest in my coming to Notre Dame. So I decided against staying close to home and I headed to Notre Dame.

I liked Notre Dame from the start. But it was different. The weather and the food were different, but the studies were as tough as they had been at Jesuit. The discipline didn't bother me that much.

Notre Dame had had two very solid years in 1954 and 1955, but we weren't a very experienced team after that. We had a few stars like Paul Hornung and Jim Morse in the backfield, but that was about it. I was 5′10″, 190 pounds when I won a starting right guard job as a sophomore in 1956, and I was one of three first-year players starting in the line.

The 1956 season opened at night in Dallas against Southern Methodist, and they were pretty good. Hank Stram had taken over as head coach, and we fell behind. Hornung made a long run from punt formation on fourth down, but SMU came back and won [19–13].

Al Ecuyer (left), pictured with Jim Schaaf, followed two other New Orleans prep stars—John Petitbon and Joe Heap—to Notre Dame.

Unfortunately, it got much worse after that. The only bright spot in the dismal 2–8 season was Hornung's Heisman Trophy and the fact that we knew we would be better in 1957. We just made up our minds that we would not lose games like we did in 1956. We got together, worked hard in the off-season, and were ready for some revenge.

We got some revenge in the first game at Purdue [a 12–0 victory], and we beat Indiana [26–0] and Army [23–21] in Philadelphia on a late field goal by Monty Stickles. We got some revenge against Pitt [a 13–7 victory], but not against Navy [a 20–6 loss]. They ended our streak at 4–0, and then we lost at Michigan State [34–6] before heading to Oklahoma, which was No. 2 in the nation.

That game against Oklahoma was a great defensive struggle. Our coaches, especially Bernie Witucki [tackles] and Bernie Crimmins [backfield], insisted all week long that we could win. And it worked out the way they said. We could stop them, but we had to score, and we finally put together an 80-yard drive with Dick Lynch scoring to give us a 7–0 win. We lost again to Iowa [21–13], but beat the Trojans [40–12] for a great comeback [7–3] season.

After the 1958 season [6–4], the coaching staff was fired. We were sorry for them. They worked hard with us, and we had only the one bad season.

I went on to play professional football for 12 years after Notre Dame, and then I moved back to the South. I don't get back to Notre Dame much because my wife suffers from ALS. When I heard [former Irish player] Pete Duranko was suffering from the same disease, I called to extend him good wishes. He was so upbeat and determined that it really made me feel good.

That's why I think so much of Notre Dame. They all think of each other and reach out to help. That's what's great about being one of the Fighting Irish.

Even by late-fifties standards, Al Ecuyer from New Orleans was small. But that didn't stop the 5'10", 190-pounder from earning a starting spot as a sopho-more on the 1956 team that struggled in the won-lost column but helped Paul Hornung claim the Heisman Trophy.

As a junior, Ecuyer was a consensus All-American while tying teammate Jim Schaaf with a team-leading 88 tackles. Ecuyer, who weighed 205 pounds by his senior season, went on to earn cocaptain honors with Chuck Puntillo in 1958.

JIM SCHAAF

1956–1958

Getting a good education was one of my goals when I was attending a Catholic high school in Erie, Pennsylvania, and as a football lineman with some ability, I had a few choices.

Should I accept an appointment to West Point and become a career officer in the military? How about attending Purdue? Or, closer to home, Pittsburgh?

Then there was Notre Dame. I had grown up listening to Irish games on radio or in the limited television of the early fifties. Monsignor James Gannon got involved in the process, too. He was a close friend of Notre Dame athletic director Ed "Moose" Krause, and the monsignor urged me to think about Notre Dame.

Assistant coach John Druze dropped by on a recruiting trip and set the stage for a visit to the campus, and from then on, I was convinced. It was Notre Dame for me. My line coach in high school was Tony Zambroski. He had played for the Irish a few years earlier, and he thought it was right for me, too. When I put it all together and added it up, everything pointed to Notre Dame.

Notre Dame was riding high in football when I was considering schools. In the previous two seasons, the team had lost only one game, and new coach Terry Brennan was trying to build a good squad despite a university-ordered cutback on recruits the previous year.

I made a pretty good impression as a guard during my freshman year in 1955. I worked against guys like Heisman Trophy winner Paul Hornung, so

I certainly was practicing against the best. And in 1955, Paul led us to an 8–2 record.

Everything seemed to be bright for the future, but I think coach Brennan knew otherwise. We were short of experience and sophomores had to man the offensive line. Al Ecuyer was ahead of me at guard, but I got to play in quite a few games.

Nothing seemed to go right for us in 1956. Plus, in October, we played No. 2 Michigan State [a 47–14 loss] and No. 1 Oklahoma [a 40–0 loss].

But as bad as the 1956 season was, the 1957 season was just as gratifying. Early in the year we had a great comeback victory over Army in Philadelphia [23–21]. Then in November, there was the 7–0 upset of Oklahoma to end the Sooners' 47-game winning streak.

Those were the highlights of my career. We finished 7–3 and seemed destined for even better things in 1958. But it didn't happen and Brennan and his staff were fired.

80

Jim Schaaf helped anchor the 1958 Notre Dame line that paved the way for the No. 5–ranked offense in the country.

During my playing days, I was stricken with bouts of dizziness and spent a lot of time under a doctor's care. It was diagnosed as Ménière's syndrome, which was a malfunctioning of the inner-ear canal that caused dizzy spells and fainting. Fortunately, the doctors were able to stabilize the condition with medicine, and there were no lasting effects.

The losing was difficult, but I really benefited from the complete Notre Dame experience. I made some off-campus friends. One was a businessman, Harry Baker, and another was Charles O. Finley, a Gary, Indiana, insurance agent who was a rabid Notre Dame fan and went on to own the Kansas City/Oakland Athletics.

I remember him saying to me, "Someday I'm going to buy a major sports franchise and you're going to be part of it." I liked Charlie and I didn't know whether the sports franchise idea was just a dream for him, but I listened.

He tried to buy the Chicago Bears from George Halas, but that didn't work out. Finally, he called me one night and said, "I've bought the Kansas City Athletics and you're going to be the team's traveling secretary." I didn't even know what a traveling secretary of a baseball team did, but I knew that Charlie meant business. My Notre Dame connection had landed me a good job.

The Athletics weren't very good when he bought them, but at least it was the major leagues. Charlie soon became well known in the Kansas City area, and that eventually helped lead me back to football. I became the public relations director under one of his former coaches, Hank Stram. Hank, of course, turned the Chiefs into a Super Bowl winner.

All the positive things that happened to me early in my career were a result of my Notre Dame experience. Going to Notre Dame was a great experience for me, and it's helped me immeasurably with contacts across the country. It's just a great place.

Jim Schaaf from Erie, Pennsylvania, was listed as a fourth-team right guard during his sophomore year at Notre Dame in 1956. One season later, he moved into the starting lineup at left guard, a position he would man during the 1957 and 1958 seasons.

In 1958, the 6'0", 203-pound Schaaf and the rest of the Irish offensive line paved the way for the No. 5–ranked offense in the country.

BOB WETOSKA

1956–1958

I remember head coach Terry Brennan and line coach Bill Fischer really making a strong push for me to come to Notre Dame. Minnesota wasn't a prime recruiting area for Notre Dame, and at first, I had not heard anything positive from Notre Dame.

Minnesota was right here at home, and I signed a Big 10 paper to become a Golden Gopher. That was long before the national letter of intent came into existence, so I was not bound to Minnesota.

When Notre Dame showed an interest, I met with coach Brennan and coach Fischer. They seemed to really want me, so I was tempted to change my mind from Minnesota.

I played in the All-Star Game, and I met two other Notre Dame recruits— Jim Colosimo and Bronko Nagurski Jr., who was the son of the former Golden Gopher and Chicago Bear great. Naturally Minnesota was recruiting Nagurski, and they were after Colosimo too. The three of us got to know each other pretty well, and we exchanged thoughts about schools. We decided that we'd all go to Notre Dame.

Bill Fischer kept calling us and sending us letters. I think it was Colosimo who broke the ice first, and then he persuaded Nagurski and me to go with him to Notre Dame.

Fall practices that freshman year [1955] were tough. The freshmen, of course, were unable to play, but we scrimmaged quite a bit against the varsity, which was led by Paul Hornung. They put together a fine season [8–2].

In 1956, however, the recruiting cutback of 1954 took its toll. We were inexperienced, particularly in the line. Nagurski and Frank Geremia, both sophomores, had to play tackle. Another sophomore, Al Ecuyer, was a guard, and I not only played a lot [215 minutes] at end, but quite a bit [102 minutes] at right tackle.

I remember that first game at Southern Methodist at night [1956]. We played fairly well, but lost a close one [19–13]. At home, we beat Indiana [20–6], but then had to face three tough opponents in a row at home. We lost to Purdue [28–14] and then got clobbered by Michigan State [47–14] and Oklahoma [40–0]. Things were pretty tough. Even though Hornung won the Heisman Trophy, it was a really bad year [2–8].

We came back strong in our junior year [1957]. Some new coaches were added, and we started out strong, winning the first four games.

I remember the Purdue game [a 12–0 victory] on a hot day down at Lafayette. I caught a fairly short pass and was in the clear. I ran as hard as I could but was running out of gas pretty fast. I was even hoping someone would catch me. But they were tired, too, and I scored.

We played Army in Philadelphia, the first game against West Point in 10 years, and Monty Stickles kicked a field goal to win it [23–21]. That was a great thrill because we finally renewed the series against them after a long layoff.

Our streak came to an end against Navy [a 20–6 loss], and then Michigan State beat us [34–6]. We were 4–2 heading to Norman to take on national champion Oklahoma.

I'll always remember that game. No one gave us a chance, but our coaches made us believe we could win. I was hurt early in the game and replaced by Colosimo. He made a couple of good catches, but we couldn't score. On defense, we shut out the Sooners' ground game, and it was a real struggle until we put together a long [80-yard] drive in the fourth period.

On fourth-and-3, Dick Lynch scored the only touchdown, and that 7–0 victory was the highlight of a 7–3 season.

My senior year didn't go as well. I remember catching a pass late against Southern California in the L.A. Coliseum that helped us win the game [20–13]. But we finished the season 6–4, and anybody that went to Notre Dame in those days expected more on the football field.

After graduation, I was drafted by the Chicago Bears in the fifth round and made a 10-year career out of it.

Quite large by late-fifties standards, Bob Wetoska parlayed his stint with the Irish into a 10-year NFL career.

I still love to get to Notre Dame as often as I can. I come to one or two games a year and go to the alumni and reunion functions. The games are great and it's a great place. I do wish they had more close-up parking for these old pro-football legs.

Minneapolis native Bob Wetoska was supposed to end up at the home-state school like most young men in Minnesota did. But the lure of Notre Dame, most especially the strong pull by the Irish coaching staff, brought him to South Bend where he experienced the ups and downs of the Terry Brennan years.

Wetoska, quite large by fifties standards at 6'3", 225 pounds, was a backup right end behind Gary Myers and Monty Stickles in 1956 and 1957 before moving into the starting lineup in 1958. He went on to a 10-year career as a tackle with the Chicago Bears.

KEN ADAMSON

1957–1959

As a lineman at a small, Catholic, military high school in Atlanta, it seemed only natural that the ideal place for me was Georgia Tech.

Georgia Tech head coach Bobby Dodd persuaded me to sign an agreement to play for the Yellow Jackets, but then Notre Dame intervened. Playing for the Fighting Irish was too appealing, and I changed my mind.

My father was an army officer overseas in Korea at the time. When I called him to tell him that my plans had changed, he insisted, "You must dress up in a coat and tie and go talk to coach Dodd." And so I did.

When I told coach Dodd, a great gentleman and one of the most respected people in college athletics, he tried to talk me out of it. He said, "You'll be away from home; you live in Atlanta and you should stay in Atlanta; you have many friends here; Notre Dame is up north and you won't like it there. . . ."

But I was convinced Notre Dame was right for me, and he wished me well. That was one of the hardest things I had to do, but when I got to Notre Dame, I knew I had made the right decision. Sure, the discipline and the academics were tough at Notre Dame, but because of my military school background, it wasn't a problem.

In my freshman year [1956], the team won only two games, but the prospects were bright for the future. In 1957, I worked my way into the lineup as a reserve guard and won my letter. Al Ecuyer and Jim Schaaf were the regulars.

We had a great season in 1957, beating No. 1 Oklahoma [7–0] in Norman, and everything looked brighter for 1958. But early in the year we lost to

Army [and Heisman winner Pete Dawkins, 14–2], Purdue [29–22], Pittsburgh [29–26], and Big 10–champ Iowa [31–21]. We finished 6–4, and Terry Brennan and his staff were replaced. I never thought coaching was the problem. I thought they were good coaches, particularly my position coach, Bill Fischer.

The new Irish staff came from pro football, but before they arrived I was elected captain by my teammates, and I was really proud of myself. Not only was I playing good football but now I was captain. I thought that was really something for a boy from a small high school in the South.

Ken Adamson (right) captained Joe Kuharich's (left) first squad at Notre Dame in 1959.

I thought [head coach] Joe Kuharich and the new assistants were good, too. My line coach was Dick Stanfel, a real pro, but we finished 5–5. One of our losses was at home to Georgia Tech [14–10], and I played really well. After the game, coach Dodd sought me out on the field and gave me a big hug and said, "Ken, we are really proud of you." That meant a lot to me.

Another one of my best games was at Iowa, where we upset the [No. 16–rated] Hawkeyes [20–19], who had won three straight over us. I was determined they weren't going to beat us a record four times. Everyone played a great game, and we ended the season by upsetting Southern Cal [16–6] in my final game.

Notre Dame was a great place for me. To this day I'm close with some of my former teammates, such as [end] Mike Lodish and [quarterback] Donnie White.

I'm in Sacramento, California, now, so I don't get back to Notre Dame very often. But one time when I went back, I put my running gear on and ran around the track on Cartier Field. I was thinking to myself, "This is the first time I ran this track when I wasn't forced to."

But it's always great to be back in a familiar place, even though the campus is so different. There are dozens of new buildings, and I have trouble finding my way around. But the church, the Dome, and the Grotto are still familiar places.

My experience at Notre Dame was really great. We didn't win all the games, but I really thought the coaching was great, too. Perhaps coach Joe Kuharich was a bit predictable, but he was a good guy, always looking out for his players.

Those were great days, and I hope the players today have the same feelings. I wouldn't trade that Notre Dame experience for anything.

Ken Adamson, from Atlanta, Georgia, was the starting right guard and captain of Joe Kuharich's first Notre Dame squad in 1959. The 6'2", 205-pounder emerged as a consistent performer along a line that also featured future NFL standout Nick Buoniconti and 6'4", 225-pound end Monty Stickles. Although he was not drafted by an NFL team, Adamson hooked on with the Denver Broncos of the AFL and became a starting guard from 1960 to 1962.

The
SIXTIES AND
SEVENTIES

BRIAN BOULAC

1960–1962

I GREW UP IN SPOKANE and went to Gonzaga Prep, a Catholic high school. In our neighborhood, I followed Gonzaga Prep when I was a kid and listened to Notre Dame football games on the radio. When I was in the eighth grade, Gary Myers, who played at Gonzaga, received a football scholarship to Notre Dame.

I remember telling my parents that that's what I wanted to do: get a football scholarship to go to Notre Dame. I went to Gonzaga and played for two years before my father was transferred to state patrol in Olympia. So I went across the state to Olympia High. My father had contacted some people who had Notre Dame interests, and Notre Dame ended up finding me way out in Olympia, Washington.

I had made up my mind that if I got a scholarship to Notre Dame, that's where I would go. There was a period of time during the coaching transition from Terry Brennan to Joe Kuharich when I didn't have contact with the university. Hughie Devore picked up that contact as an assistant with the new staff. My visit came late in the process, after basketball season.

There was some deemphasis in the midfifties when the university cut back on the number of scholarships. But I think with my class that was signed, maybe we gave Joe Kuharich a little more opportunity. In 1956 they fell to 2–8, but it turned around to 7–3 the next year. In Brennan's period, there were some good classes, but we didn't have the national title–caliber team.

When I came to Notre Dame, we had players, but again didn't have the success. When Ara [Parseghian] came to Notre Dame in 1964, he took the same players—plus the 1963 freshman class, which included Kevin Hardy, Alan Page, Jim Lynch, Don Gmitter, Larry Conjar, and that group—and was able to transform them into something special.

As freshmen in 1959, we didn't even play other freshman teams. We were told as freshmen that we were here primarily to get an education. So that first year, we learned our skills football-wise and came to practice. But if you had a test or a paper due, all you had to do was come to the coaches and say, "Hey, I've got an academic project." There were times when we had just 7 to 10 [freshmen] at practice.

It was a learning experience. Monty Stickles was an All-American, and we got in a scuffle at one practice. Ken Adamson, the team captain, had to pull us apart. When Ken was here for captain's day in the [2003] Washington State opener, he remembered that incident. I broke a tooth in that scuffle, so I remember that more than anything from my freshman year.

The 2–8 season in my sophomore year [1960] is something I have kind of blocked out. It's become selective memory. We were never really out of many games, other than the loss to Purdue [51–19]. I remember that game more than any other loss during my period at Notre Dame because I thought we were a pretty good football team. It was like being at a racetrack, watching them run up and down the field. It was our second game after we won the opener, and I'm sure it affected us the rest of the season because we lost eight in a row.

There wasn't this feeling of, "Oh God, we're horrible!" We felt going into every game that we were going to win, and we practiced that way. We had some great talent. Myron Pottios was the captain, a great linebacker who played a long time in the pros. Nick Buoniconti was a linebacker, and Daryle Lamonica was a quarterback in my class.

I was amazed by the spirit on the campus even though we had such a poor record. Today when you're not successful, the press and the alumni seem to make it even more apparent. From 1956 to 1963, we had only two winning records and it was the most dismal time, won-lost-wise, in Notre Dame history. But I don't think we as players ever went into a game feeling we were overmatched, that we were going to get blown out or didn't want to play.

One of the strengths of Notre Dame is that your roommates are not varsity athletes. When we walked into the dorm, we were part of the dorm. We were every bit a part of the student body: we went to class together and went to eat together. There was no, "You're a football player and you guys are

91

Brian Boulac, an end for the Irish in the early sixties, has gone on to a lifelong career at Notre Dame, first as a coach and then as an athletic administrator.

lousy." They may have said that in the dorms when we weren't there, but we never sensed that. We knew we weren't successful, but I don't think that diminished our love for the game or the way we practiced and played.

One of my favorite memories was the first game I started as a sophomore. It came against Navy when they had [Heisman Trophy winner] Joe Bellino. I remember vividly in the second half how the guy across from me said, "You're the biggest 195-pound guy I've ever seen." I was actually 225, but that was a [sports information director] Charlie Callahan thing. I weighed 195 one day as a freshman after I had the flu, and that's how I was listed most of my career. I was 240 as a senior, but still listed at 200.

In 1961 we felt we were back. We opened with victories over Oklahoma with Bud Wilkinson, USC with John McKay, and Purdue with Jack Mollenkopf, the year after our 51–19 loss to Purdue. We moved up to No. 6 in the polls and had already won more games—three—than we had the year before. We had a lot of talent and a lot of competition. Angelo Dabiero and George Sefcik were two very competent backs, and a lot of things were going our way. We never felt after the 1960 season that we couldn't rebound and be as good as we should be.

When we lost to Michigan State [17–7] after starting 3–0, it was very deflating. We felt we were riding the crest and were a good football team. But Michigan State was a very good football team that day. I had no complaints about the schedules we were playing and didn't think we were overmatched. Michigan State was really good then, and you knew when you stepped on the field they were a step above USC. We were beating USC regularly then, and even beat them 17–0 out there when we were 2–8.

I really don't know why we couldn't get over the hump. But as an assistant coach sitting in on meetings in 1964, I felt Ara's approach was different than coach Kuharich's. He was maybe more at ease in communicating with young kids, whereas Kuharich was used to working with the professional athlete. Kuharich knew his *X*s and *O*s, and he and his staff worked hard. But I felt the difference immediately when Ara arrived, with his enthusiasm and preparation, the way we approached the game, and the way you could pick that up as a player.

Prior to Ara, we competed and were rarely out of games. When Ara came, they competed, they were in games—and they won. He got us over that hump. I guess coaching at times does make a difference. Prior to Ara, the talent was there, the spirit was there, but it took the master chef to put it together.

It wore on us players. You asked yourself, "Why weren't we more successful?" We felt we should have been better and probably should have been.

There's no question you could see this job wear on coach Kuharich. Having been a professional coach and coming here to work with teenagers again, maybe it was different. And then there's the feeling that everyone here wants to be successful and every alumnus thinks Notre Dame should win the national championship every year. So there was immense pressure.

Even with Ara, we would beat a team 14–10 and the mail and correspondence he would get would say, "How come you didn't beat them by three touchdowns?" Just look at the pictures of Ara when he came to Notre Dame in 1964 and as the years progressed, and he was still a young man [51] when he finally had to leave.

I felt unfulfilled when my football career ended. I don't think I reached what I could have done or should have done. When I had an opportunity to work as a grad assistant, I jumped at it. It was an opportunity to stay close with the team, and when Ara came I knew I really wanted to coach.

I have no regrets. Maybe it's because I've blocked out that period as a player, but when I look back on it, I had a lot of fun, we had great camaraderie, and our class has stayed close for 40 years. When we come back to reunions, my teammates, my roommates, the guys in my hall . . . these are the people I still remain in close contact with, and the lasting friendships are what become important.

94

Recruited out of Olympia, Washington, as an end in 1959, Brian Boulac played all four years under Joe Kuharich when the program was at its nadir and then was a graduate assistant from 1963 to 1965 when Ara Parseghian restored the glory.

Boulac was an assistant for the Irish freshmen in 1966 and 1967 and was hired by Parseghian as an offensive line coach in 1970. He served on three national title staffs and became the recruiting coordinator while also instructing Dan Devine's offensive line.

After serving as a defensive line and special teams coach for Gerry Faust in 1981 and 1982, Boulac opted to move into athletic administration at Notre Dame in 1983 and is currently the Joyce Center manager.

DARYLE LAMONICA

1960–1962

WHEN IT CAME TIME FOR ME TO CHOOSE A SCHOOL, it was between Southern Cal and Notre Dame. I knew more about USC and I wasn't sure I wanted to be as far away from home as I would be at Notre Dame.

Coach Kuharich had come from the pro ranks and had been in San Francisco a few years earlier, so both he and line coach Dick Stanfel, who also was a California native, knew the talent in the area.

In the end, I picked Notre Dame because it was a prestigious school and its football program was well known.

But for most of my freshman year, I had doubts whether I would ever see action for the Irish varsity. I had suffered some torn ligaments in my leg and was sent to see a specialist in Chicago. The specialist said my leg would be all right but that I would never be able to compete in sports again.

Needless to say, that wasn't the opinion I was looking for, and I asked to see another doctor. The South Bend doctor had been an athlete himself and had suffered a similar injury. He prescribed a walking cast, and for several months I hobbled to and from classes and eventually to the football field.

Once I got back on the field, I started to have some doubts about playing football for Notre Dame. School was great. I liked it, but on the football field, I began to have some doubts. I wasn't getting the coaching that I thought I would get.

In high school, I had a great head coach and we had a great line coach, too. But at Notre Dame, there was no quarterback coach and about all the strategy we ever got was in team meetings. I decided to make the most of it and became the starting quarterback in 1960.

My first game was against, ironically, the Cal Golden Bears from back home. We won [21–7] and everything seemed to be settling in nicely. But it got much worse after that. We lost to Purdue [51–19], and that was the first of eight losses in a row. We pushed North Carolina all over the field in Chapel Hill but still lost [12–7].

Finally, in the last game of the season in Los Angeles in a driving rainstorm, we beat USC [17–0]. After that game, we were determined never to have a season like that [2–8] again.

We started fast in 1961 with wins over Oklahoma, Purdue, and Southern California, but Michigan State, Northwestern, and Navy beat us after that. We had a good group of players with people like [end] Jim Kelly and [linebacker] Nick Buoniconti. But we never seemed to put it all together and finished 5–5.

We started fast again in 1962 with a win over Oklahoma [13–7]. I think I called more automatics in that game than we even had. But the following

96

In and out of the lineup at Notre Dame, quarterback Daryle Lamonica went on to a successful professional career with the Buffalo Bills and the Oakland Raiders.

week against Purdue, I didn't play; [halfback] Ed Rutkowski didn't play. . . . As I recall, about five or six players who helped beat Oklahoma weren't even used against Purdue [a 24–6 loss]. I think coach Kuharich's explanation was that he thought [quarterback] Frank [Budka] had a much better week of practice than I did. We ended up 5–5 again.

I ended up being selected to play in the annual East-West Shrine Game in California. A year later, Ara Parseghian was brought in at Notre Dame. I would have given anything to have played for him.

Everything worked out pretty well for me, though, when I went on to professional football. I was drafted by the Buffalo Bills, where I played for four years. And then I played eight years for John Rauch and John Madden of the Oakland Raiders.

Even though I was back home in California and was known as a player for the Raiders, it was great to have the prestige of a Notre Dame degree and to have played football for the Irish.

I get back to the campus about every five years or so for class reunions. I hardly know my way around campus now. There have been so many changes. There are new buildings everywhere. But football has been better than in my days. I wish it could have been better when I was there, but Notre Dame was still a great experience.

97

Due in large part to Notre Dame's 12–18 record during his three-year varsity career, quarterback Daryle Lamonica is known more for his exploits with the Oakland Raiders (Super Bowl II) than with the Irish. Lamonica was truly a diamond in the rough at Notre Dame.

The 6'2", 205-pounder split time with Frank Budka during his last two years with the Irish, but he managed to complete 64 of 128 passes for 821 yards and six touchdowns in 1961. After a four-year stint with the Buffalo Bills, Lamonica came into his own as a Raider under John Rauch and John Madden from 1967 to 1974.

JOHN HUARTE

1962–1964

Dick Coury, my high school coach at Mater Dei in Santa Ana, California, was a Notre Dame graduate, as was my older brother David. For me it was a clear decision that I wanted to go to Notre Dame, with not only my family's influence but also the enormous, rich tradition.

As a teenager growing up and listening to Notre Dame on the radio, I remember the team ending the win streak of Oklahoma. I remember names like Joe Heap and Ralph Guglielmi. Those traditions made it a dream for me to go to Notre Dame. It didn't matter to me what the team's current record was. Going to Notre Dame was a simple choice.

I remember being on my first flight going to Notre Dame and telling the people sitting next to me that I had never been to the East before. South Bend sure was east of California without me ever realizing that you had to keep going to actually get to the East. I was just a farm boy from California.

I remember our first practice my freshman year in 1961. Joe Kuharich called everybody out and then started dividing players into position groupings and told the linebackers and quarterbacks to come with him and to bring a football. I thought that was a little unusual, but I grabbed a football and ran over to where he was standing.

I was told to put a couple of tackling dummies five yards apart. Then when the whistle blew, you had to pick up the football and run through a confined area. He used the quarterbacks for tackling practice, and when you're just a young kid out of high school, you don't know what to think.

Kuharich would just stand there and grumble about how quarterbacks had to be tough. Of course, he was exactly right. It was a surprise to go through that in your first practice, but if you're going to play football at Notre Dame, you had to learn how to hold on to the ball.

My first three seasons at Notre Dame were very discouraging. All I did was scrimmage. I played a lot of football, but it always came on Tuesdays, Wednesdays, and Thursdays.

[When I was] a sophomore, Kuharich had his structure to practices, and in my mind he really had a good eye for talent. But we were not a smoothly running team. I think he expected more maturity from us as players. [Backfield coach] Don Doll always stood out to me as a clear-eyed disciplinarian. But that year I didn't get to play, other than in scrimmages.

My junior year was just a really poor season. I started near the top of the quarterback depth chart, moved to second string, and then through a 10-week cycle I think I went down to third, fourth, then fifth string. For one game, I didn't even travel.

Then I started moving back up. I wound up playing a little bit in the first and last games, including the Syracuse game in Yankee Stadium [a 14–7 loss]. Going into the House That Ruth Built to warm up made for some great memories. Unfortunately, we were a poor football team at 2–7.

I absolutely believe that team had some talented pieces with Nick Rassas and Jack Snow and Paul Costa. We had some backs that could catch the ball, and I knew I could throw the ball. One game against Northwestern I was stuck leaning on my helmet on the sidelines watching their quarterback throw the ball into the flat and moving the offense. I knew I could do that, but I didn't get the chance. Little did I know that that same Northwestern coach was going to be on my side of the field one year later and off we'd go.

When Ara [Parseghian] arrived that winter you had the sense that things were going to get pointed in the right direction in a hurry. During the spring we could advance the ball and were able to do some things right off the bat.

When the coach is new you're sensitive to what he's thinking. At some point I did something that was OK, and I glanced over at Tom Pagna and Ara, and I couldn't hear what they were saying because I was 15 yards away. But I knew it was good. It seemed like they thought whatever I was doing was going to work.

Ara was another guy who would test his players. During one scrimmage in a spring practice, he stopped play and put me in at middle linebacker. It was a goal-line defense situation, and I had never played linebacker in my life. The coaching staff just wanted to see if I could hit somebody. We ran about six plays and I did all I could, diving onto the pile. And then they pulled me

Quarterback John Huarte went from college football anonymity to greatness when he claimed the coveted Heisman Trophy in 1964.

out. They just wanted to see if their quarterback could hit. Ara didn't know what kind of players he had, so that was a good way to figure it out.

When I talk about the job that Ara did, I mean Ara and his assistants. The jobs that John Ray [defensive line/linebackers], Paul Shoults [defensive backs], Doc Urich [offensive line], and especially Tom Pagna [offensive backs] did . . . this was a management team that came in. They all knew each other and they made a lot of decisions as a group on moving guys around from the year before, breaking up the elephant backfield, for example, or lining Jack Snow up at end.

To me, Tom Pagna was the key guy on that staff when it came to my success, along with Ara of course. Tom spent a lot of time with me. Every time I see him I tell him how lucky I was to have him as a coach. He of course tells me how lucky he was to have me as a player.

Tom was very skilled at handling young college kids. Tom's style was very fundamental and reassuring. He wasn't a rah-rah cheerleader, but more of an execution guy. He really drilled the little things, like the importance of getting deep off the line and staying precise with your footwork. That was a particular point that Tom really worked with me on. He was a gently encouraging coach who was a fun guy but serious at the same time.

About four days before the first game in 1964, I was walking into a meeting with Ara and a couple players. Ara put his arm around me and said, "John, this Saturday I want you just to relax and play like you can. If you make a mistake, don't worry about it. I'm going with you." Those words were really, really important to me. Ara had enough experience handling young kids to tell me that, especially after the year before when I had been bounced around and just shattered.

We were starved for leadership in 1964. But keep in mind that we had the talent to win and that Joe Kuharich brought in talent. You look at that team in 1964, and there were about 20 guys who played in the pros. Maybe a lot of them didn't play more than a year or two, but that shows how much talent we had on that squad. We won most of our games that year going away. Other than Pittsburgh [a 17–15 victory] and USC [a 20–17 loss], we pretty much dominated.

I don't know if we surprised ourselves as much as we were just doing what we were told to do and listening to the instructions of a maestro. We weren't strategists; we were just young kids blocking and tackling. At the time you're just playing football—you're not thinking about grand strategy.

We treated the USC game just like another game. We knew we could move the ball on them and we did. We got them down 17–0 at halftime, but they came back in the second half and played like a hang-loose outfit. They had some players and a few things happened that got them believing they could win after catching a ball here and a ball there. Then all of a sudden they passed us up and nipped us, and we finished the season 9–1.

The pep rally when we returned home had a phenomenal turnout. To see that kind of appreciation was remarkable. It capped a very dramatic year for everyone. It was an emotional reception that really marked a return to prominence. It was unbelievably uplifting to see how excited the student body was for us to have such a strong team. Maybe because we got nipped in the last game, maybe they felt like they wanted to show us that we were *the* team.

Winning the Heisman Trophy that year—it's hard for a young kid to realize the power of that award. My parents were treated so well, flown in and shown the red carpet. I was excited that my folks were treated so well.

It was an unbelievable moment, and coming from being an unknown at the beginning of the year made it special. There's a lot of luck and a lot of fate in sports. There are a lot of guys who struggled, but I experienced a Cinderella story my senior year.

A Heisman Trophy winner in 1964, Huarte took home college football's top honor before picking up his first varsity letter. In leading Notre Dame to a 9–1 record during his senior season, Huarte set 12 Notre Dame passing records to become the sixth Irish Heisman winner. Huarte passed for 2,062 yards and 16 touchdowns in 1964, shattering the previous school mark by nearly 700 yards and tying the school standard for touchdown passes.

Huarte played professional football with the Boston Patriots, Philadelphia Eagles, Kansas City Chiefs, and Chicago Bears from 1966 to 1972.

BOB MEEKER

1963–1965

As a kid living in the heart of Ohio, we never went to an Ohio State game or even an Akron University game. My father took me to Notre Dame games. He built my interest up at an early age.

When I had a chance to go just about anywhere I wanted to coming out of high school in Akron, I took some trips, including one to Northwestern, where Ara Parseghian was coaching. I really liked [backfield coach] Tom Pagna when I took that trip and admired Ara so much. In those days you didn't sign a letter of intent with a school; you signed a letter of intent with a conference, so if I went to the Big 10 I had to play at Northwestern.

When I took my visit to Northwestern, Ara and his staff gave me a lot of attention. But when I visited Notre Dame, the entire weekend went by and I never saw Joe Kuharich until a half hour before I was scheduled to leave. I went in to meet this kind of sullen, really dry guy, and he goes over my grades, sighs, then says, "We have fourteen tackles we're looking at and we're going to take seven. You're one of the seven we want. If I'm in a position to offer, are you in a position to accept?" I immediately said yes and accepted, which made for about a 10-minute conversation just before I left the campus.

I was a guy who was deep into tradition and knew a lot about the history of Notre Dame. I watched Notre Dame break Oklahoma's winning streak and was well aware of the great players and teams under Frank Leahy. I wasn't bothered by Joe Kuharich or the current team's record. I picked the institution and the academics, not the coach. My high school was the Fighting Irish, so I'd always been aware of Notre Dame. We even had an All-American center go to Notre Dame before me in the fifties, Art Hunter.

The players who were coming to Notre Dame during my time were so talented that every guy seemed like he was all-state or an All-American, yet our sophomore year [1963], we were 2–7 under Hugh Devore. The squad had good athletes and good players. We just didn't know how to win.

Then to look back at some of the practices we went through, comparing Joe Kuharich to Ara Parseghian, Joe would have these five-hour scrimmages with 22 guys on the field and 80 guys on the sidelines. Then Parseghian comes in and every guy is moving for every second of two hours. It made for such a contrast in organization. Ara could have been the president of General Motors or could have been a great general. He was just totally organized in every aspect.

When I arrived in the fall of 1962 we reported to the practice fields, where some stands were roped off so the freshmen and their parents could watch a varsity scrimmage. My mother and father were sitting on either side of me watching the offensive team punt the ball as one of the tackles ran down the field trying to make a tackle. The return man called for a fair catch at the last second, so the tackle stopped short of hitting him and went down screaming in pain.

Here comes Kuharich yelling, "Get up, get up! You're not hurt! Get up!" This guy was not getting up and ended up with a cast from ankle to thigh. I think he fractured his leg, tore his ACL, and never played again. My mother got one look at this and was ready to head east with me in the car.

One of the tough things was to go home and face the music when you're not playing as a sophomore and your team isn't winning. My first year with Ara, I led the team with almost 300 minutes. There were a lot of guys who weren't starting or weren't in the right position in 1963 and then burst onto the scene the next year.

The year under Hugh Devore was just a crazy season. He brought Leon Hart back to work with the ends during summer ball. Every night Leon would keep one of the ends out, and about a half hour later, the door would pop open and in would walk Leon with a mean look on his face and spit running down his mouth. About 20 minutes later in comes the end Leon had out there, with his jersey ripped because he just got the hell beat out of him.

When I first heard that Ara was taking over I was traveling back home for Christmas and a radio report came on. I was thrilled that Ara and Tom Pagna were coming. It brought such great hope for all of us.

My first start came in the spring of my sophomore year in the old-timers' game. I played over Hart. The two middle linebackers were Myron Pottios and Nick Buoniconti. That was my initiation. To be around those people, it made you do your best. You had to do that much just to survive. Those games were such a history lesson for me, and I enjoyed all the stories, from the Four Horsemen to the Seven Rocks of Granite and all those players.

Once the 1964 season started with a guy like John Huarte at quarterback, I think if you asked most guys they thought Tom Longo should have been the quarterback because he was such a great athlete. But Ara saw some magic in Huarte, who of course went on to win the Heisman Trophy.

Then there's the story of Jack Snow, who went from a 230-pound running back to an All-American wide receiver and had a wonderful senior year. Ara had a way of finding talent in guys across the board, plus developing a lot of young guys who helped out in a big way on that 1964 team.

As much as I'll remember that 1964 season as one where guys came off the depth chart to play huge roles, the year, to me, was about how strongly we believed in Ara Parseghian. It was a total commitment to him.

When we went out to Los Angeles for the USC game at 9–0, we knew that we could beat them. We had beaten them the year before with a much lesser team, so there was no lack of confidence. *Life* magazine was doing a major cover story on us, a piece that ultimately didn't run on the cover, but there was still a lot of excitement about that. We stopped at Arizona State on the way to get acclimated to the weather before moving on to Los Angeles. The night before the game we watched the first screening of *Goldfinger.*

We broke out to a 17–0 lead by halftime before USC closed the gap to 17–7 by the start of the fourth quarter. We drove down to the six-inch line, bringing up second down with the ball on the left hash. We called for an off-tackle play to the left side, where I was lined up. The play called for me to post block. That meant I'd stop the penetration of the defensive tackle, our tight end would wipe him out, and then our fullback would follow into the hole.

As I stepped to the line, the Southern California defense was in a veer, and the guy over me stepped away and I missed him totally. As I stepped and missed, I fell to the ground. I can't remember who blocked him, but our fullback scored anyway. That touchdown should have iced the game. But there was a flag.

Known for a controversial holding call against USC in 1964, tackle Bob Meeker helped lead the Irish to a No. 2 ranking in total offense and a No. 3 mark in scoring offense in 1964.

I've looked at this film 50 times because I wanted to know what really happened. On tape you can see before the play that the field judge, whose job is to watch the wide receivers and defensive backs, had a hand on his flag. Remember that I'm the left tackle on the left hash, so there's no way that field judge should be watching me—ever!

The USC defensive back came up and smacked Jack Snow right in the mouth, and we thought the flag was for unnecessary roughness. But that field judge comes running up to the referee and tells him that No. 75 made the hold. Not only didn't I hold anyone, I didn't have any contact with a player. When *Life* magazine ran its story it had a picture of me crying on the bench, noting that it appeared I didn't have any contact with anyone on the play. That call moved us back and we didn't score.

There were two other plays in that game that helped make the difference. One was when the guard next to me, John Atamian, was called for a hold on a punt, and the difference in field position between where the referees spotted the ball and where the hold was amounted to about 40 yards.

Then the last play when USC scored to take the lead, there were three players in motion and one of their receivers pushed off. Those three calls were really crucial, but the one that's always talked about was the holding penalty called on me.

107

On my wall I have a letter from Ara in which he writes, "You were the victim of the worst call in the history of college football." When we had a get-together in 1994, our line coach, Doc Urich, took the microphone at one point and made sure everyone knew that Bob Meeker was not holding.

There was a guy from my high school who was a longtime field judge in the NFL named Fritz Graff. He was at the game because he was in town to do the Rams game the next day. The first call I got when I got back to the hotel was from Fritz, telling me that it was such crap that a field judge would ever make that call. I felt badly that I was involved in this play at all, but I knew and my teammates knew that I was the victim of a classic case of home cooking.

The next year was a great year too after we opened up by beating California and then moved up to No. 1 heading into Purdue. That game went back and forth with the lead changing hands. We were up 21–18 and Purdue was facing fourth-and-11 on its own 9. Bob Griese threw a pass out in the flat that moved the ball up to the 35. Then Griese threw a bomb down to the 5 before they eventually scored.

That game made for a long bus ride back to South Bend. We won our next six before losing to Michigan State in South Bend, 12–3, after throwing interceptions twice in their end zone. Bill Zloch was our quarterback and a fine runner, but we didn't have much success in the passing game.

When USC came to Notre Dame for our revenge game earlier that season I noticed on tape during the week that one of the Trojans' defensive linemen changed his feet when he was veering to the inside or the outside. So when Zloch would come to the line of scrimmage he could call an audible, depending on which way the USC line was going. It was the easiest block in the world for me to make because I just had to drive him with his momentum. We scored all four of our touchdowns in that hole because we knew what was coming. All four of our backs outgained Mike Garrett in that game, even though he went on to win the Heisman Trophy. That fact was a source of pride for our line.

People don't seem to remember that the 1965 team came really close to winning another national championship. That Purdue game was one of the only times when a John Ray defense let down. Against Michigan State, it could have gone the other way with those interceptions in the end zone. If we had gone down to Miami at 9–0, I feel that game would have been a lot different.

It felt great to leave the program at a high point. This isn't a knock on Kuharich, but it's a great feeling when you feel the way we did about our coaches. We had tremendous respect for Ara and his staff.

108

A two-year starter at left offensive tackle, Bob Meeker helped lead Notre Dame on a national title run in 1964 before a perfect campaign was spoiled by a loss to Southern California in the final game of the regular season.

Meeker, a 6'2", 235-pounder from Akron, Ohio, is best known for a controversial holding penalty at USC that prevented the Irish from extending their 17–0 lead against the Trojans, who rallied for a 20–17 come-from-behind victory.

Yet Meeker was part of an offensive front that helped lead the Irish to a No. 2 ranking in total offense and No. 3 mark in scoring offense in 1964, as well as the No. 9 scoring offense in 1965.

PHIL SHERIDAN

1963–1965

I WAS INTO NOTRE DAME PROBABLY BEFORE a lot of other people were because my father went there and played football [1939–1940] with Johnny Kelly, who was from our hometown [Rutherford, New Jersey] and captain of the 1939 team. I was indoctrinated into Notre Dame football as a kid listening to the radio broadcasts of games from Franklin Field in Philadelphia. I was a really rabid Notre Dame fan because my family was made up of Notre Dame people.

Another aspect that led me to Notre Dame was the fact that Hugh Devore was the freshman coach and a New Jersey native. He had a very successful playing and coaching career that started in New Jersey, and he kept those roots and connections alive. He was the main recruiter in my area, and not coincidentally we had quite a few people at Notre Dame in the early sixties who were from the New Jersey area. Tom Longo was from the next town over from Rutherford, and I knew him because we went to Bordentown Military Institute, a local prep school. There's a whole list of guys who went to Notre Dame out of Bordentown. On the 1964 team I think there were four starters, two on offense and two on defense: John Atamian, myself, Tommy Longo, and Paul Costa. Having all those local guys come to Notre Dame made the transition much more comfortable.

Joining the team as a freshman was very, very difficult. You were the fodder for the varsity under Joe Kuharich, who had very long practice sessions. Every position went six or seven people deep, and you were left wondering how you were going to get a break or how a coach was going to notice you.

My father kept me persevering more than anything. You make those phone calls home to talk about how things aren't working, how you're the fifth-team end, and how you don't see any daylight. My father, who didn't letter until his senior year, had the experience to tell me to stick with it because somebody was going to get hurt, somebody was going to flunk out, and somebody was going to get in trouble with the coach. He told me I just had to hang with it.

When Hugh Devore took over as interim coach in 1963, he walked into a situation where the coaching staff had been decimated because of the time frame of Joe Kuharich's leaving. There was no real immediate action by the school to hire a coach, and Hugh had trouble finding assistants. When spring practice started that year Hugh called in all his cards, talking to players he had played with and known throughout his career.

Working with the end position were Pete Pihos from the Philadelphia Eagles and Leon Hart. Leon was one of the biggest guys I had ever seen at 6'4" and a legitimate 285 pounds. In those days that's saying something. I remember watching him playing with the Lions on Thanksgiving Day as an all-pro end that had won the Heisman Trophy. When the Lions would get down to the 1-yard line, they'd put him in the backfield and run the Refrigerator Perry play—that all started with Leon Hart.

As a coach, Leon would dress in football spikes, football pants with no padding, and a T-shirt, then take the ends out and have live contact with us. He'd set you up in your stance, he'd play the defensive guy, and you had to block him. It was like playing with a toy for him because he was so strong and had huge hands. He was a tough coach, probably the sternest coach that we had in my whole career. He was also a guy who didn't smile a lot.

Like everything in life, it was timing that helped my career get going. When Ara Parseghian came in, I had two years left in my career. He looked at me and knew there was time to turn me into something. If I was a senior in 1964 maybe I wouldn't have played while he was changing everybody's position and instituting the platoon system. Without as many guys going two ways, it created opportunities for people because the coaching staff was looking for 22 players, not just 11. Again, going back to knowing guys from prep school and spending a year away from home before Notre Dame, my experience helped me through the coaching transition.

Ara's arrival was like flipping a switch. He had his rules, but he didn't make a big deal out of them. Ara told us that if we didn't live by his rules, we'd be gone. He made a couple examples out of guys who tested him. That let you know that Ara meant business.

He was so organized. For example, we might spend exactly 22 minutes on the offensive line, then we'd run to a new drill with everything done by whistle. Before, the ends would be down at one end of the field and the coach would be doing a demonstration while everyone else took a knee. Ara believed in entire units working through drills as a group with everyone moving. Our practice time went from three and a half hours to an hour and a half. Everybody knew you'd be on the field at a certain time and off the field at a certain time.

Ara not only organized the program, he upgraded it too. The first thing he said was we were going to get lighter shoulder pads, new pants, and new shoes. Everything was geared to make the uniform lighter with an emphasis on speed. Ara made a big deal out of the shoulder pads because the old ones must have weighed 12 pounds and you wanted to get them off after a half hour of practice.

That first game against Wisconsin was fantastic. We went up there knowing that they were a good team from the Big 10, but honestly it wasn't that hard of a win. We won, 31–7, and it was just like being in practice, probably easier. Everything seemed to work. Teams hadn't seen us, nobody knew [receiver] Jack Snow or [quarterback] John Huarte. We were so thoroughly prepared that it wasn't a difficult game. The prior year it seemed like we were in every game but would lose by less than a touchdown. We'd been giving it our all, but we didn't have the confidence or ability to get the job done. That all changed with Ara's preparation.

Games turned into no big deal because we knew things would work. If things didn't work in the first quarter, we'd change it up and things would work in the second. We could run the ball successfully with our backs and it opened up the passing game off play-action. There was never a lack of talent on our teams; it was just a question of finding out where to play these guys and giving them confidence that they could win. We had the same players from 1963; we just got some confidence.

We got to the point in 1964 where we were 7–0 and the bowls started looking around for teams. We had a rule where we didn't go to bowls because of travel and exams, but Ara indicated that he might be able to talk to Father Hesburgh and present a good argument that a bowl game would be good for the university, not just the football program. Before he did that, he wanted

111

112

Phil Sheridan was a two-year starter at end and captain of Notre Dame's 7–2–1 squad in 1965.

our input. We organized a vote after a meeting and Ara told us that before the plan could fly, he wanted to know if we'd be interested in going.

From our perspective a bowl game meant we had to stay at school and practice through our vacation, and we didn't have an indoor facility. We'd practice with baggies on our feet to keep the snow out, and we'd be wearing three sweatshirts. We felt so confident that we'd be 10–0 at the end of the year and No. 1 that we voted against the bowl. It wasn't worth the extra time to us as players, practicing through our break and coming away with a watch or whatever the bowls gave you.

I didn't think I had much of a chance to be voted captain in 1965 because there were more well-known seniors on the team. It's not something you campaign for. I was particularly thrilled because it goes back to the history I had with Johnny Kelly and his friendship with my father. I don't think there have been too many Notre Dame captains that came out of the same town.

Being captain was a great responsibility, a great honor, and a great privilege. My dad flew to every game during my senior year. I'm the oldest of eight, and many of my brothers and sisters came to the games, some driving from New Jersey. Everybody came to the Miami game at the end of 1965. I know my father enjoyed watching my career, and that made me feel good.

113

As captain your role on the team changes on a day-to-day basis. There was no room to slack off because you knew everybody was looking at you as the example. You can't take a day off in the preseason routine when you're running around the stadium. Everybody's eyes seem to be on you. There was a tremendous responsibility not only to the players but to the coaches too.

We went into 1965 with the idea of showing people that Notre Dame was truly back in the national picture. We were hurt in several positions because we didn't have the explosiveness to score points that we had the year before. When you lose a Heisman Trophy winner [Huarte] and you lose Snow, it's hard to fill those voids. On top of that, we also lost the element of surprise because people took us seriously. That made the schedule even more difficult.

Look at our two losses from 1965 and they stand out as unbelievable games. The Purdue game had Bob Griese putting together an 80-yard drive in the final minutes, and we lost, 25–21. Michigan State probably had its most talented team ever. I think that 1965 team was actually better than the 1966 squad. Running back Clinton Jones was a hell of a runner and scored the touchdown that beat us on kind of a controversial call when he stuck the ball over the goal line in the pile. Michigan State was such a physical team, when you look at guys like Bubba Smith. On first and second downs Michigan State would play him at defensive tackle to stuff up the middle. When the Spartans got you in passing situations, they'd line him up on the outside and he was a hell of a pass rusher at 6'8", 290 pounds. Throw in Gene Washington at wide receiver and George Webster at linebacker, and their talent level was unbelievable.

It was really nice to leave the program on the upswing because it felt like part of a rejuvenation. You knew things were only going to get better for Notre Dame because of Ara. It was gratifying to know that you were part of a revitalization because the football program's rise made the whole campus more alive. Everything was better, even going to class.

Ara's organizational skills were what made him such a success in my mind. He could have been successful in whatever avenue of life he wanted to get into. Put his organization with his ability to gain the respect of the people around him, whether players or assistant coaches, and you really had something. Ara had a knack for obtaining the respect of everybody around him, and that made you want to work hard for him. We weren't used to seeing assistants up to all hours working like that staff did. You knew he was going to be successful. If you have a program that's so well organized and everything is so well timed, it gives you the feeling things are going to happen. Then when you add in hard work, the bottom line is going to be success.

114

Phil Sheridan, a 6'4", 215-pound right end from Rutherford, New Jersey, followed in the footsteps of his father, Phil Sr., who played at Notre Dame during the Elmer Layden years in the late thirties and early forties.

The younger Sheridan played for the Irish during the early years of the Ara Parseghian regime, when only one player per season served as captain. Jim Carroll was Parseghian's first Notre Dame captain, followed by Sheridan in 1965, Jim Lynch in 1966, and Rocky Bleier in 1967. The Irish had multiple captains beginning in 1968 until Rodney Culver was the lone captain in 1991.

Sheridan was a two-year starter, beginning in his junior year when the Irish finished 9–1 and made what many considered an improbable run for the national title. Sheridan then captained the 1965 team that finished 7–2–1.

Sheridan was a third-round draft pick of the Atlanta Falcons in 1966.

PETE DURANKO

1963–1966

I FIRST BECAME AWARE OF NOTRE DAME when I was in the sixth grade. One of the priests gave out report cards and told me that I'd end up going there. He'd tell me that every time I got a report card from sixth through eighth grade. When he started mentioning Notre Dame I didn't know what it was, so I started listening to games on the radio, all the way back to the teams with Ralph Guglielmi. The first time I saw the movie *Knute Rockne: All-American*, it got me really excited.

When I started playing football in eighth grade I never thought I'd be able to go to Notre Dame. But as I started to gain a little more respect, my high school started pushing Notre Dame, as did Leroy Leslie, who was an All-American basketball player during the fifties, and the high school basketball coach.

Notre Dame was my number one choice, but I wanted to look at Pittsburgh and Kentucky. In the end, tradition was so big for me that it helped keep Notre Dame at the top, even though the Irish were coming off a 5–5 season. I knew things could turn around quickly because when my high school coach arrived we had won only two games before getting pointed in the right direction.

During my freshman year all we did was practice. We did what we had to do, which meant playing the guys on Monday who didn't play that weekend. Those were some real battles because those guys were always mad that they didn't play, and they weren't going to let the freshmen beat them. It's amazing what motivation can do for you. When you put a piece of meat

115

in front of someone they'll go after it. During my freshman year, we were the meat.

Making the first team as a fullback during the spring of my freshman year was one of the top thrills of my life. I remember waiting in the tunnel before the game and feeling nervous as hell. I was wearing No. 32, a jersey the equipment manager gave me because I was a Pennsylvania guy. I remember John Lujack wearing that number, which made me proud to wear it. We played the old-timers, who weren't in bad shape, but they weren't in good shape either. In the back of their minds they thought they were tough, and I was hearing Lujack, Lattner, Guglielmi, George Izo, Hornung, and Hart over the loudspeaker, names I'd heard on the radio. My back got so chilled that I had goose bumps coming out of my head. I thought I was going to pass out!

I scored two touchdowns in the game and earned a little bit of respect. The story that I heard was that Lattner heard people talking about me during the game and he wanted to knock the hell out of me. So one play a hole opened up and he saw me coming. He put his head down to tackle me and the next thing he knew, he was on the bench looking up at the sky. I thought, "Oh my God, I knocked out a Heisman Trophy winner!"

116

That fall I stuck at fullback during Hugh Devore's one season. That squad had too many assistants who wanted to be head coach, making everything disorganized. Hugh called in old Heisman Trophy winners and ex-players to show us how to play. Leon Hart showed up and beat the hell out of the linemen.

We won a couple of games in 1963 and came close against some top teams. We knew we had some talent, but we just didn't have the organization to get us over the top. We used five different backfields and four different quarterbacks. It was so frustrating to see we had talent but weren't able to turn it into something on the field. We called that time "the Winter of Discontent," winning two games and having John Kennedy die. I remember practicing for the Iowa game and Devore telling us to say a prayer for the president.

We really had to hang in there during the off-season until Ara Parseghian came in and changed everything. When I heard him talk I knew we had something. Right away Ara cut out drinking and smoking and organized the entire program.

The first week of spring we were playing all sorts of different positions. I moved from fullback to linebacker at first. It was amazing how organized Ara was with everything planned to the minute, like we were in the Marine Corps.

Ara put us through a lot of mental gymnastics, running us from one end of the field to another for drills and working us into shape. The coaches took their time between stations, but we had to beat them there. We would have done whatever Ara told us because we wanted so badly for something good to happen, and it did from the start against Wisconsin in 1964.

That first game I worked as a second-team linebacker with Jim Carroll, and luckily, as it turned out, I hurt my wrist. Ara decided to hold me out for the rest of the season. For me that was devastating, but I agreed to do whatever he said. I probably could have come back that season because it was just a hairline fracture. At the time my friends Bob Meeker and Phil Sheridan were still playing and going to every road game. I just got to practice. Watching the team win made that a tough year for me because I wasn't really a part of the team. I went to the Grotto every day hoping something good would come from my injury, and of course it did, two years later in 1966 when I was allowed to play in my fifth year.

The 1965 team was a good one too. Nothing against Bill Zloch, but he wasn't the quarterback that John Huarte was. Losing to Purdue in the last minute [25–21] when Bob Griese went crazy and then losing to a Michigan State team [12–3] with a great defense was difficult.

117

Even though we didn't have a great passing game, that was a pretty good team. The Miami game at the end of the year [0–0] was just a fluke in my mind because it was hard to get into the game right after Michigan State. If we had been undefeated heading into Miami, we would have beaten the hell out of them. We were disappointed at 7–2–1, but the program was still in good shape heading into 1966, even though we didn't have a quarterback. We knew Ara had his own ideas.

Right from the spring you could see that the 1966 team had great camaraderie and didn't have one star. But Ara kept us in a one-game-at-a-time mentality. After that Purdue game [a 26–14 victory] we started rolling.

George Goeddeke was the comedy leader of the offense. I was the comedy leader of the defense. Jim Lynch was our cerebral captain. We had a lot of fun during that season, but only because we were disciplined. You knew that Ara was always watching you from the tower. It was like God up there watching down.

That was such a disciplined team, and people noted that during the Michigan State game. Even in the second half of the hardest-hitting game of my life, the defensive linemen were down on their knees and the defensive backs had their hands behind them. It looked like the marines in terms of a disciplined approach to every play. We came out of the huddle and set ourselves the same way every time so we never showed any sign of fatigue. That discipline ran from start to finish that season, and it was a huge part of winning the national championship.

We had fun too, and that extended to the coaches. In practice [defensive coordinator] John Ray would always stand in the middle of the scrimmages and [offensive line coach] Jerry Wampfler would tell the offensive linemen to run right at him. One day coach Ray told me to make a run at Wampfler

Pete Duranko benefited from the arrival of head coach Ara Parseghian, who converted him into a defensive lineman who later became an 11-year NFL performer.

and swipe him. I didn't want to, but Ray said I had to, otherwise I'd have to run laps.

Wampfler knew I was running straight at him, so he stepped in front of Ara. I had no choice but to pull up. Ara knew we were playing games in practice and that let us release some of the tension of staying undefeated.

One of the most important points about the 1966 team was our sense of tradition as players. It was one of the things that drew me to Notre Dame in the first place, and I think it was important to a lot of players on that team. There's always going to be that Notre Dame mystique during good times and bad times, and it's more important than anything that I know of.

There's tradition at schools like Michigan and Miami, but there's something special about Notre Dame. I think players from my era understood that. When you understand tradition, you understand what it means to fight for it. We wanted to make the players who played at Notre Dame before us proud. That's an important part of Fighting Irish football.

119

Pete Duranko from Johnstown, Pennsylvania, enrolled at Notre Dame as a fullback before Ara Parseghian moved him to linebacker and ultimately defensive tackle. It was a move that would help propel the Irish to a national title and Duranko to a successful professional career.

The 6'2", 235-pounder started along the defensive line as a fifth-year senior for the 1966 national champions. Joining him on the line were steady Tom Rhoads and standouts Alan Page (right end) and Kevin Hardy (right tackle).

Duranko then parlayed his position move into an AFL/NFL career from 1967 to 1974 with the Denver Broncos.

KEVIN HARDY

1964–1967

I GREW UP LISTENING TO NOTRE DAME FOOTBALL and watching the reruns on Sunday, but I never played football in high school, so the Notre Dame football program wasn't what drew me to South Bend.

I was never recruited by Notre Dame and was set to go to Stanford to play basketball and baseball, but my mother and my high school principal somehow got in touch with someone in the program and asked if they'd like a 6'5", 270-pound kid who was an All-American basketball and baseball player. My mother pushed Notre Dame, and around April I got a call from the football staff to come out and visit South Bend.

In a lot of ways it didn't make any difference to me where I went to school. Because my mother was pushing Notre Dame, that's what I decided to do. It wasn't that tough a sell for a lifelong Catholic who had nuns pulling for him.

My first memory of Notre Dame football is clear: Alan Page. I had never been around anyone that big before. I might have been even bigger than he was, but you don't look at yourself like that. When I walked into the room with Page, I didn't know what I was getting into. Of course all these other guys were probably looking at me thinking about how I was one big SOB.

I've tried to put into words what my feeling was trying to learn how to play football at Notre Dame, and I don't know exactly how I felt about it all. I just put my head down and got to work. During some of the first practices the coaches asked me what position I played, and I just went over with offensive guards and started running with them. Eventually I was weeded over to defensive tackle where I was better suited.

The entire first year was a blur in the sense that I never thought during practices: I reacted. Defensive linemen don't have to be rocket scientists.

The problems didn't start until my sophomore year during training camp because I had never gone through a training camp before. I didn't mind the physical part of football, even though it was tougher than anything I had ever done. But the mental part of coaches yelling at me was unique. My mentality was just not a football player's mentality at that stage.

I was a star in high school and nobody ever had to yell at me. I just did everything naturally. About a week into training camp my sophomore year I was threatening to transfer to Stanford to go play basketball. I had already made the call to the coach there.

[Assistant coach] Brian Boulac found out about my intentions and came in to talk me out of it. He was only a few years older than me and could identify with what I was going through, and he convinced me to stay. I wasn't a prima donna; I just didn't need to be called names. If coaches wanted to question my manhood, my attitude was, "Come get me!" Once I figured out that's just how football coaches were, it was never a problem again. I really wasn't being treated any differently from anyone else.

By the time we got out of camp I was feeling better about my position on the team and managed to play the fourth quarter in the 1964 opener against Wisconsin [a 31–7 victory], then the second half a week later against Purdue [a 34–15 victory]. After that, I started the rest of the way.

It was an all-sophomore defensive line, and at that point we figured it was natural that we started. Ara was smart enough to know that we were just about as good as some of the older guys and we'd be around for three more years. I don't know how well that set with some of the older guys, but it worked for us up front. [Editor's note: listed behind Hardy on the depth chart in 1964 was future Notre Dame athletic director Michael Wadsworth.]

Playing three sports is something I could never do again. I had an understanding with the coaches that as long as I kept up with all my class work and didn't try to play two sports at once, they would allow it. Playing baseball got me out of spring football, other than during my freshman year. The coaches weren't thrilled about it, but we had an understanding that that's what I wanted to do. They would have loved to have had me concentrate on one sport, but the decision was mine as long as I maintained grades.

Two of my four years at Notre Dame I roomed with a guy who had my exact same schedule, and he was a good note taker. It wasn't that easy, and I

121

had to carry books on trips. I probably didn't lead a normal college life because I was busy all the time.

Going into 1965 we had the same personnel except for [quarterback] John Huarte and [receiver] Jack Snow, and as it turned out those were pretty big losses for the program. I got hurt that season when a couple disks ruptured in my back, and my expectations were lowered quickly after playing just one half of the first game.

Standing on the sidelines was difficult because after my surgery I felt fine and started playing basketball again. But then the football coaches told me that if I played basketball, I'd lose a year of eligibility for football. The basketball coach, Johnny Dee, agreed that it would be a good career move on my part to give up basketball.

By the time 1966 rolled around I was ready to go. We knew we were going to be really good with my class coming back for its senior year. That defense had a ton of talent, and the offensive line had been there for two years. It's incredible how much talent was on that team. But no one could have expected the effect that [quarterback] Terry Hanratty and [receiver] Jim Seymour would have. We basically had the same team as 1965, but we were able to throw the ball.

The old cliché is that you never look ahead, but a couple of weeks before the 10-10 tie against Michigan State, we knew what was coming. We were so good that it was assumed we would be No. 1. There was no reason to think we'd be anything but No. 1. There wasn't the kind of hype that would make you think the game was the "Game of the Century." We were just reading the *South Bend Tribune*, which always had stories about half the opposing players who wanted to come to Notre Dame and couldn't, so they really wanted to beat us. That happened in every game.

The stadium was so packed in East Lansing that we couldn't even sit on the bench. There were people all around us. There must have been ten thousand sideline passes. If you were a running back headed out of bounds, you weren't going to hit the ground because you were going to land on three bodies.

I had a friend come out for the Duke game the weekend before, and he loved the experience, so I gave him one of my tickets and he hitchhiked up to East Lansing. He wound up watching the game on the field standing next to me. Everybody was so wrapped up in the game that I doubt any usher noticed him climbing over the railings to get down on the field.

Kevin Hardy didn't play football in high school, but he grew into a powerful defensive tackle, where he helped form one of Notre Dame's all-time great lines in 1966.

I don't think anybody on the defense was all that concerned with the outcome even after Hanratty went down and [running back] Nick Eddy and [center] George Goeddeke were out too. We never thought about losing, and it wasn't an issue on the sidelines.

Looking back at that game, I really thought we should have won it, and the decision that sticks with me wasn't sitting on the ball at the end. It was after Tom Schoen's interception that he took it down to the 15. We tried to run a sweep and lost eight yards. We weren't a real sweep team anyway, and Eddy was hurt. That ended up pushing the field goal try back to 42 yards, and [Joe Azzaro's attempt] just missed. I think the game could have been won there if we had run the ball up the middle instead of trying to call a sweep.

We beat some good teams that season and shut out a lot of people. It never surprised me that we blew out USC [51–0] the very next week. The surprise of the season to me was that we didn't score more against Michigan State. With Hanratty and Eddy out, there were physical reasons for us not scoring more, but I really believe we should have won that game. And yet we were still the national champions and deserved to be.

My fifth year [8–2 in 1967] was hard. I really didn't know many of the guys below me because you tended to bond with the guys in your class, and the 1966 team was senior dominated to begin with. We lost the defensive line and some of the backups, so there wasn't much left.

When I got hurt in the first game, that set a negative tone for the year for me. Socially it was tougher for me than physically. On the field I could concentrate on the task at hand, but off the field, I don't want to say I was lonely, but I felt disenfranchised. I was almost an outsider as a fifth-year senior, something I found to be true in basketball and baseball too.

Was it the right decision to stay for the fifth year? I would have been $30,000 richer if I had left. It was kind of a blind decision for me. If I had stayed healthy and I had done what I could do and the team had done what it could do, 1967 probably would have been a great year. But when Purdue set up a play to take me out of the game, [running back] Leroy Keyes came up from behind and clipped me. I played with guys later in the pros from Purdue, and they finally admitted to me that they worked on that play to get me out of the game. I knew it right away.

I played six years of pro ball wanting to get a shot at Keyes. What he did was totally unconscionable. The Big 10 wrote Ara a letter apologizing for not throwing a flag on the play. I told their coach that if he ever coached in the pros, he had better be on his toes.

I missed four games in 1967, and it put a damper on the whole year. I was already disenfranchised, and being injured made it even more so. I just went through the motions.

No matter how it ended, I wouldn't trade my Notre Dame experience for anything. I wish I had gotten more out of college than I did in terms of a social life, but I don't ever regret my decision to go to Notre Dame. I'm still close with my teammates, and we get together every year. We're still a close group and I wouldn't trade that for the world.

If the term "multifaceted athlete" applies to anyone in the history of Notre Dame sports, it's 6'5", 270-pound Oakland, California, native Kevin Hardy.

A football, basketball, and baseball player at Notre Dame, Hardy excelled in all three sports. He was a first-team AP and UPI All-American football player in 1967. He was part of the top eight players on John Dee's 15–12 basketball team in 1964–1965. And he was a career .330 hitter for Jake Kline's baseball squad.

As a member of Ara Parseghian's football team, Hardy teamed up with defensive linemen Alan Page, Pete Duranko, and Tom Rhoads in 1966 to form one of Notre Dame's all-time best fronts, helping lead the Irish to a No. 2 ranking in scoring defense and a No. 4 ranking against the run.

Hardy played with the San Francisco 49ers, Green Bay Packers, and San Diego Chargers from 1968 to 1972.

125

JOE AZZARO

1964–1967

I WAS A ONE-YEAR ATHLETE IN HIGH SCHOOL because as a freshman I was in an automobile accident and suffered ligament damage in both ankles. I had a tough time getting around from then on, so I decided to take up swimming just as a way to compete and strengthen my ankles. I got to a point where I thought I could give football a shot during my senior year.

I was lucky enough to have a high school coach who had been with the Steelers and saw me kicking the ball. After that he took me aside and started mentoring me. After one two-a-day practice the coaching staff pulled everyone aside who wanted to try out as a kicker, and that was the end of my career as an offensive lineman right there. I wound up having a successful year kicking the ball and drew attention from more than a handful of schools. But for me, it was always a love affair with Notre Dame.

The first game I ever saw was Notre Dame against Pittsburgh with Ralph Guglielmi. Every time Notre Dame would come to town, I was down at Pitt Stadium looking for the players. Some of my first memories were watching Notre Dame on television when I was five years old.

When Notre Dame showed some interest I wound up turning down more than 20 other schools just to get a shot in South Bend. Notre Dame had already given an offer to Jim Ryan, who was a running back/kicker, and there wasn't a need to take on two kickers, which I understood. I was confident enough in myself to give Notre Dame a shot, and things worked out.

Our freshman class in 1963 was an interesting one in that we had a lot of talent. Of course when you scrimmage the varsity on the first day of practice that makes for a real eye-opener. I think they stuck me in at defensive back in those types of drills, but I got through it. I knew I had what it took to compete, so I was never discouraged that fall or in the spring when Ara Parseghian arrived.

During fall camp in 1964 was when I really started to blossom. Ara watched me for several weeks and finally gave me a shot in the UCLA game to kick off a couple of times. My dad was listening on the radio, and when he heard how deep the kickoffs were going, he said he knew it was me. I don't think the announcers knew who I was.

Not many people get to do what they want to do in life, and Ara really made me earn those moments. He timed the hang times of my kickoffs with a stopwatch for three weeks before he let me kick one off in a game. My first kick went nine yards deep in the end zone, and I was in good shape from there.

I dealt with Ara more than any other coach. Every day he'd bet me milk-shakes in practice when he'd kick alongside me, but he never paid off. It took him a long time to gain trust in me, but once I had that, there wasn't much that could take it away. He'd work with me every day, throwing stuff at my feet, telling the snapper to snap it poorly, and trying to get me off my game. He wanted to make sure I could handle the pressure, and that's something he tried to do with everybody.

I was injured in the Navy game in 1964 when I got speared on the top of my thigh and tore my right quadriceps muscle. I tried to gut it out for a couple more weeks because, like most college kids, I thought I was indestructible. But my muscle kept tearing and tearing and tearing.

The morning of the Michigan State game that year I got out of bed and couldn't walk. The coaches didn't know anything about it because I was on a little bit of a roll and didn't want to sit down. But that injury sidelined me for the rest of the year, and then I pulled it again in fall camp of 1965. I tried to start kicking left-footed, but finally I broke down and had surgery halfway through the year.

When you're injured there's not much you can do about it. In those days there wasn't much in the way of rehab, except for maybe one leg machine in the weight room. You just had to wait, but at the same time you wanted to push it, and that's where I'd get into trouble.

Before the 1966 season started we all knew how good of a team we were going to have. That team was an example of everything coming together. We had a great class and the group behind us was very solid too. All we lacked was a quarterback. When Terry Hanratty and Coley O'Brien came in and started throwing the ball to Jim Seymour, who was something special, and Curt Heneghan, who was pretty darn good too until he got hurt, we were able to get it all together.

We never had any question about whether or not we were going to win; it was just a matter of by how much. I think that was everybody's attitude, and it wasn't that we were cocky; we just had a pretty good team. That defense was so good that I don't know that I've seen one on that level since. And on offense, even though we had the great breakaway passing game, the running backs always seemed to come out on the other side of the pile. They weren't flashy, but they just beat you with Larry Conjar, Rocky Bleier, and Nick Eddy. That group was about as good as it got. There was never any doubt that everyone was going to do his job. Everybody knew how good everybody else was on that team, so you knew people were going to make plays.

Even during the Michigan State game there was never any doubt that we were going to win. That game was easily one of the coldest days that I've ever played football in.

Before the game I was practicing kicks and [Michigan State head coach] Duffy Daugherty came up to me and started talking, but I didn't know who he was. Duffy was from my neck of the woods and started talking about Western Pennsylvania. Trying to keep my mind on my business, I just didn't realize it was Duffy until a half hour later when I saw him standing on the sidelines.

That stadium was so packed that there was no room on the sidelines. I don't know how all those people got in, but they were down on the field, which made for a lot of disorganization. We had fans sitting on our bench.

I don't remember much about the 28-yard field goal that I made to tie the game at 10–10. What stands out to me is the one that I missed from 42 yards. It didn't seem like a big deal at the time because there was time left in the game. That kick couldn't have gone more than a couple of inches wide right, and the wind even took it a little bit at the end. I thought it was going to go right down the middle, but then it started veering a little bit at the end and just missed. There's no question that if we hadn't lost eight yards on that drive before the field-goal try, that kick would have been good. I still felt that we'd get a shot to kick another one, but that never happened.

Joe Azzaro's 28-yard field goal put the Irish on the board in the famous 10–10 tie against Michigan State in 1966.

When that game was over you looked around and wondered when you were going to play the rest of the game. Somebody had to win, right? There was a sense of emptiness, which I'm sure the Michigan State players were feeling too.

That said, I think Ara made all the right decisions in the end. If one of us had won that game instead of it being a tie, I wonder how much people would still be talking about it. Michigan State had a team of great athletes and deserved a lot of recognition. It would have been a shame if someone had lost that game, so maybe it's better that no one did.

There was no emotional letdown that next week at Southern California. I don't know if I ever saw [backfield coach] Tom Pagna as focused as he was that week. He was really a ball of fire! Maybe that focus kept us from having a letdown. Normally when you're going out to Los Angeles to play the Rose Bowl representative there's a little bit of apprehension because they were a pretty good team. I don't want to say it was men playing against boys, but we just took them apart.

There was no doubt in my mind that we were the best team in the country in 1966. I'm sure there were some doubts in some people's minds, but looking at the entire body of work, that was one of the great teams to ever play in South Bend.

Lou Holtz had some great teams and I loved the 1988 team and maybe the team with Kevin McDougal [1993] even more. I loved the 1973 team with Tom Clements and those guys, but I think in terms of a body of work and the way that defense was put together, 1966 was something special.

> The kicker for Notre Dame's national championship team of 1966, Azzaro connected on a 28-yard field goal on the first play of the fourth quarter in "the Game of the Century" that ended in a 10–10 tie in East Lansing.
>
> A walk-on from Pittsburgh, the 5'11", 190-pounder returned for a fifth season in 1967 and paced the Irish in scoring with 61 points, including eight field goals and a school-record 37 extra points.

BOB GLADIEUX

1966–1968

M Y DAD WAS A NOTRE DAME FAN for 75 years and saw his first games in 1929–1930 when they won national titles under Knute Rockne. So while I was growing up, Notre Dame was like a golden arch, a dream you never really thought you could realistically attain, especially because I came from a small town [Louisville, Ohio] of about six or seven thousand people. As my high school football career evolved, I began to draw the attention of the major colleges, but the decision was cut-and-dry once Notre Dame came into the picture.

The only other school that interested me was Ohio State. Woody Hayes recruited me pretty heavily for two years. He was a speaker at our football banquet one year, and another year it was Lou McCullough, his defensive coordinator. Woody would sometimes show up at my basketball games unannounced.

I told coach Hayes that Notre Dame was my number one choice, and if Notre Dame didn't want me—and it seemed like they didn't—I'd play for Ohio State. He said he respected that. That's the way it was said, and that's the way it was left and done. In the final week of recruiting, I finally got the call from [backfield coach] Tom Pagna that Notre Dame would offer. I don't know what they were waiting for. I was kind of perplexed, but what did I know about recruiting?

Notre Dame was intimidating to me academically more than anything. You could almost smell the knowledge when you toured the campus. Even on a football Saturday, I was getting a tour of the buildings before the game and there would be classes and people studying. I'm thinking, "How can I compete academically at this level?" My brother assured me if they didn't think I could do it, they wouldn't have recruited me. The academic tutoring system they had in place also helped me feel a little more at ease.

I visited during my senior year for the [November 21] Iowa game in 1964 [a 28–0 victory]. Notre Dame was ranked No. 1 with Ara as the new head coach. I sat in the stands on Coca-Cola cartons because there must have been 10 inches of snow. What I also remember from the game is it looked like the Notre Dame defense was the one that had the ball because they pushed Iowa backward all day. When I went into the locker room, I was intimidated again, seeing some of the defensive and offensive linemen who were 250 and 260 pounds at the time.

When you enroll as a freshman, you have to tread water for a while, but you recognize that the other freshmen are in the same boat. I can still distinctly see my parents' Plymouth station wagon pulling away after they dropped me off. I took one step toward Notre Dame—and I took another toward that station wagon. Finally, I just said bye-bye: it's time to go into the dorm with the rest of them. That's where we had everything in common and took one day at a time.

It was every bit as challenging as I anticipated. I was fortunate to get off to a good start with Father Tom Brennan in philosophy and Professor Jake Kline in math. They were great teachers who cared about you as people.

It's a bigger jump from high school to college than from college to the pros. You go in a boy and come out a man in college, and it's really tough to compete in your freshman year. Every Monday we would have a "Mud Bowl," which was a scrimmage with most of the varsity players who didn't see much action in Saturday's game versus the freshmen.

One Monday afternoon we beat them, 7–0, and [linebackers coach and assistant head coach] John Ray was really upset. It was the first time the varsity guys had been beaten. That was a feather in our cap when a freshman class can beat sophomores, juniors, and some seniors, but we had a pretty good nucleus with guys like [Terry] Hanratty, [Jim] Seymour, [Coley] O'Brien, [George] Kunz, [Bob] Kuechenberg . . .

My sophomore year I was behind Nick Eddy. When he was injured prior to the 1966 Michigan State game, I looked at it as an opportunity. Nick was graduating after the 1966 season, so this was a way for me to prepare and gain experience. Without a doubt, the defining moment of my career was the touchdown catch at Michigan State. That's how I get introduced all the time: "This is Bob Gladieux. He caught the touchdown pass in the famous 10–10 tie with Michigan State in 1966." We never had the opportunity to review the film of that game. The coaches went right into preparation for USC the next week because it would be for the national title.

I thought I was lined up in the slot on that touchdown [against Michigan State], but when I recently saw the ESPN Classic broadcast of that game, I was in a twin formation. In the style we played, the halfback was a flanker too. When Rocky [Bleier] and I weren't in the backfield, we'd be flanked out. All I know is I wasn't the primary receiver on the play. I was supposed to go deep to tie up the safety, but they blew a coverage and Coley got me the ball.

I got injured later in the game, and it was the hardest I've ever been hit. I had been doing pretty well in the game up to that point with my pass catching. My recollection is we got into the huddle and came in with the play. When they called the formation, I thought, "What the heck is that?" But I was told, "Harpo, get open." As soon as I released, I didn't recognize the coverage so I ad-libbed an inside route, which was a no-no. I kept going inside, running against the grain, and Jess Phillips hit me while I was in the air. I got hit in the head and in the leg. My quadriceps muscle was splattered into hamburger meat and my thigh pad busted into four pieces. I couldn't walk. I missed the rest of the game plus the USC game, and I was sidelined the entire spring.

I'm remembered most for the 1966 Michigan State game, but my best game at Notre Dame was my last, at USC in 1968. [Gladieux carried 19 times for a career-high 121 yards, including a 57-yard touchdown, as Notre Dame outrushed the O. J. Simpson–led Trojans, 277–52.] We kicked their butts physically, but they scored two second-half touchdowns on passes to tie us, 21–21. They had been unbeaten and were going to play Ohio State in the Rose Bowl for the national title.

We had two weeks to prepare, and I just sensed during that time we would have a good game and it would be my best game.

During my freshman year I roomed with Bob Belden in Keenan Hall. Ronnie [Dushney] was in Stanford, which is the other wing, and he roomed with Frank Criniti. Every day at 5:00, Dush played "Five O'Clock World" by The Vogues. After about four months, Frank had had enough. Ron moved

Bob Gladieux's touchdown against Michigan State as a sophomore in 1966 was
Notre Dame's lone six-pointer in the famous 10–10 tie with the Spartans.

in with me the next year; we had a great three years in Sorin Hall—and there was no more "Five O'Clock World." We made good friends in the hall with the upperclassmen—friendships we still have today.

The social life at Notre Dame was nonexistent. You'd go to St. Mary's for their annual spring panty raid, and then you had the townies for social activities. So Terry, Dush, and I went out often, and they had a few pubs around town. We liked to socialize with the ladies, have a dance and a chat—plus a little libation. Word got around and [former Irish trainer] Gene Paszkiet would tell us, "The owls would howl at night, but they could still soar with the eagles in the day." The message was if you party at night, you better be an eagle too and be ready to answer the call in the day.

I got called into Ara's office a few times, and it wasn't a place you wanted to be. He could put the fear of God in you because he was so demanding and had such a commanding presence. You wouldn't dare screw up—and I still watch my behavior around him now.

One day in practice, I'll never forget how the world seemed to stand still for a few seconds when John Ray yelled back after Ara yelled at the defense. Nobody talked back to Ara—and here was Johnny yelling back at him. There was dead silence, and we thought all hell was going to break loose. But Ara yelled back to him about a guy who didn't do what he was supposed to do, practice went on, and Ara got it straightened out with everybody.

135

One night I guess I was a bit frustrated about some things as I was coming back to the campus, and there were a bunch of bicycles at the LaFortune Student Center . . . I kind of stacked them up and was jumping on them. I don't know why. A priest saw the whole thing and said, "I'm going to let Ara handle this one." And I'm going, "Oh my God, no!" Just before I went in to see Ara, coach Pagna told me to expect the worst. Ara said, "I've got no choice. I've got to let you go."

I pleaded my case, and he left it up to the team and captains [George Kunz and Bob Olson]. I was eventually reinstated, and I was on a 9:00 P.M. curfew the rest of the semester as a junior . . . but not in my senior year.

We had one particularly great evening after my senior season in 1968. Dush, Terry and I were at The Linebacker talking to the owner, Stan "the Man" Piestak. Stan belonged to a flying club out at Michiana Regional Airport, and it must have been about 10:00 one night when we said we wanted to go with him to Fort Wayne [Indiana]. Ron was the "copilot" on the flight, but Stan let him have a hold of the [stick] too.

We landed in Fort Wayne, where Stan was like the mayor, and we hit every pub and bar in town. Ernie Terrell and the Heavyweights were there, and we were on the stage with the band playing the drums and the saxophone . . . we didn't know what we were doing, but we had a great time doing it.

There's no question those were the best four years of my life. You were never more proud than to say, wherever you went, you were from Notre Dame. It was a special place then, and it's special now. It was not so much that you played football at Notre Dame, but that you were from the University of Notre Dame.

I was ready to move on after my senior year, but you don't realize how good you have it. When you look back you think, "Boy, I must have been nuts to go to a place like that!" It was strict, no women at the school, academic standards were tough . . . but that's why I went there. I knew I would be better for it.

As a senior in 1968, Bob Gladieux became the first Notre Dame player to amass more than 1,500 all-purpose yards in a season when he totaled 1,512 in just 10 games (717 rushing, 442 receiving, 262 on kickoff returns, and 91 on punt returns). That standard lasted 15 years, and the only ones to have surpassed it since then are Irish superstars Allen Pinkett, Tim Brown, Raghib Ismail, and Autry Denson.

Gladieux's 37 receptions and 442 yards receiving in 1968 remain as the single-season standard at Notre Dame by a running back, and he scored more touchdowns (26) than any other Irish player during Ara Parseghian's 11-year reign at the school.

Nicknamed "Harpo" because of his resemblance to the Marx brother with the curly hair, the 5'11", 185-pounder from Louisville, Ohio, also earned the moniker "Owl," along with fellow classmates Terry Hanratty and Ron Dushney, for their love of the nightlife.

Gladieux spent three years playing professionally with the Boston (later, New England) Patriots.

TERRY HANRATTY

1966–1968

I WAS ALMOST SIGNED, SEALED, AND DELIVERED to Michigan State coming out of high school because of [Spartans head coach] Duffy Daugherty, a wonderfully charismatic person who was hard to say no to. Who knows, I could have been on the other side of that 10–10 tie.

I had a high school coach who told me not to go to California or Florida because back during my high school days, to go that far for school was almost unheard of. My coach told me to be true to these college coaches who were recruiting me, so Michigan State was a local favorite with Daugherty's Pennsylvania ties.

I visited Michigan State a couple of times and the Spartans' coaches came to see me at Butler High School. Woody Hayes came to Butler too, but at that time he threw the ball twice a game if Ohio State was down by 30 points. I had a real fatherly comfort with Duffy, even though John Ray was recruiting me for Notre Dame. But after Ara Parseghian saw my film he told John to call me and set up a meeting.

We met at the Hilton Hotel in Pittsburgh in a little dining room, and I remember looking at the menu and seeing the steak sandwich, which was $3.95. I said to myself, "I can't get that because they'll think I'm trying to gouge them." So I went for the club sandwich that was $1.25. Just spending an hour or two with Ara right then was all I needed.

Duffy had told me that if I didn't start at quarterback by my sophomore year I could start at wide receiver. All Ara told me was that I had a good chance to play as a sophomore. That's all he could guarantee.

Now, I'm 17 years old here and they talk about what recruits are getting today. Well, it was unbelievable back then. I won't mention schools, but some talked about houses for my mother, cash, and cars. It was amazing what these guys got. I know it's true because guys from my hometown went to those schools and didn't get the big stuff, but only because they weren't the star quarterback. They were linemen. Notre Dame offered you nothing.

Being poor at 17, how I made the best decision of my life to go to Notre Dame, I'll never know. I'll never forget the night that I picked Notre Dame. I called Ara, but then I had to call Duffy and tell him. For the next hour Duffy went on and on about how great Notre Dame was and what a great guy Ara Parseghian was. He made the call so easy for me, and I always had the utmost respect for Duffy Daugherty from then on.

But for me to go to Indiana from Pennsylvania after not going as far as Pittsburgh until my junior year in high school, I knew it was going to be an adjustment. Then when you arrive and can't play as a freshman, all you have is practice and you get beat up by the varsity every Monday. It was a grueling year and not fun.

138

I remember sitting in the stands during the Michigan State game in 1965 when the Spartans played a nine-man line and won, 12–3. I was chomping at the bit thinking that I would kill to be in that game. [Notre Dame quarterback] Bill Zloch was a great guy and a great leader, but he just didn't throw the ball well. I would have loved to have had the chance to start throwing the ball in that game.

Freshman year was a frustrating time because you were just cannon fodder for the varsity and you had no football life. It was just a year of limbo. Not until the spring of my freshman year when I won the starting job did playing football at Notre Dame start to become fun. We had some scrimmages and I got hot, which was the key to it all.

Jim Seymour and I used to practice in that old field house, and in there, if I had to throw the ball 40 yards, I'd have to arc it over two or three rafters. The lighting in there was horrible, but we got our timing down. If you could catch the ball in there, you could catch it anywhere.

Heading into 1966 we only had two questions: quarterback and wide receiver. Sure, Jim and I played well in practice and we played well in scrimmages, but until you get under fire, you don't know. Of course we took fire immediately against Purdue in the opener.

Quarterback Terry Hanratty was the trigger man for Notre Dame's 1966 national championship squad, which finished 9–0–1.

They tell the story, which I guess is true, that before the game some of the upperclassmen—Pete Duranko, George Goeddeke, and Jim Lynch—were watching me come through the chow line, where I had loaded up with steak, baked potatoes, scrambled eggs, toast. . . . I had this mound of food in front of me because I had never eaten this well before in my life. I had my head down, shoveling it in, and little did I know there were 50 sets of eyes watching me. Some of those big guys would just take two bites and then they'd be too nervous to eat before a big game. They couldn't figure out what I was doing.

My philosophy coming from a big high school that won was that game time was supposed to be fun. You practiced your butt off and you did all the mental work, all the physical work, and then you played. If you had prepared, that's all you could do and sometimes you'd win and sometimes you'd lose. Come Saturday morning I was ready to eat because I had all my mental and physical work done.

After that Purdue game my sophomore year [a 26–14 victory, with Hanratty throwing for 366 yards], I went back to the dorm and called my mom, and the first thing she said was how great [Purdue quarterback] Bob Griese was, what a classy kid he was, and how I should try to be like him. She was even calling him Mr. Griese.

140

I tried to tell her that I had just thrown three touchdown passes, but she didn't seem to care. Then Sunday night we watched the film of the game with my chest pumped out, and for the next two hours the coaches just rode me on my footwork and everything. I walked out of that meeting room thinking I had played a terrible game. Ara was just making sure that Jim [Seymour, who caught 13 passes for 276 yards against Purdue] and I didn't get bigger than the team just from one good game. We realized the team wasn't about Jim and me; it was about everybody.

You look at that team and the offensive line was fantastic, the defense was fabulous, and the running game was great. That 1966 team had everything. Jim and I were just the missing links.

The [10–10] Michigan State game that season was probably a matchup of the two most talented teams on one field in college football history when you look at all the All-Americans out there.

In what I remember as our third series, in comes a play from the sidelines calling for a quarterback draw on a drive that was marching. I couldn't figure out why Ara would call for that because we hadn't run it in a couple of weeks. So I took my three steps back and started to go forward into a sea of green. I knew I wasn't going anywhere and I'd be lucky to get back to the line of scrimmage.

A couple Michigan State guys wrapped me up, and out of the corner of my eye I see Bubba Smith just bearing down the line. I knew that wasn't a collision I was going to win. He buried me, and when I got up my left shoulder felt a little weird. So on the next play Ara calls for a pass, a down-and-out to the left side. The second I threw my left arm up the pain just shot through it because my shoulder was separated.

So as I'm coming off the field the first thing Ara says is, "Why the hell did you call that draw?" I told him that he sent it in, but Ara said, "No, that was supposed to be a halfback draw!" So as it turns out it was a screwup in communication that knocked me out of the game.

After that season we lost so much that we weren't that good of a football team during my junior and senior seasons. We lost a ton of people, including a couple of fifth-year guys in Pete Duranko and Nick Eddy.

We still had good teams that finished in the top 10 in 1967 and 1968, but we never vied for the national title. We knew right away in 1967 that people were going to be gunning for us. We ran into a couple buzz saws, including Purdue [a 28–21 loss].

141

It's amazing when you play at Notre Dame, and people don't believe me when I tell them this, but people always play their best game against you. You can walk out of film sessions during the week thinking games will be cakewalks. Then Saturday rolls around and you don't know who you're playing against. People love to beat Notre Dame.

I think Ara was an extremely warm and caring person. He graduated all of his players and that was a big thing to him. He took care of you and wasn't going to put you in harm's way.

During my senior year leading up to the Pittsburgh game everybody was screwing up in practice, and he told us if we couldn't do it right we'd scrimmage. Then on the first play of the scrimmage someone slipped through the line on an option play and tore the ligaments in my knee. From then on quarterbacks weren't open to live hitting, so everybody after me should thank me for giving them those red shirts.

Ara couldn't believe it when I stood up and my leg was all wobbly. They flew in the New York Jets' team doctor to take a look at my knee because [the doctor] had a kid going to Notre Dame at the time. I was out for the last three games of my senior year. Talk about anticlimactic endings, I didn't even get a chance to hear the roar of the crowd in my last home game.

But to show you how caring a person Ara was, he was devastated about my injury, and even though my career was over at Notre Dame, he wanted to get me ready for the pros. He wasn't going to try to win at all costs by pushing me.

From consensus All-Americans to the guys who never got in a game, nobody could ever say anything bad about Ara. He was an extremely fair and caring person. He helped make my Notre Dame football experience very special.

Terry Hanratty, a native of Butler, Pennsylvania, stepped into the Notre Dame spotlight in his first game as a sophomore by leading the Irish over Purdue and earning a spot on the cover of *Time* alongside fellow sophomore receiver Jim Seymour.

Hanratty went on to help Notre Dame win the national title during that 1966 season. He ranks as Notre Dame's fifth all-time leading passer with 4,152 yards and 27 touchdowns.

Hanratty finished sixth in the Heisman voting as a sophomore in 1966, ninth in 1967 and third in 1968, two spots behind winner O. J. Simpson of USC. He was a second-round selection by the Pittsburgh Steelers, where he played from 1969 to 1975.

MIKE McCOY

1967–1969

I CAME OUT OF ERIE, PENNSYLVANIA, from Cathedral Prep High School, which was an all-boys Catholic school known for academic and athletic excellence. I didn't go there until my sophomore year, after spending my freshman year in the seminary studying to be a priest. I thought that's what God called me to do, so I spent a year at St. Mark's, a local seminary in Erie. I can probably give you 10 reasons why I left, but I still really don't know why. But when I decided to leave I couldn't get into Cathedral because it was full.

I planned to go to a public school, but somehow word got to Monsignor McDonald that there was a seminarian who had some football experience and a size-15 cleat, or at least that's the story that I've been told. I had never played a down of football. But after spending less than a month on the junior varsity and averaging 15 yards a carry as a fullback, I moved up to the varsity on Labor Day back in 1963. They put me at nose tackle because I had no experience at all, and I started working with Tony Zambroski, who played under Frank Leahy and was my high school line coach.

I was playing both ways by my junior year, which was about the time Zambroski started asking me where I was thinking about playing in college. I didn't know what he was talking about. I was so naïve it was incredible. When Tony mentioned Notre Dame, I didn't even know where it was.

I wound up visiting Penn State, Syracuse, and Indiana, while getting hundreds of letters. Then I went back to Notre Dame on a visit and sat down with Ara [Parseghian]. That meeting pretty much sealed it for me.

Where Notre Dame was headed at that time after Ara's first two years of winning, as well as the academics, just fit for me. I think I was the first freshman to sign that year so I could get it out of the way. I still have the picture on my wall that Ara gave me. He wrote on it, "Mike, welcome to the Notre Dame family." The great thing about Notre Dame is that you really felt like that was the truth. You felt the whole Notre Dame mystique right when you walked on campus.

Big Mike McCoy (6'5", 275 pounds) was the anchor of Notre Dame's defensive lines in the late seventies, and eventually became the No. 2 overall pick in the NFL draft by the Green Bay Packers.

The two players who showed me around campus during that visit were Terry Hanratty and Jim Seymour. I didn't know this at the time, but they got some spending money to take the recruits around and they asked me what I wanted to do. They suggested pizza at the Morris Inn and a movie, which was fine by me. Little did I know they probably pocketed the rest of that money.

My first practice on the freshman team consisted of getting killed for about an hour and then Wally Moore calling out 11 guys and sending us to go scrimmage the first-team defense. I was working at offensive tackle, and on my first play I had to trap Alan Page. Then I had to block Kevin Hardy. On my third play Pete Duranko went right by me and knocked out Tom Nash. Those were my first three plays, and they left me with three stitches under my eye and I couldn't talk that night.

I got up at 6:00 the next morning, went to class, and for the next four weeks that was the schedule. I got a lot of encouragement from the coaches to hang in there because sometimes with younger players you're taken aback by all the things you didn't see during the recruiting process. For example, I remember Johnny Ray had told me that Notre Dame didn't recruit junior college guys, and the first person I met was Bob Jockisch, a defensive tackle bigger than me from a junior college.

145

Looking at the success of Ara, there were several things that made him such a great coach. One aspect was the combination of his hands-off style when we lost and how hard he would work us after we won. Another was his knowledge of the game and how he could be up in that tower and before the snap of the ball he could tell if the middle linebacker, Bob Olson, was too far to the left or if I wasn't lined up right. He knew everybody's position and assignment because he wrote the book.

Another strength was Ara's ability to change a game plan on the run, something all the great coaches do. If you've got a drop-back quarterback and try to make him an option passer, that's never going to work. He knew how to mold the players and suit them to the system, which for him meant putting the best athletes on defense.

Through his personality Ara developed an atmosphere where you could go in and tell him things. You knew he wouldn't put you down to third team because you did something wrong. He drew the line short of being your buddy, and you knew he wasn't following you around checking up on your work all the time. But he let you know what was expected of you. You knew if you didn't get those things done that you wouldn't play. He had the authority, but you knew you could approach him too.

I'll never forget my first game against Cal in 1967 [a 41–8 victory] and hearing the band playing. Johnny Ray came up to me beforehand and put his hands on my head and just told me to do my best and play hard. The butterflies were going pretty good during that game. On the flip side, I'll never forget those Purdue games either, not to dwell on the negative. In three years we never beat them, and that still hurts today. They'd always wind up losing to Wake Forest, so you never knew with them.

Tying USC my junior year [21–21 in 1968] was another big moment because we held O. J. Simpson to 55 yards on 21 carries and made the cover of *Sports Illustrated*. That was his last game for them. That was a game that showed Ara's coaching ability because we designed a defense to combat their running game by taking away the cutback lanes. We didn't go in there and try to force our base defense and make it work. We did something to stop that guy and adapted.

146

Playing in the Cotton Bowl after the 1969 season was something that stirred mixed emotions in me because I wanted to get home after getting picked to play in the East-West All-Star Game, and we had tests after Christmas. Ara said we were going and whoever didn't want to go didn't have to, and unfortunately a couple guys didn't.

Ara made it very clear why we were going to a bowl. Obviously there was the money factor, and if we wanted to stay competitive in recruiting, it was time to change the policy. I had to take some of my books down to Texas because a couple days later we had tests. I wound up skipping the Shrine Game.

We probably should have beaten Texas [Notre Dame lost, 21–17] after recovering a fumble on the 2-yard line, but the refs threw a flag as a Texas player was running onto the field. The refs said that made the play dead, so the fumble we caused and recovered didn't count. To Texas' credit, they drove down and converted their third downs and then punched it in.

After the game a few of us seniors were sitting in the training room, devastated, and in walks Lyndon B. Johnson with the big 10-gallon hat, the belt buckle, and the boots. He was the last person I wanted to see.

What my last year helped teach me was the responsibility of the veteran players to carry on the Notre Dame tradition. Younger players such as Greg Marx, Walt Patulski, and Fred Swendsen were lining up next to me during my last year. I felt a responsibility not in terms of showing them what to do, but in terms of teaching them to play hard. I think that sense of responsibility was passed on down to us from guys like Nick Eddy and Jim Lynch, and now the torch was passed down to my class. We had to carry on what was started in 1964. I think that's a good pressure. I'd rather have that than start with something new.

I think the importance of tradition and expectations started back with Father Edward Sorin and carried on down through the years. That's what Notre Dame is about, and there's a faith on campus that's important. That faith pushes people to be better. At a place like Notre Dame, when you put expectations in front of people, they're going to do everything they can to meet them.

One of Notre Dame's most imposing players during the sixties, Mike McCoy started at defensive tackle during his junior and senior seasons and helped the Irish to a bowl berth against No. 1 Texas in the 1970 Cotton Bowl—Notre Dame's first bowl game in 45 years.

The 6'5", 275-pounder from Erie, Pennsylvania, helped form an imposing left side of the defensive line in 1969 when he teamed up with Walt Patulski, who would become the overall number one pick in the 1972 NFL draft.

McCoy was drafted second overall by the Green Bay Packers in 1970 and spent twelve years in the NFL—seven with the Packers, two with the Oakland Raiders, two with the New York Giants, and one in Detroit.

Ironically, after spending his football career knocking people down, he has devoted his postfootball life to helping people up, so to speak, with his positive attitude and motivating words.

JOE THEISMANN

1968–1970

I WAS 5'10", 152 POUNDS WHEN I ENTERED COLLEGE. I weighed 172 when I graduated, and I played almost my entire 15-year career in professional football under 195.

When I arrived here on a recruiting trip, [defensive coordinator] Johnny Ray kept looking for this Joe Thees-man kid. He thought I was a student manager or water boy. [Defensive line coach] Joe Yonto, who recruited me, said, "No, that's the quarterback." Johnny said, "You gotta be kidding me!"

I was interested in Penn State [Joe Paterno's first year as head coach], Notre Dame, Wake Forest, North Carolina, and North Carolina State. Wake's campus is very similar to ours the way they configured the quadrangles. I signed with North Carolina State because my high school coach was a guy named Ron Wojcicki, who played behind Roman Gabriel at North Carolina State [1959–1960]. I was impressed with that.

I didn't enter college, in all honesty, for an academic reason. I was a good enough student to get by in high school, but I really wanted to play ball. Even though I signed a grant-in-aid, the fact that Notre Dame was an independent gave me the opportunity to change my decision back then. Had I gone to another conference school, I would have lost a year of eligibility.

The reason I switched was I made another trip to Notre Dame. It was a typical November day in South Bend: rainy, overcast . . . dismal. Rocky Bleier was my chaperone. I flew back home and got off at Newark, New Jersey; my mom and dad were there, and my dad said, "What do you think?" I said, "I have to go to Notre Dame!" He said, "Why?" I told him, "I can't tell you why." I just felt like that was where I belonged. I'm sure you've had feelings where you're someplace and it's where you have to be—with no real logical explanation. That's what happened to me.

One of the reasons I didn't go to the University of North Carolina was as we were driving on campus, they pointed out a house that was a sorority of blondes. I said, "I can't go here. I know my frailties. I know what I'm incapable of doing. I'm not capable of focusing with beautiful women around." That automatically eliminated UNC—to their benefit, not mine.

Notre Dame was an all-male institution where I could concentrate on athletics and academics. That was it. I knew I had to be a better student. I went to study hall and I graduated as an Academic All-American. I went out on two dates my first two years at Notre Dame.

The thing I appreciated about the university was that the standard for athletes was higher than for regular students. You had to carry a 2.0 to stay eligible to play football. The student body needed something like a 1.8 to stay in school.

My youngest son, Patrick, graduated from Notre Dame [in 2003], and what I told him was you have to find a routine that works for you, and then you manage your time to get your studying done. It's a great time to learn how to deal with life without Mommy and Daddy taking care of you. That's what it meant to me.

149

When I arrived, Terry Hanratty and Coley O'Brien already had quarterbacked a national title, and a third guy, Bob Belden, would be drafted by the NFL. However, Ara gave me the chance to play, and part of it was by moving Coley to halfback. When Terry got hurt in the latter part of my sophomore season [1968], that's when I got the chance to start.

It wasn't until the final game [at USC in 1968] that I felt I could play bigtime college football. I always used the University of Southern California as the barometer of excellence, just as I did the Dallas Cowboys when I played as a professional. When I played well against those two teams, then I felt I belonged.

The first pass I threw in the 1968 USC game was picked off by Sandy Durko and run back for a touchdown. As I walked by Ara I said, "Don't worry about it. I'll get it back." Ara told me later that it was at that moment he became very comfortable with his decision to have me be his quarterback. We went ahead 21–7 and ended with a tie against the No. 1 team in the country.

I've always had great belief in my abilities because I'm willing to outwork anybody. I've never been the most talented person; I've never been the biggest person; I've never been the fastest person. But if you want to match me work for work, I'll work you into the ground. You can't stay with me. I'll work harder than anybody until I get it right, until I feel comfortable with where I am in my ability to do my job the best I possibly can.

The change in pronunciation for my name . . . I believe it happened when a reporter was watching spring practice and kidded [sports information direc-

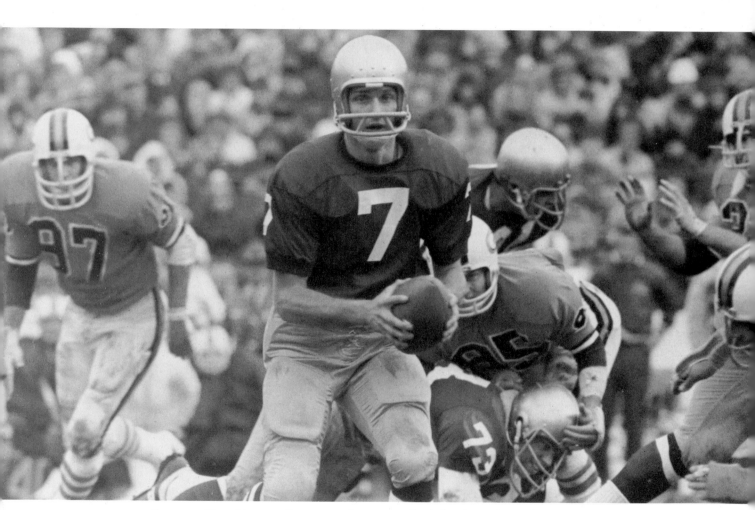

Once considered too small to succeed at quarterback for the Irish, Joe Theismann set numerous Irish passing records and went on to lead the Washington Redskins to a Super Bowl title.

tor] Roger Valdiserri, "Is that Theismann like in Heisman?" Roger stored that away and called me into his office to ask if we could change it from Joe Thees-man. I asked my dad how we pronounced our last name, and he wanted to know if I was nuts.

Roger changed my name; Ara changed my life. He has a reverence about him that is regal. We were so prepared, and he was willing to take chances too. He gave me all the freedom in the world. I called a lot of the plays during my senior season. He would give me a block of four or five plays, and I could make decisions about what I wanted to do at the line of scrimmage.

Whenever someone would come up to me and say, "Coach wants to see you," I would get a big knot in my stomach. Sitting in front of Ara was, to me, like having an audience with the pope. You get a feeling when you're in his presence that this is not just another football coach, this is not just another man, this is someone who is bigger than everything else.

He used to sit in the tower, offense on one side, defense on the other. I'd run a play, screw up, and I'd quickly look up to see if he was looking—and he'd be facing the other way. I'd think, "Whew, I dodged a bullet!" I'd break the huddle, come walking out, and he'd say, "Joe, don't make the mistake you just made!" I'd think, "How did you know?" To this day, I'm uneasy in his presence.

151

The 1970 team was the right group of guys in the right situation, and I happened to be lucky enough to be the driver of the Cadillac. We had grown together in 1968–1969, and we had a great defense. Today, teams recruit differently. We recruited athletes and made them into something else. We recruited a lot of quarterbacks and made them into linebackers, defensive backs, receivers. . . . Now, you recruit specifically for a position. There was a special chemistry in 1970, and we received great leadership from Ara and his staff.

There's no question the 1970 USC game was the most memorable even though we lost [38–28]. I didn't find out until years later that [Washington Redskins head coach] Joe Gibbs was USC's offensive line coach. He was amazed at how I was able to grip the football and pass for so many yards, but for some reason I've always been able to throw a wet football.

People talk about the class of 1983 quarterbacks who went to the NFL as the best ever. There were six who were picked in the first round, including John Elway and Dan Marino. But I'd put my class of 1971 quarterbacks with any group. You had Jim Plunkett [Stanford], Archie Manning [Mississippi], Dan Pastorini [Santa Clara], Ken Anderson [Augustana], Rex Kern [Ohio State], Lynn Dickey [Kansas State], Dennis Dummit [UCLA], and Chuck Hixson [SMU].

Everyone said, "Wasn't it great to be the runner-up for the Heisman Trophy?" There's nothing great about finishing second. It's an honor to be mentioned, but it's like losing in the Super Bowl. There are 31 teams and one champion. There's one Heisman winner and a whole bunch of other guys who didn't make it. I've never been comfortable settling for number two.

If one had to name the most famous player during the Ara Parseghian era (1964–1974), 1970 Heisman Trophy runner-up Joe Theismann likely would garner the most votes. The two-and-a-half-year starter rewrote the Notre Dame record books in passing and total offense, and his 1970 campaign is considered the greatest ever by an Irish quarterback.

In 1970, the 6', 170-pounder from South River, New Jersey, led the Irish to a 9–0 start before passing for a school-record 526 yards in a monsoon during the 38–28 loss at USC. He then propelled Notre Dame to a 24–11 victory over No. 1 Texas in the 1971 Cotton Bowl, leaving the Irish No. 2 to Nebraska.

The Irish offense averaged 510.5 yards per game that season, a school record that still stands. Not one starting offensive lineman from that team played in the NFL, and not one of Notre Dame's top five running backs was picked either. Theismann's skills and confidence compensated for the shortage of marquee athletes.

Theismann would go on to lead the Washington Redskins to a Super Bowl title and was elected to the College Football Hall of Fame in the spring of 2003.

TOM GATEWOOD

1969–1971

I WAS CONSIDERING GOING TO YALE because my high school quarterback, Kurt Schmoke, went there and later became the mayor of Baltimore [1987–1999]. He became a Rhodes scholar and we were pretty close. A chance to go to Yale on an academic scholarship can be enticing. Like most players at Notre Dame, I was recruited by hundreds of schools.

One of the more interesting ones was Alabama. They were looking for me to be a groundbreaker because the SEC wasn't integrated. A letter came from them and I basically ignored it. I didn't even consider visiting, let alone going to the conference. My father had been stationed in the military in Alabama and Mississippi during World War II, and he had a horrible, horrible experience in Alabama, so it was a bad name in our household.

I was recruited very late by Notre Dame and didn't take my visit until February. The Maryland area wasn't a hotbed for recruitment, but I was a Parade All-American and got some attention. My high school coach, George Young, who would go on to become the general manager of the New York Giants, was very progressive and strongly connected.

George had a great deal of ambition and was very smart. While he was coaching at my high school, he was working with the [Baltimore] Colts and Don Shula during his off time. That was good for us because the benefits rubbed off: we had game footage, our practices were taped, we had pro sets, and all kinds of things were highly influenced by the NFL. I'm pretty sure he sent my tape to Notre Dame because I wasn't really sure how they found out about me.

My high school was all male, and six hundred boys came out for football. It was a college prep school and highly integrated. We dominated the
state championships in every sport. I was a three-sport athlete, and we won
the state in football and basketball, and we had a very good baseball team.
Therefore, Notre Dame was a very attractive school because it had a similar allure with academic status, graduating athletes, and a national ranking
in football.

My host was Tony Capers, one of three black football players there at the
time. There was Larry Schumacher, who was a linebacker; Tony, an offensive guard and place-kicker; and a defensive back named Ernie Jackson. The
only one who ended up starting was Schumacher. Tony flunked out and
Ernie suffered a knee injury that ended his career. He graduated but never
played beyond his sophomore year.

The lack of black faces at Notre Dame didn't frighten me. The balance on
my teams in high school was about 30 percent black and 70 percent white, so
in terms of race relations and getting along, it was a smooth transition. It
wasn't like I was coming from Selma, Alabama, with a chip on my shoulder
and all kinds of baggage.

154

What I was looking for was: 1) an opportunity to be independent by being
away from home, and 2) getting a strong enough education to go anywhere
in the country. I wanted a national presence. My degree was more important
to me than football. I had heard of too many cases where players who had
injuries or other problems didn't finish school and people just forgot about
them. I didn't want to be a statistic.

I spent most of the time on my visit with academic advisers and counselors
and talking to students on campus to find out what it was like at Notre Dame.
What locked it up was Ara Parseghian. I didn't see Ara until the last two
hours of that weekend. We had about 20 minutes together. Basically he said,
"We've seen film of you, I've got feedback from people who have talked to
you and know your personality and how you would blend into the Notre
Dame program, and we'd like to offer you a scholarship to play with us. We
think you would make a contribution and be a proud addition to our family.
We feel certain we can offer you things that will help you with your future."

When I think about it now, he said just what I wanted to hear in comparison to what I heard from other coaches around the country. Those places
told me I was guaranteed to be an All-American, guaranteed to be a starter.
. . . That's nice stroking for a kid who's 17 or 18 years old, but I've got to tell

you, I was like a 22-year-old analyzing what people were saying. Woody Hayes was telling me he was going to change his offense to a high-powered passing attack. Ben Schwartzwalder [Syracuse] said the same thing. It went in one ear and out the other. I was not immature enough to buy it.

Parseghian wasn't guaranteeing I would be an All-American—he wasn't even guaranteeing I would be a productive part of the team! He never called me again, and I didn't have people from Notre Dame on the phone harassing me, whereas I had high-pressure tactics from several schools. I guess in some instances players take that as ego strokes and feel good about it. I would have felt it annoying, so I was the right personality for that low-pressure sales pitch. But it was a quality sales pitch, and it answered the questions I needed to know. I was the right fit at the right time for the right coaches.

In high school, I was a tight end in a two-tight-end set. They would throw me a 2-yard pass and I would run 90 yards for a touchdown. But when I was recruited by Notre Dame, it was strictly as a running back. I didn't know that at the time because nobody said, "Hey, you're going to be a great running back at Notre Dame." The tip-off for me was when I arrived in August. They gave me my jersey and assigned me No. 44. I said, "Why am I 44? Don't they have any 80s left?" They said, "We don't give 80s to running backs." I said, "No, you must have me mixed up with someone else." Next thing I know I'm in line with the halfbacks and fullbacks, learning how to take handoffs I had never taken in my life.

155

Learning the skills and techniques at running back felt mechanical. I was trying to develop the instincts that other guys who had been playing running back since they were in Pop Warner—like Bob Minnix and Ed Gulyas—already had. I didn't have that cutback instinct, and I was trying to learn. That's something you can't really teach. You have to figure it out and feel it.

When our scout team played the varsity [in 1968], I wore No. 32, meaning I was O. J. Simpson when we prepared for USC, Leroy Keyes from Purdue . . . I was all these top-name backs, except I was getting slammed around by Bob Olson, Mike McCoy, and all the varsity guys. Once we were done with that, we would get to do our regular freshman practice.

I became my own best salesman. I kept telling the coaches, "You're missing the boat here. I'm a really good receiver." Every day I went out early to practice and was in line with the receivers so I could have quarterbacks throw balls to me. I kept trying to demonstrate myself to the coaches. I was thinking, "Please look! Please look!"

Finally, they got tired of me nagging them. They lined me up, sent me out wide, and said, "Theismann, throw long to this guy!" I just took off and Joe lofted one that I caught over my shoulder. They wanted me to do it again to see if it was a fluke, and we did the same thing. That's how it started in the spring of 1969. Jim Seymour was graduating and his spot was open.

I don't think there was anything immediate in my chemistry with Theismann. He had a very, very accurate arm. He could get you the ball in the area it had to be. It didn't always have a full head of steam, it didn't always have the perfect spiral, but it was always where I had an opportunity to get it.

The first year we played [1969], Joe was maybe 170 pounds. He didn't have the strongest arm, but he really worked at it. He came from a working-class family like I did. He was always out early, always willing to stay late. His senior year [1970], his arm was much stronger and even more accurate—plus he could run. Because he was always a threat to take off, it made my routes easier. The chemistry evolved and after a while we could just read each other.

He could do check offs, and we had a signal system where I could tip him off what I was going to do by using certain gestures. We could read each other and communicate in a stadium with seventy thousand people, and we would know exactly what was going to happen. It was fun. It was magic.

156

There have been all kinds of different offensive schemes since that year, including my senior year when I caught only 33 passes, but I don't think Notre Dame has had the kind of passing attack we had in 1970. I was the same body in 1971, but we were running kind of a wishbone offense with Theismann gone.

The things I had going for me when I caught 77 passes in 1970 were Ara was very innovative and we had a quarterback who could hit me anywhere. I wasn't just lined up on the left as a receiver or a wing on the right. If you did a grid of where I made those 77 catches as far as where I started out in the formation and where I caught the ball, you'd find I was all over the field. When they evaluated my footage in high school, they said, "This guy is a good broken-field runner, so he can line up at a lot of different spots."

Sometimes I would line up in a formation where I would get linebacker coverage. So now I could outrun a linebacker and put him at a place where he wasn't comfortable. Then I could line up on one side, go in motion, and take a guy who was used to playing left corner to an area he wasn't used to. Ara saw me as versatile and said, "You've got the whole field, young man.

The epitome of the Notre Dame student-athlete, receiver Tom Gatewood not only caught an Irish-record 77 passes in 1970, but also was a two-time Academic All-American.

You can go anywhere you want in our offense. We're going to get you open because they can't double-cover you on this side or they'll get mixed up with personnel. We can use you as a decoy on one play, and then when they fall asleep we can throw to you."

The most disappointing game for me was at Southern California in 1970 because I felt we were the best team in the country that year. We lost [38–28] to a team that was not that good [USC finished 3–4 that year in the Pac-8 conference]. It wasn't our day. We got behind early and couldn't come back in the rain. Later we won the Cotton Bowl and knocked off the No. 1 team [Texas, 24–11], but we fell short [finishing No. 2]. That was the one thing I felt got away. I would have loved to have had that championship ring on my finger. That USC loss was the low point, the worst defeat for me as an athlete.

The high point was probably being named a captain in 1971. The coaches did not appoint captains: it was a team vote. So when your team elects you, it's one of the greatest honors you can get because it's your immediate peers. I was a silent leader. I didn't bang lockers, I didn't scream. If I was out working after practice, I hoped others were watching. I was doing it for myself, but somewhere along the line maybe a few more teammates would stay and work too. If I went in early, they were going to go in early. I did it by example, not by telling someone, "Hey, you have to stay out a little later."

I was the captain of the freshman team too, but that was different. That was a group of strangers electing a guy they didn't really know yet. You don't get to know someone in three months. You spend three years with the same core group and add two more classes of strangers who get to know you . . . now you're elected by familiar people and it's family. Being elected captain my last year had more meaning because I had a sense of, "OK, people have been watching me, and now I've achieved the ultimate reward."

Recruited as a halfback in 1968, Tom Gatewood carried only 10 times for 24 yards in three games with the freshman team. The former tight end from City College High in Baltimore, Maryland, implored the coaching staff to shift him to receiver, and he got his wish in the spring of 1969.

To this day, his 157 receptions remain the Notre Dame standard, highlighted by his school-record 77 for 1,123 yards and seven scores in just 10 regular-season games in 1970. The closest anyone has come since then is Arnaz Battle with 58 catches in 2002—and that was in 13 games (bowl game included).

Besides earning consensus All-America honors in 1970 and becoming the football program's first black captain in 1971, Gatewood excelled in the classroom, where he was a two-time CoSIDA Academic All-American who earned postgraduate scholarships from the NCAA and National Football Foundation. He went on to play two years of professional football with the New York Giants.

WALT PATULSKI

1969–1971

I SPOKE AT A PEP RALLY WHEN NOTRE DAME played Syracuse up here [in 2003], and the topic was why I chose Notre Dame. Here's what I said. First of all they have a fight song that brings you up no matter what frame of mind or mood you're in, and you never get tired of hearing it.

Second, they have an Alma Mater that is so comforting and beautiful that it brings tears to your eyes every time you sing it.

Third, they have meaningful symbols like Touchdown Jesus, No. 1 Moses, a Golden Dome, leprechauns, shillelaghs, green jerseys, and a Grotto where candles burn 24 hours a day, symbolizing eternal hope.

They have tradition and academic excellence where all students graduate. They have fans, not just any fans, but superfans who plan their weddings, vacations, and travel schedules around Irish home games. Finally, they have a spirit that defies description; it can only be experienced. There is a sense of community that melds people together from different races, different faiths, and different economic circumstances in life.

I took a really hard look at nearby Syracuse University because they were going to play me at fullback. That's when Ben Schwartzwalder was there and they had a great tradition with the running game. But they were in the twilight of Ben's years, and that figured into my decision.

Michigan State was kind of the same with Duffy Daugherty. Duffy told me to go to Syracuse just to keep me away from Notre Dame, who he had to play every year. My goal was to play fullback. Duffy told me, "At Syracuse, you will play fullback; at Notre Dame, you won't." He was right.

The other school I looked at pretty hard was Boston College. I narrowed it down pretty quickly to Notre Dame, Syracuse, and Boston College even though I was a high school All-American and recruited all over the country.

The Notre Dame coaches said I would get a good look and opportunity at fullback, but I lasted all of two weeks. I was 6′6″, 235 when I enrolled. Being the good foot soldier that I was, I took it OK. There was room at defensive end and there wasn't a hell of a lot of room at running back. The competition was less severe and things opened up right away at defensive end. The starters in my freshman year [1968] were Bob Kuechenberg and Chick Lauck, and they were both seniors.

The coaches told me I was a natural to play defensive end, that I would get much bigger, and that there was nobody who was going to be in my way. I could start right out of the gate. [Defensive line coach Joe] Yonto told me, "You're still at fullback, but we're lining you up on the opposite side and you have to go get the ball." The logic didn't quite work, but it was amusing.

160

When I was with the freshman team [1968], we played Michigan State twice and Tennessee once, and I played a little tight end too. Today, kids are much more ready for early action and are more sophisticated than we were at that time. The offenses and defenses have become more complex; the players have more coaches and are better instructed. I think it's easier to play with the varsity today than in my time. When we played, it was better to have the transition time with the freshman team. The level of sophistication is so much higher now than when I played.

It was interesting the way coach Yonto would handle us. Fred Swendsen was the guy who couldn't do anything right in his eyes; Mike Kadish was kind of a Golden Boy, while I was just someone you would tell something and I would do it. So all these personalities just blended together and we started to jibe as a defensive team.

There was a lot of pride defensively. Regardless of what the offense was doing, we knew we could limit what another team could do against us. It was more of a defensive game in our era. We played LSU at home in my junior year [1970] and won 3–0—and that was with Bert Jones and Joe Theismann as the quarterbacks. I don't know if you hear about great defenses as much as you used to.

Reflecting back, what Ara Parseghian did was put the best athletes on defense, and that enabled us to be in every game. The offense is more of a regimentation where you can be more disciplined.

When the school broke its bowl ban in my sophomore year [1969], it was a great, great opportunity because I went there thinking they didn't go to bowls. The experience of travel and staying at a different city for a number of days . . . that's what college is all about.

When we lost in the final minute to [No. 1] Texas [21–17], I don't think Ara was out of the shower before he told us, "We'll be back here next year, and the score is going to be different!" In spring ball, we put the "mirror defense" in, and we worked on it all spring. He knew we were going back to play Texas in the Cotton Bowl. He knew how the defense worked, and he couldn't wait to use it. He put in new wrinkles that I don't think Texas had seen. Once the game arrived, we were so ready.

After we won [24–11], we were excited at the prospect that we might be national champions. The problem was letting someone else do your work for you. We were 9–0 before losing at USC, but we still had a chance. The [Orange Bowl] between Nebraska and LSU started at 9:00, and we had already gone to the awards ceremony for the Cotton Bowl. When LSU couldn't beat Nebraska at the end, we felt very let down. We were so close. The door was wide open and we had a legitimate claim.

Because we had virtually everyone back on defense in 1971, we were the preseason No. 1 in *Sports Illustrated*. I think we knew we were lacking at some skill positions, and Theismann was just too much to replace. Those kinds of players don't come around often. The defense had a lot more pressure than it ever had.

161

We were 8–1 with just the game at LSU to go, but that was the week the players voted to turn down the invitation to the Gator Bowl. We were kind of egotistical because we were the preseason No. 1 and we weren't playing for the national championship. We had played the No. 1 team the two previous years in the Cotton Bowl.

There was a lot of sentiment of people wanting to go back home to their families, and the bowl wouldn't really prove anything. It was free will and we exercised the right to choose. As the cocaptains, Tom Gatewood and I had to tell coach Parseghian that we weren't going—and that wasn't fun. He was livid, so we went back and revoted. When the count came back, it was closer the second time, but we still voted it down. You look in the annals of sport and I don't know if that has ever happened at any other place.

I think there was a disconnection between the coaches and players at that point. I remember the coaches' wives and kids were picketing us. They had

Defensive end Walt Patulski was the No. 1 pick in the 1972 draft while two other teammates (Mike Kadish and Clarence Ellis) were selected in the first round.

little signs out in front of the practice field about going to a bowl. The coaches couldn't believe our decision. They couldn't understand why the players were saying they didn't want to go. Some of the players who hadn't been playing weren't buying in. It was kind of strange. The attitude was, "If we're not at a certain level, then there's just no point."

That kind of affected us when we went to LSU in the final game and lost [28–8]. I had never experienced such noise in a totally foreign zone. It was parochial and I wasn't part of the parish. It was very different. It was something like playing in a game that was rigged, like running into a buzz saw. They were ready, and we weren't ready to deal with it.

The Lombardi Award was special because that's like a Heisman Trophy for a lineman. The award was presented to me in Houston by George Bush [the first], who was an ambassador at the time.

I don't think anybody was more disappointed in my pro career than myself. I've put it in perspective that it was a good pro career. However, in light of the expectations of being drafted number one, I could see where people would say I didn't live up to expectations.

Put it this way. Whereas I was a natural in college, I had to start thinking about it in the pros. When I played in college, it was totally without thought. It was automatic. When I got to the pros, I got tight and I started thinking.

It's like Yogi Berra said: "How can you hit when you're up there thinking about getting a hit?" In a nutshell, that's what happened.

The 1971 recipient of the Lombardi Award, Walt Patulski started every game at defensive end during his three-year collegiate career on the varsity level (1969–1971). The 1971 Irish cocaptain (along with Tom Gatewood) is the last Notre Dame player to be the number one selection in the NFL draft.

The 6'6", 260-pounder was a headline performer for one of the greatest defensive classes recruited in one season at Notre Dame. The 1968 haul included fellow first-round picks Mike Kadish and Clarence Ellis, as well as other top linemen such as second-round pick Greg Marx and third-round choice Fred Swendsen.

In 1970 and 1971, that nucleus limited the opposition to seven or fewer points 14 times in 21 games, and the "mirror defense" helped snap No. 1 Texas' 30-game winning streak (24–11) in the 1971 Cotton Bowl.

The shift in 1968 as a freshman from fullback to defensive end paid off for the Liverpool, New York, native, who played four years with the team that drafted him, the Buffalo Bills, and another with the St. Louis Cardinals.

FRANK POMARICO

1971–1973

NOTRE DAME WAS A SIMPLE CHOICE FOR ME. When I was growing up in New York, Gerry DiNardo and I were classmates in grade school and high school, and his brother, Larry, was someone we looked up to.

Larry was a great baseball player, and then when he went to St. Francis Prep, he was a model for us to look up to. He was a great student, a great shot-putter, great rugby player. . . . He was three years older than me, so when he was a senior, I was a freshman. Larry was just the model that we wanted to be like. He did everything the right way. He was a sound individual; he did well with adjustments; he did well with his own classmates. . . .

So now I get to high school, Larry goes to Notre Dame, Gerry and I are sophomores in high school, and Larry comes back talking about this guy named Ara Parseghian. Of course, Larry could have gone to any school he wanted. All the academies, Harvard . . . but he picked Notre Dame because I think he thought that was his greatest challenge athletically as well as academically. Our goal was, "Maybe someday that can happen to us."

I had a pretty good senior year at St. Francis Prep, and remember, I modeled my stance, the way I approached things, everything was geared to being like Larry. Finally, I had achieved my goal!

I was on the all-city team, and when I went to Notre Dame, the other players asked me, "Were you all-state?" And I said, "No, I was all-city." All-city doesn't sound like much, but when there are nine million people in the town, it means something, and I didn't realize that until later on.

No one epitomized spirit and love for Notre Dame more than 1973 captain and left guard Frank Pomarico.

165

My senior year I was recruited by North Carolina and Notre Dame. The other tackle, a guy who was in Larry's class, went to North Carolina and he became the All-ACC tackle at 209 pounds. That was Paul Hoolahan, who then went on to become the athletic director at Vanderbilt and is now the executive director of the Sugar Bowl.

Paul is a real fiery Irishman and was always competing with Larry. So he went to North Carolina, Larry went to Notre Dame, and there weren't too many schools that wanted me. Places like Villanova said I was too small. Most other schools thought I was too small. I was 6′1″, about 235 when I came to Notre Dame.

Ara took a shot on me. He had success with Larry and thought, "Let's see if we can have a warm body with Frank." Gerry went to a year of prep school because he left St. Francis at 200 pounds. He came back at 240, and we were staggered by a year at Notre Dame.

I knew all about Ara before I got there. Ara was a very, very impressive guy. He's got these piercing eyes that make you stand at attention, and everything he said was gobbled up because we felt if we wanted to be successful as a team, as individuals we were going to try to emulate his intensity, his character. That was something that we believed in. Even if you lost games, you would still win by showing your character and strong will.

Ara instilled in us that the game may be over and we may have lost the battle, but we didn't lose the war. We were always trying to achieve and improve on the athletic field, as individuals, or in the classroom. So it was never really lost: time just ran out. He used to talk about not having a breaking point.

I loved every day at Notre Dame. I guess I was really living a dream. Coming from New York with a very ethnic background, Notre Dame was just a dream. And then to start as a sophomore was unbelievable to me. . . . I get a little emotional every time I talk about it.

166

And then to get Larry's number [No. 56], wow! It wasn't as much the number itself as it was the fact that [the coaching staff] knew how much it meant to me and gave me the number. He was the left guard in 1970, and I was the left guard in 1971. So from 1968 to 1973, the left guard at Notre Dame was from St. Francis Prep.

When I think of the greatest memories at Notre Dame, the first one was my sophomore year [1971] against Northwestern when we came out of that tunnel. It was more than just coming out of the tunnel. It was also the feeling and emotion that was shared with me by guys like Walt Patulski, Dan Novokov, John Dampeer, Andy Huff, Ed Gulyas, John Cieszkowski. . . . They were all very supportive. These guys were saying, "You're going to do it; it's going to be easier than practice!" So we go out, score the first touchdown over my hole, and go on to win, 50–7.

The Monday before that game, Ara had told me that Northwestern's best defensive tackle was a guy named Jim Anderson. He said, "Frank, you're going to be playing against him. We're expecting a lot from you." That was such a great feeling, and I had a great game.

Then we slipped by Purdue [an 8–7 victory], but before we played Michigan State the next week, they moved me to tackle. Here I was with just two starts under my belt, and I'm changing positions!

[Left tackle] Jim Humbert had a bad knee, and I was playing against a guy named Wes Josephs, who was a big, strong, heavy guy. I think they thought that I could block a little stronger on the runs than Jim. Jim was real quick and got real good leverage on guys, but to drive a guy out? I was a better choice, plus Jim had a bad knee. We beat Michigan State [14–2], and the next week I was back at guard.

The most satisfying game was the Southern Cal game in 1973 [a 23–14 victory]. They were national champs in 1972 and 1974, and when we played them in 1973, we were 5–0. The first four games of that year I had ripped up my ankle and I was in a cast for about a month. I came back for the Rice game and only played on an extra point. I started the Army game and I probably wasn't ready, but I wanted to come back. I knew if I didn't come back for the Army game, I probably wouldn't play against Southern Cal.

We had such intensity playing against Southern Cal in those days, mostly because they were the essence of athletes. They were big; they were strong; they were fast; they were talented. The thing they had too was this air about them coming from California. You know, good weather, Hollywood, everything at their fingertips as far as the good life was concerned . . . that was how we thought about them.

167

Back in South Bend, it was cloudy, it was dingy, it was disciplined as far as school was concerned. We had all this snow in the winter. . . . It was just a contrast in lifestyles, and we represented more of the middle class, hard-working individuals, not the flashy athletes.

We had a strong ground game. We were going to grind it out. We weren't going to win on the big play. The buildup to that game after Anthony Davis had scored six touchdowns the year before was intense. Playing against them was an emotional, electric time.

Anthony Davis had been on the cover of *Sports Illustrated*, and somebody made copies of that cover and put them all over the crosswalks at Notre Dame. Every time the students at Notre Dame would come across one of those pictures, they'd spit on it or stomp on it. So the intensity wasn't just with the team; it was with the whole university. When Southern Cal came in here it was like the anticipation of a heavyweight fight.

Remember I said we were going to grind it out against them? Well, we did, but we also had an 85-yard touchdown run by Eric Penick, so we did beat them with the big play as well while limiting Anthony Davis.

My college career culminated with the [24–23] victory over Alabama in the Sugar Bowl to win the national title. It was overwhelming. The culmination of seven years of dreaming ended in the locker room with my father, my grandfather, and my little brother, not yelling and screaming, but just watching everybody go crazy. I don't think we had the intensity toward Alabama that we had toward Southern Cal, but it was a humongous victory for us.

That year, Ara had broken precedent by making three of us captains. I think it was very close in the voting between me and David Casper as the offensive captain. So Dave was the team captain, I was the offensive captain, and Mike Townsend was the defensive captain, so to speak. We all had different roles. I was more of a quiet leader. I tried to lead by example through hard work during the off-season and tried to do the right thing.

One time Ara said, "I don't want you going down to the bars. If you get caught, you're going to get thrown off the team!" So I didn't go down to the bars. That was the kind of respect we had for him.

Ara concentrated on ball control and always gave us an advantage as far as blocking rules were concerned. Tom Clements was Ara on the field. He was the fulcrum of the offense because he understood what Ara was talking about, and you could recognize it on the field.

I think the closest we could get to what Ara did was having Tom out there. He had such a command of Ara's offense, and it was a very complicated offense. We had guards pulling one way, backs going the other way; we were always screwing up the defense.

As far as the school is concerned and what Notre Dame means to me, it has become more crystallized as I have gotten older. When my daughter graduated from there, I realized not only that Notre Dame is a great place but that it is a great place because it has good people there.

The thing that makes it great is the kids who go there. The kids I met with my daughter, I recognized that these were the same kind of kids I went to school with. They were good kids who wanted to give back to the community and supply hope to the community in the future. That makes it different from other places, and that's what it's all about.

Notre Dame is about the people; it's not about the bricks and the mortar and the Golden Dome per se. Notre Dame was a special place to me because of Ara Parseghian, because of [academic adviser] Mike DeCicco, not because of the Golden Dome. That's not what makes it great.

One time somebody asked me if the tradition of Rockne and Gipper helped us in our games, and I said, "The tradition here is the guys I'm with right now that make it such a special place. They're the guys who help me." Because of the people, there is no place in the world quite like Notre Dame.

Frank Pomarico, from Howard Beach, New York, moved into the starting lineup at left guard during his sophomore year in 1971 at Notre Dame. He remained a fixture for the Irish through the 1973 season when he was named tri-captain of the Irish, along with Dave Casper and Mike Townsend.

There were bigger players for the Irish, faster players, and players who went on to stellar professional careers. But no one cherished his role as a leader of the Notre Dame squad more than the 6'1", 250-pound Pomarico. His journey to and through Notre Dame truly was a labor of love toward his alma mater.

The 1973 starting offensive line of (from left to right) Steve Neece, Pomarico, Mark Brenneman, Gerry DiNardo, and Steve Sylvester, along with tight end Dave Casper, helped pave the way for an offensive unit that averaged an incredible 350.2 yards rushing per game.

TOM CLEMENTS

1972–1974

I DIDN'T ALWAYS THINK I WAS GOING TO NOTRE DAME, at least not until my senior year in high school. Up until that time I felt I was going to be a college basketball player instead of a quarterback. I had played basketball longer than I had played football by at least four years. I felt I was a lot further along in basketball and a better basketball player than football player. But of course, I had a lot more room to improve in football.

I had an older brother who went to Notre Dame but didn't play football. I started following the football program when he was there. Then when Ara arrived and Terry Hanratty decided to go there out of Western Pennsylvania where I'm from, that added to my interest in the program and the university. When I was recruited by Notre Dame and visited the campus, it fit my mental picture of what a college was supposed to be like with the trees, the buildings, and the campus beauty.

I didn't visit a lot of schools because playing basketball in the Pittsburgh Catholic League meant games on Wednesday and Saturday nights. I had interest in a lot of other schools, but I couldn't visit many places until after the basketball season.

I narrowed it down to Notre Dame, Pittsburgh, and North Carolina. If I picked North Carolina it was going to be to play basketball, and if I picked Pitt I was going to try to play both. It was a tough choice between Notre Dame and North Carolina.

My first year wasn't a frustrating one in part because we had freshman games against Michigan, Michigan State, Tennessee, and then a Mexican

All-Star team in Mexico City, an interesting experience in itself. We were down there for about four days, and it was like a mini bowl trip.

We played in Aztec Stadium, which at the time held about 120,000 people, and about 90,000 to 100,000 fans showed up for this freshman game. We ended up beating them 82–0 with our roster of about 32 players, so there wasn't much substituting we could do. The one thing that really was funny to me was listening to the Mexican players call out signals in Spanish. The game didn't do much for international relations.

That year really let you get acclimated to college football and let you learn the ropes. The varsity in 1971 had a good ranking going into the year [No. 2 in the AP] with a good defense, but the offense struggled a little bit at times with different quarterbacks playing. I just concentrated on what I was doing on the freshman team and the prep team.

We had what we called the Toilet Bowl on Mondays, where we scrimmaged against the varsity players who didn't play the previous Saturday. One afternoon we beat them, and of course the next week, they put it to us pretty good. As a freshman you were part of Notre Dame football, but not that big of a part just yet.

I'll never forget going out as freshmen and wearing those white football practice pants. Everyone on the varsity wore gold pants, and when you graduated from the white pants to the gold pants, you knew you were stepping up. But there was still a growth process in moving up to the varsity.

171

Spring practice during my freshman year was my chance to win a spot on the varsity roster. The quarterback job was an open competition during that spring, and I thought I played well. But going into the fall Ara hadn't named a starting quarterback. It wasn't until the week before the [1972] opener [versus Northwestern] that I finally won the job.

Sometimes things went well that season and sometimes they didn't, as you might expect for a team with an inexperienced quarterback. We were up and down in 1972 [8–3]. We had some good games but we lost a few too, and then in the Orange Bowl, Nebraska beat us badly, 40–6.

The USC game was a little different because up until the last quarter we had played pretty well and they were No. 1. They scored a number of points in the fourth quarter and beat us handily [45–23], but it was a good game for three quarters. The Trojans were just a better team than we were and deserved to win. You never like to lose, but the feeling there was different from the one we had against Nebraska. In that game the Cornhuskers just put it to us, and they were better as well. Everyone was just waiting for the spring to try to improve.

Any time you lose your last game in the fashion we did, it makes for a long off-season for everyone. The winter workouts were harder, and there wasn't much levity around the team. Spring practice was serious business. We knew we'd be better in 1973, and we obviously ended up being very good. After we beat USC and we were unbeaten and halfway home, we knew we had something special in front of us.

I remember the week before USC we beat Army 62–3 on the road, and you could sense the excitement in that locker room as if we had just won a big game. We knew what was next, and the anticipation started immediately after Army. With all the pep rallies and the posters of Anthony Davis on the sidewalks, every day you were reminded in some way that there was a big game coming up. It built up all week.

When Luther Bradley put that big hit on Lynn Swann early in the game, that set the tone for the day. The most memorable play was Eric Penick's [85-yard] touchdown run at the start of the second half. That was probably the loudest I've ever heard Notre Dame Stadium. The reaction to that run was unforgettable. Once Eric got outside the line, you knew that he was going to go all the way.

172

The atmosphere around the Sugar Bowl was very special too because we knew it was going to be for the national title. That's why you come to Notre Dame in the first place, to play in big games. That's why you go to Alabama, USC, or Ohio State. Add in two Hall of Fame coaches [Parseghian and Paul "Bear" Bryant] and there were so many elements that made the game exciting. The buildup over the course of a month made it all the more intense.

Through my career Ara and Tom Pagna coached me very well. Ara had a unique system that put a lot of responsibility on the quarterback's shoulders to call different blocking schemes and figure out which passes you could go to based on what the defense gave you. You could change things at the line of scrimmage just by a word or, in some cases, by the inflection of your voice. Notre Dame is the only place I've ever been where you could go right or left on not only the word, but how you *said* the word. It was an intricate system, but it was very logical and the more I got involved in it, the more comfortable I became.

Heading into my senior season [1974], we lost some players to off-the-field problems, but we thought we had a chance to possibly repeat. Getting upset early in the year by Purdue [31–20] was bad, but at least it came early.

Cool under fire, quarterback Tom Clements helped direct the Fighting Irish to the 1973 national title. *Photo courtesy of Dennis Luczak/Notre Dame Sports Information Department.*

We won a lot of close games, including that Navy game [14–6] when Ara made the decision to retire at the end of the season. Then we lost a strange game at USC [55–24] when we couldn't stop them in the second half. It was gratifying to beat Alabama again [13–11 in the Orange Bowl] and end up with a respectable ranking [No. 6 AP, No. 4 UPI].

I never saw Ara's retirement coming. When you're 21 years old playing football in college, you're just concerned with yourself, life in the dorms, and going to school. It would have been hard to make an assessment of how Ara was feeling at the time. When you're that young as a player, you thought Ara would be there for a long time. My first reaction when Ara decided to step down was shock, followed by the fact that I was glad I was a senior and wouldn't have to work with a new regime.

We wanted to send Ara off in his last game with a victory over a tough Crimson Tide team that had the motivation of revenge on their side. Ara handled the situation so well. We practiced for the Orange Bowl over on Marco Island in the morning and then enjoyed the afternoons. Then three days before the game we went over to Miami, got down to business, and were focused. Ara planned the practices very well, and he went out like the champion that he was.

174

A three-year starter at quarterback, Tom Clements helped Notre Dame to the national title in 1973 and was Ara Parseghian's last starting quarterback during his Irish coaching career.

Listed at 6'0", 190 pounds, the McKees Rocks, Pennsylvania, native spearheaded Notre Dame's incomparable 1973 ground attack that averaged 350.2 yards rushing per game, a mark that no Irish team has come within 60 yards of since. Clements, who cocaptained the 1974 squad with linebacker Greg Collins, finished his Notre Dame career with 3,594 yards passing and 24 touchdown passes.

After a sterling professional football career in Canada, Clements played one year for the Kansas City Chiefs (1980) before embarking upon a career in law. He returned to Notre Dame as an assistant coach (1992–1995) under Lou Holtz before moving on to the coaching ranks in the NFL, where he remains today.

LUTHER BRADLEY

1973, 1975–1977

T<small>HE MAJOR</small> B<small>IG</small> 10 <small>POWERS</small>, Michigan and Ohio State, weren't recruiting me at all when I was a senior in high school. Where I really wanted to go was the University of Tennessee because they were becoming a national powerhouse. My high school coaches sent my films down to Tennessee, but the Volunteers weren't interested. That kind of hurt my feelings.

Then my dad talked to the Penn State coaches because he was a graduate of the school. My coach sent them films—and the Penn State people said they weren't interested either! So when we played Penn State in the 1976 Gator Bowl [a 20–9 victory], I was pumped big time.

The schools that recruited me—Indiana University, Purdue University, the University of Minnesota, and the University of Cincinnati—looked at me mainly as a running back. All Ara said was, "We want you to be a defensive back because we have real needs there."

The other school that kind of wanted me to be a defensive back was Indiana. That was the same time they had Quinn Buckner, who was the point guard for the basketball team. But he was also a defensive back. They tried to entice me by saying I might have a chance to play on the basketball team as well.

Purdue had a selling point of me playing a multiple role. They had an All-American by the name of Leroy Keyes [1966–1968], who played both sides of the field as an offensive back and defensive back. They said I could be like him. But I didn't want to be a running back. I figured my long-term football future would be as a defensive back, and it fit my personality better too.

Notre Dame wanting me as a defensive back was one of the reasons I signed there. Second, they were always on the hunt for national championships and major bowls. The Big 10 back then sent only one team to a bowl. It would either be Michigan or Ohio State going to the Rose Bowl, and the rest were "wannabes." I wanted to play in big bowls and for national titles.

The third thing was the quality of education. One of the things Notre Dame did that other schools didn't was send a coach to look at me in track and field. I was probably in the top five in the state and had run a 9.7 in the 100-yard dash. I don't think the other coaches or schools even knew I ran track, but Notre Dame was amazed at how fast I was when the coach—I think it was Denny Murphy, the freshman coach—saw me compete.

After a couple of weeks on the practice field at Notre Dame, it all started to fit. I didn't feel uncomfortable; I didn't feel like a fish out of water. I felt like I deserved to be there and was pretty good at what I did.

After the first week, Ross [Browner], myself, and a bunch of freshmen—Willie Fry, Al Hunter, Tim Simon, Marvin Russell—were put on the second team. After the second week, Ross and I were with the first team, and Willie alternated with Jim Stock at right defensive end.

176

A week before our opener, the freshman team had a game up at Michigan. Ross and I were standing on the sidelines and watched them as they were preparing to go to Michigan. We said to one of the coaches, "Why don't you let us go up to Michigan and play this weekend to get the bugs out?" He said, "Are you kidding? If something happened to you two, I'd get fired!"

My most fond memory is the 1973 USC game. That's probably the best game I ever played, and certainly the most intense. [USC wide receiver] Lynn Swann was an All-American, so you get pumped for that challenge. You see him on tape and just know he's a superstar. He was like the guys you see today—Larry Fitzgerald [Pittsburgh] and Mike Williams [USC]—the best in the United States. I was just ready to play.

The Sugar Bowl was a consummation of the season, from losing 40–6 to Nebraska in the Orange Bowl the previous year to winning the national title. But the highlight for me was that USC game in 1973. I remember Ara telling us the week before the game, "They always have more talent than we do, but we're going to outsmart them and play better football than them," and that's exactly what we did.

I went to Indiana–Purdue University at Fort Wayne in 1974–1975 during my suspension from Notre Dame. The only school that called my dad was Ball State, in my hometown, and Dave McClain was the coach at the time. He lived a block and a half away from us. He called my dad but also said, "It would be a disservice if I took him. I'd only take him because he's out there. But he deserves to be at Notre Dame playing against big-time people."

I wanted to go to the best; I went to the best and I knew what the best felt like. So there was no way I was going to go somewhere else during that time. I would have had to have gone to Southern Cal, Oklahoma . . . somewhere just as powerful as Notre Dame. But even then, I still didn't feel they had the prestige Notre Dame did.

I have a son now who just got accepted into Stanford. For me, it's kind of a double-edged sword. As a father, I'm proud because it's one of the best schools in the United States, but it's also $40,000 a year. I told him of my own experience. When you have an opportunity to go to the best, if you go somewhere else, you'll feel like you're with a second-rate organization.

Ara was a different kind of guy in that he knew everything about football. Dan Devine was basically a recruiter, and he had a great staff. Parseghian was a little more demanding than Dan Devine was. The bottom line was the staff was still there to say our goal was to win football games and a national championship.

177

My 99-yard touchdown return at Purdue [in 1975] was a favorite moment because it was such a tight game [a 17–0 victory]. Another reason it stood out was my mom was there even though she was not a football person. She was just a Luther Bradley fan. After the game, all the reporters were around me, and when I finally walked away, she grabbed my hand and said, "Wow, you caught that ball and ran all the way down the field—what do you call that?" It was kind of cute. All she knew was she was supposed to clap.

We weren't tight at the start of the 1977 season. We just didn't gel, particularly offensively. We knew we would be real good on defense, and that's the main reason most everyone picked us No. 1 in the preseason. It always takes about two or three weeks for the offense to catch up with the defense. We carried the offense the first two or three weeks but still lost at Ole Miss [20–13]. By the middle of the year, the offense finally caught up and became a machine.

Joe Montana lining up as the third-team quarterback in practice was something we talked about all the time as a first-team defense. We had to go against

Notre Dame's talent level began to rise in the early seventies with the arrival of players such as defensive back Luther Bradley.

this guy on the scout team, and he made us look bad. But he wasn't playing, so we knew it was more of a political thing than the fact that he didn't have the talent to play. Eventually, the cream rises to the top, and he did.

I never approached the staff about Joe not playing, but Willie Fry was one of the captains. We were good friends, and I'd go by his room once in a while and say, "Man, you ought to tell Devine to let Joe play!" He'd say, "Yeah, I know, it's pretty sad. Maybe I'll say something to him." I don't know if Willie ever did say anything.

The green jersey game [versus USC in 1977] was a favorite memory. We weren't privy to the information that we were going to change jerseys. But I remember walking with Willie to the dorm that week and he kept telling people who were passing by, "Make sure you wear green [for the game]!" So when we got into the locker room after warming up and saw the green jerseys hanging there, it was pretty exciting, all the yelling and screaming. That put us over the top.

I was really close to Willie, but he never said a word about it to me. After the game, I said "Willie, how did you know? When did you find out?" He said the captains had been told about a week earlier, but Devine had said, "Don't tell anybody because if it gets out and everybody knows, it's not going to have the same impact."

During my senior year, I was selected to attend the Heisman Trophy dinner. It was the first of its kind where they had the best players from each position participate and get an award. A couple of months prior to that, the professor in one of my classes had said no one could get out of a certain project we were doing, which was a team project.

I had to go to New York for the Heisman dinner on a Thursday night, and the presentation was going to be on Friday. So I told the professor I had to do this Notre Dame thing for the Heisman, and he said, "I told you there is no way anybody can get out of this. If you don't come to my class, you're going to fail!"

I said, "What do I have to do?" He said, "Go to the dean and the athletic director." I thought, "These people are really serious about education!"

I had to first go to the athletic director's office. After I sat down and talked with [Ed] "Moose" Krause to explain what happened, he said he'd make a call over to the dean of the business school. Then the dean had to call the professor to permit me to go to the function. But he told him I was still

179

responsible to do what everyone else did. That sticks out because it epitomizes what Notre Dame stands for.

Other than Georgia's Herschel Walker in 1980, one would be hard-pressed to find two freshmen in college football history who made a greater immediate impact on their squads than defensive back Luther Bradley and defensive end Ross Browner did for Notre Dame in 1973. The duo became instant starters as freshmen and helped lead Notre Dame to the 1973 national title. Bradley paced the team in interceptions (6) and passes broken up (11) while starting at strong safety.

After serving a school suspension during the 1974–1975 academic year, the duo returned to Notre Dame in August of 1975 under new head coach Dan Devine, and they would help the Irish to yet another national title in 1977.

Bradley, who lined up at cornerback under Devine, holds the Irish career record for interceptions (17), earned consensus first-team All-America notice in 1977, was a first-round NFL draft pick by Detroit, and never missed a start in four seasons for the Irish.

The 6'2", 205-pound Muncie, Indiana, native played four years of professional football with the Lions.

ROSS BROWNER

1973, 1975–1977

DURING THE RECRUITING PROCESS, I evaluated the school, education, coaches, and the publicity the school was receiving. Notre Dame had TV and radio going, and I grew up watching Theismann-to-Gatewood on the highlights. But it was one man who did it for me: Ara Parseghian. I really liked his leadership. He had genuine honesty and strong character.

Woody Hayes made a lot of trips to our house and I said, "Coach, I just met a very impressive gentleman at Notre Dame who was a player of yours." And he said, "Yeah, Ara Parseghian . . . a good kid! But I'm the coach you should be playing for! Ohio kids should stay in Ohio! Look at Archie Griffin! We gave him a chance to start as a freshman [in 1972, the first year the NCAA made freshmen eligible for the varsity again], and look at what he's done!"

I was at Archie Griffin's first start against North Carolina [1972] when he ran for 200-plus yards, and I had a chance to meet him. I was impressed because they weren't shy about playing rookies. Ohio State has a very impressive campus, but eighty-six thousand students or whatever it was really concerned me, compared to just six thousand at Notre Dame.

The night before my signing, I had to hide at my Aunt Mary's house. She lived about two streets away, and I told Notre Dame to meet me there. Michigan, Ohio State, Michigan State, and, I think, Nebraska were at my parents' door the next morning. They were pretty surprised when I wasn't there and they confronted my mom and dad. My parents talked with all of them and said, "Ross has made a decision we allowed him to make on his own. He's decided to go to Notre Dame." The schools weren't too happy about that because they all thought I would go to their place.

Ohio State, Michigan, and Michigan State wanted me as a tight end. Michigan State was graduating an All-American in Billy Joe DuPree, and they told me I could follow in his footsteps. Ara said he was looking at me as a tight end because I had good speed, good hands, and height, but he also asked me what I wanted to play.

I said, "Coach, if you're going to give me a choice, on offense you have to kind of accept the punishment, whereas on defense you get a chance to dish it out. I prefer to dish out. I like tackling people. If you would, I'd love to play defensive end." He just said, "OK, that'll be a good position for you."

I just loved destroying offenses. I loved catching people in the backfield, throwing the whole thing off, and giving our defense an advantage. For my freshman year I was just thinking of being a kamikaze guy on the kickoff team and showing them I could hit. After a couple of days of practice, [defensive line coach] Joe Yonto told me, "We're looking at you a little more than just being on the kickoff team, Ross. I want to start you."

After our first scrimmage with the varsity, that's when they moved up about six freshmen, mostly on defense. Our offense had Tom Clements, Wayne "the Train" [Bullock], Dave Casper, Steve Sylvester, Gerry DiNardo . . . so many great players, but they weren't able to do anything against our freshmen.

After Willie Fry and I made a couple of tackles in the backfield, Ara's eyes lit up and he said, "Hey, we've got a good corps of freshmen here. We can't let these guys just play freshman ball. They've got to play varsity." [Defensive back] Luther [Bradley] and I started with the first team from then on. Winning the national title that year was the most tremendous award we could give back to coach Parseghian.

After I was suspended the next year, I decided I would not run away from anything because I did not do anything wrong other than have a young lady in the dormitory after hours. A school disciplinary action had to happen because of that. My mom and dad had an extensive talk about it, and then I had a real extensive talk with Ara, Father Hesburgh, and Father Joyce. I came out of that thinking, "Hey, this school still wants me."

They did have to do something to discipline us. It was like being a father. You teach your kids that this is not right and we had to be set as examples. They said, "Unfortunately, due to the publicity and circumstances, we have

Many longtime Irish followers believe end Ross Browner is the best to ever play defense for Notre Dame.

to do something to rectify it." I was thinking something like having to stay on campus and they said, "No, it's got to be something stricter than that. We have to suspend you for one year of school."

I really didn't want that, but coming from a strict upbringing, I understood you have to do things to your child to make him understand right and wrong. Plus, we were examples for the whole school, the eyes of the nation were on us, and the university had to be a little stricter with their disciplinary rules.

I could have gone to Ohio State, Michigan, Nebraska . . . they had contacted my mother and father and told them they were still interested if I was willing to go to their school. I told them Notre Dame was still the school I wanted to attend. I didn't enroll anywhere for the 1974–1975 school year. I went down to the School of Hard Knocks and did construction work in Indianapolis with Bob Welsh's development agency. I just stayed hard-nosed and took my knocks.

I didn't know what to expect when I came back and there was a new coach. Once I met coach Devine, I was impressed with his professionalism and how he handled players. I also had the same position coach, Joe Yonto. We still had Father Hesburgh, Father Joyce, [Ed] "Moose" Krause, Colonel Jack Stephens, and Roger Valdiserri at the same positions. To me, Notre Dame hadn't really changed other than the head coach.

184

My biggest adjustment was prior to my junior year [1976] when my father died during the summer. I had five brothers and a sister underneath me. My mother was a wonderful, strong woman. I told her, "Mom, it looks like I have to quit school and go to work for the family." She said, "Nope, you're going to stay in school and you're still going to work for the family by being the first in our whole family to graduate from college. You need to show your younger brothers and sister how important that degree is."

That put a large lump in my throat because I had thought I was going to have to give up something I loved to do, which was play football and go to college. I had convinced myself that if I had to, I'd bite the bullet and support the family. I was going to make a major sacrifice. I was just thinking of being the oldest, the man of the family, and taking over my father's position.

What changed my life at Notre Dame were the people I was involved with on and off the campus. On the campus were my coaches, friends, and professors. Emil T. Hoffman was one of those professors, and my dean was Mike DeCicco. He also happened to be the fencing coach, and he kept a sword in his office. He told me, quite seriously, "I'll put this sword where it's not going to feel good if you mess up any of these classes!" I was like, "Yes, sir!" He was a very good influence.

Roger Valdiserri was tremendous to me. A wonderful sports information director, plus quite a person to know and talk to who would keep you straight. You add in [athletic directors] Moose Krause and Colonel Stephens, and I had a lot of fathers there—other than Father Hesburgh and Father Joyce.

Off campus there were Paul and Sharon Harvey, plus Mr. Ed Smothers and his family. Paul was the captain of the police force in South Bend. They gave me a lot of leadership and guidance.

Back then, Notre Dame had a program implemented in which black families in South Bend served as hosts for each black student-athlete. It helped us assimilate into the community and helped the adjustment away from home. It was also nice to get a home-cooked meal now and then. [Nineteen forty-nine Heisman Trophy winner] Leon Hart was also one of my mentors.

Joe Yonto is a strong Italian product. He never let you get too big for your shoes. He kept you where you needed to be, was always very honest, and always worked you very hard. No matter what we did the previous Saturday, by Monday it was, "OK, we have to start from scratch. Let's fall on the ball. Let's do our bear crawls. Let's do our monkey rolls. Let's get down and dirty, and get your hands in the mud." We didn't change our practice habits or his way of coaching.

185

My greatest moment in football was beating No. 1 Texas for the national title in the Cotton Bowl my senior year. Down in Texas we were told we shouldn't even have shown up because Texas was the largest state in the whole U.S.A. Everything in Texas is big, and Texas is number one in everything.

Every place we went, people just said, "You're Notre Dame. You guys are Catholic, you're small, you need to go back home." We weren't very welcome in Dallas. Even at the awards ceremony on the evening before the game, we had to sit in a balcony and all the Texas players sat on the main floor. That burned a spur in our hide. They got their [Cotton Bowl] watches presented to them on time, and we had ours presented the next day. We were upset about being treated like second-class citizens.

They didn't know who they were messing with, which is why we whipped them, 38–10. Our whole team just said, "We're not going to take this!" Coach Devine didn't have to give a pep talk or anything because we were ready to tear out the door.

I played in the Super Bowl in the pros, but every game we played at Notre Dame was like a Super Bowl. We always had packed stadiums wherever we went. We always played under a tremendous amount of pressure. Every game was important to our school's history and to the schools we were playing.

One thing I loved is we played all over the country: north, south, east, and west. A lot of universities don't travel like we do.

I would love to go into coaching or football administration, and I'm start-ing to look into those avenues. Eventually, my highest expectation would be to head back to Notre Dame. What Notre Damer wouldn't want to do that!

Enshrined in the College Football Hall of Fame in 2000, Ross Browner was one of the game's most dominant performers. He stepped into the starting lineup as a freshman in his first college game and led the defensive line of the 1973 national champs in tackles (69) and stops for lost yardage (15). He concluded his college career with another national title in 1977.

The two-time consensus All-American and Dean's List student also won the Outland Trophy (1976) and Maxwell Award (1977) and was fifth in the 1977 Heisman balloting. His 340 career tackles are an unbreakable standard for Irish linemen, with Steve Niehaus' 290 a distant second. Browner's 77 career tack-les for loss also is a figure in its own stratosphere. (Through 2003, second place belonged to Kory Minor with 43.5.) Just as impressive was how the Warren, Ohio, native remained committed to Notre Dame after serving a one-year sus-pension during the 1974–1975 school year.

The 6'3", 248-pound tri-captain of the 1977 Fighting Irish (along with Willie Fry and Terry Eurick) was a first-round pick (eighth overall) of the Cincinnati Bengals, where he spent nine years before concluding his NFL career with the Green Bay Packers.

DAVE REEVE

1974—1977

I GREW UP IN BLOOMINGTON, INDIANA, and was always a Notre Dame fan. I'm not Catholic, but I had relatives in South Bend and got hooked at a young age and was wearing Notre Dame sweatshirts in grade school and high school.

Even though I was an All-American kicker in high school and Notre Dame needed a kicker after just winning a national championship [in 1973], I really didn't think that playing for the Irish would happen. Even in February of my senior year I was waiting to hear back from the Notre Dame coaching staff while some other schools were waiting to sign me up.

Finally, I called Notre Dame and got [offensive line coach] Wally Moore on the phone. Of course he told me that he was just getting ready to call me. I felt like saying, "Oh sure, right." In hindsight they had to wait until they got all their key players lined up before they could go get a kicker, which was the last thing on the list. Back then it was rare that a kicker was offered a scholarship. In fact, I was the first kicker they gave a scholarship to straight out of high school.

Bob Thomas was there before me, but he had walked on before earning his scholarship. I had followed Bob's career at Notre Dame, and Ara Parseghian was very candid with me about how Thomas' success had showed him how important a kicker was. Timing was everything because Bob was on his way out as I was on my way in.

It was a dream just to get looked at by Notre Dame. It was my dream school from the start. I got letters from what seemed like every school in the country. Notre Dame sent me a calendar at one point, and that got me really excited because I thought maybe they were paying attention to me. What I didn't know until after I finished high school was that my high school had been in contact with Notre Dame every week of every game and had sent the coaching staff game film. My high school coach didn't tell me because he knew how much more nervous that would have made me.

So after talking to coach Moore in February, I had a visit scheduled for that weekend. At the time Mississippi State was really putting the press on me to sign, but I told them I had to see Notre Dame first.

When I arrived at Notre Dame I met with coach Parseghian in his office. He was so professional. He told me the facts and that was it. I left the office with coach Moore, not knowing if Ara had offered me a scholarship or not. I had just come from Mississippi State, Ball State, and all these other schools that were falling all over themselves to get me.

My first game as a freshman in 1974 was on national television when we opened on Monday night against Georgia Tech [a 31–7 victory]. I really didn't think playing at Notre Dame was that big of a deal to everybody else until I got to my hotel room the first day and had half a dozen telegrams from my parents and friends. That's when I realized that this was big for my community back in Bloomington.

188

So there I was in the locker room at Georgia Tech, and Ara's telling us to leave our helmets on while we were on our sideline. I thought that was some sort of tradition until we ran out on the field and Georgia Tech fans were throwing fish and bottles and pouring stuff on us as we ran out through the tunnel. That's one lesson I took out of Notre Dame: you either love the Irish or hate them, and down South you were hated.

I remember going down to Clemson in 1977 and we had a bomb scare. Ken MacAfee and I snuck out and went down to McDonald's and they wouldn't serve us because we were Notre Dame football players.

When we played Texas in the Cotton Bowl after the 1977 season, several of the players' wives went with us on the trip. They would come back after a day of shopping in Dallas and tell us all these horror stories about how they were treated by the local people. Dallas thought they not only invented the game of football, but that we had no right to be there with them. That really fired us up to play the game even more.

With Notre Dame everything started at the top with Ara Parseghian. You hear all these stories about teams where the freshmen are shunned and ridiculed. We had 10 freshmen who contributed on our team, and our captains welcomed us because they knew we were there to help them win.

How freshmen were treated shows the quality of coaches that Ara had and shows the type of player he recruited, ones that put the team first. We didn't have hotshot guys who played to become stars. We had stars in Joe Montana, Vagas Ferguson, and Ken MacAfee, but they became stars because they were team players to begin with.

Believe it or not, I never kicked a game-winning field goal with no time left on the clock during my Notre Dame career. The biggest kick I made was the opening points at the Cotton Bowl against Texas in 1978 on a 47-yard field goal. I swear if it needed to be 48 yards it would have been short. I thought that set the tone for the game [a 38–10 victory].

The closest I ever came to kicking a game-winner was a 26-yarder against Pittsburgh on the road with about a minute to go [in 1977]. That field goal put us ahead, but then Pitt fumbled and we scored again to win 19–9, so the kick didn't matter. It's strange to me that I was never put in a win-lose field-goal position in all my four years.

When I look back at the 1977 season, losing at Mississippi was truly a fluke. I could see it in everybody's face that the heat got to us. Throw in the fact that Mississippi was making all these one-handed catches, and we just couldn't do anything about it.

Losing 20–13 with Rusty Lisch at quarterback, I think everyone on the team knew we didn't have the best quarterback out there yet. We all knew that Joe Montana was that quarterback, and not until the next week at Purdue did he get that chance. Although honestly, I think [quarterback] Gary Forystek [who was injured in the Purdue game] could have won the national championship too.

When Rusty came out of the game at Purdue and Gary went in, you could sense a relief on the sidelines that with Gary in there we were going to win the game. But it wasn't long before Gary took a helmet to the chin. He laid motionless on the field for what seemed like forever as the ambulance came out. We thought he might be dead. Then Rusty goes back in, still couldn't move the team, and then Joe got his chance in the third quarter. Joe is just a winner, no matter whether it's football or tiddlywinks.

My first marital fight was over Joe Montana. My wife and I got married before my senior year and moved up to South Bend in the apartment right

Dave Reeve, the first kicker-only to receive a scholarship to Notre Dame, still ranks fifth on the school's all-time scoring list.

above Joe and his first wife, Kim. Joe and I went to school together, and our wives went to work together.

One day during the summer my wife and I were sitting around the pool, and she asked me if I wanted to go play tennis. I wanted to, but she really wasn't a very good tennis player, so I passed because I'm so competitive. All of a sudden Joe comes up riding his bike and says, "Hey Dave, you want to play tennis?" I was up out of that chair and on the court. Of course, my wife didn't like that.

That summer Joe was not a known name, even if we all knew as players that he should be our starting quarterback. That summer day at the tennis courts, a bunch of kids came up to me asking for autographs with Joe Montana standing on the other side of the court. I told them that Joe Montana was over there, but they didn't know what position he played. They asked me if he started and when I told them he didn't, the kids wouldn't even go over and bother him.

I think you can sum up the 1977 season with a show we saw during the Cotton Bowl week in Dallas. We went to a restaurant during the week and Frank Gorshin, who played the Riddler on *Batman*, the television series, came out and did a song and dance that included a tune called, "It's Not Where You Start, It's Where You Finish." We took that song to heart, and before the Texas game I went up and wrote those words on the chalkboard.

We used that thought as motivation because it didn't matter where we were ranked in September; it was where we could finish after the bowls. We kept believing from the Mississippi game on because we had the schedule on our side, including the USC game, which obviously stands out as the green jersey game.

I knew about the switch before it happened, and I can't reveal how, but about 10 guys knew. I remember the chills that went down our spines when we came back into the locker room and saw those jerseys. I was one of the last guys off the field after pregame, and when I made it to the locker room some of the guys already had the jerseys on. It looked like the game was over and we'd already won 49–19 with the jubilation in that locker room.

Of course it was all set up the night before when Digger Phelps went on at the pep rally and told the fans to show everyone the Irish colors by wearing green. When we first got to the locker room they had set out our normal game socks, but instead of the blue and gold stripe, it had two green stripes. Everyone was thinking how cool it was that we had our green.

Coming in later to see the entire jerseys, it fired up everyone. There was more emotion in that locker room at that time than there ever was during my career. Changing the uniforms was a masterful decision. Who takes credit for it, I don't know, but I think Digger Phelps had something to do with it.

A four-year starting kicker for Notre Dame, Dave Reeve owns the mark for the longest field goal kicked by an Irish player, a 53-yarder versus Pittsburgh during the 1976 season. Reeve ranks fifth all time in scoring with 247 points, including 39 field goals and 130 extra points. A native of Bloomington, Indiana, the 6'3", 216-pounder was the first kicker-only out of high school to receive a scholarship from Notre Dame.

191

JOE MONTANA

1975, 1977–1978

I GREW UP LOVING THIS PLACE. I loved where I grew up also. But one of the things I've never done a lot is look back. There were always places to go and things to do.

Now that my career is over, I have kids looking around at colleges, and it's fun to be back at Notre Dame. Hopefully there will be a lot more visits. It's one of those places that has always been very special to me from many, many, many moons ago.

We came back for a visit and just tried to get our older daughter to understand the essence of the place and what it's really all about. As much as it is the education, it's that closeness of the university that will mean a lot more to you when you're gone.

Choosing Notre Dame was easy for me. As soon as they said I had a scholarship, I was here. I had visited a few other universities prior to that, but I had always wanted to come here. It was part of a dream growing up.

When I came to Notre Dame, there were a lot of people from Western Pennsylvania here. Notre Dame was having great years in football. It seemed like Notre Dame was on TV Saturday, Sunday, Monday, and Tuesday, although it was really the game Saturday and the replay on Sunday.

I just had a love for Notre Dame from a very early age. When I had the opportunity, I took it. I canceled the rest of my visits. If it had not been for [Notre Dame], who knows where I would have been. I might have played basketball.

Winning at Notre Dame every year is not easy. Number one, this is Notre Dame, and when Notre Dame shows up on someone's schedule, you're a target, no matter what kind of year you're having.

When you're winning, they obviously want to beat you, and when you're down, they want to kick you while you're down. It's a matter of remembering those guys who are kicking you when you're down to help motivate you to get back to the other side of that table.

Being at Notre Dame, you're going to take away some great memories. You're going to take away some great friendships that will last a lifetime. And you're going to take away an education that no matter how long your career is, or if you're just coming out of college and you know your football career is over, you're going to fall back on that education at some point in time, as I've learned after my [pro football] career.

There are certain places where no matter what type of team you have or they have, there's a certain amount of respect, and Notre Dame's great rival, USC, happens to be one of those places. It's like a brother. You constantly fight, but when it comes down to it, you're best of friends when you're not in that mode.

I have the utmost respect in the world for [former USC star] Ronnie Lott. He is the godfather to our youngest son. So that tells you what I think of Ronnie, and I think the world of SC. They've got a tremendous program, it's a great university, but when it comes to being out on the field, nobody likes anyone until it's over.

193

People talk about all the great comebacks we had at Notre Dame, but my best advice is to try not to get in those situations where you have to come from behind.

When you go about trying to overcome an obstacle that sometimes seems further away than you would like it to be, or not within your grasp, people try to reach and do things that they typically wouldn't try to do and are outside of their capabilities. Where I have had the most success is trying to go almost opposite of that. I'm going to do whatever I can within my ability. There will be a certain time for desperation somewhere along the line, but most of those situations aren't desperation at all. It feels like there isn't a lot of time, but there is.

In San Francisco, when we made comebacks or would pull things out, we tried to go back to fundamentals. We stepped backward instead of trying to

Nothing in Notre Dame football annals prompts awe and excitement quite like the magical name of quarterback Joe Montana.

extend forward. Many times we'd say, "OK, we had a bad first half. Now we've got to just go back to basic football."

I guess I learned that in high school, a little more of that at Notre Dame, and then refined it when I got to the NFL with [San Francisco head coach] Bill Walsh.

Bill had a completely different approach than I'd ever seen. He didn't want you to just be good; he wanted you to be perfect. He felt if you didn't quite make perfect you'd be damn good. So he could live with that, but he wanted you to be perfect. It got to the point, every day at practice, that I strived to not have a football hit the ground. I never made it, but I tried every day to do that.

People probably ask me the most about the 1979 Cotton Bowl when we came back from a large deficit [34–12] to defeat Houston [35–34]. It was probably the coldest game I ever played in. I think there were more people watching the game in the parking lot and in their RVs than there were in the stands.

There were 69 points scored in the game, and the wind was blowing so hard in one direction that I think only 14 points were scored against the wind, one of which was a blocked punt. We were fortunate enough to have the wind in the fourth quarter and have that momentum.

195

I got a little hypothermia during that game. It was so cold . . . I didn't like going from the field to the heater to the field to the heater. But I was doing it that day. My body temperature dropped and we had tried to heat my body core with some chicken soup or some chicken bouillon or whatever was in the locker room at that time. They wouldn't let me come back out until [my body temperature] was back to normal. Fortunately I got to go back out. I wasn't sure if that's what I wanted to do at the time, but we went back and we did the simple things.

We weren't throwing the ball down the field in desperation. We just wanted to go back and end the game on a high note. Typically what coaches do when you're getting beat that badly, they say, "Let's just go back to the fundamentals and let's start showing some progress. If we end the game that way and we're progressively getting better than we were, that's a plus even if we lose the game." But in that game, things really started working in our favor, which they typically do when you take that approach.

I'm asked about my relationship [with coach Dan Devine], and even with Bill [Walsh]; people talk about how there was this battle between us. All coaches have to make a decision on a player and can never be as personal as they would like to be. People like to make more of it than there is. I don't think [my relationship] was any different [with Devine] than it was with any head coach and player who thought he should be playing and wasn't.

I've talked with Bill about our relationship through the years and how people tried to drive something between us even though there wasn't anything. It's just impossible for a coach to get too close to a player because one day, that coach has to make a judgment.

We lost to Mississippi in 1977, and Gary Forystek was the quarterback when we went to Purdue. Unfortunately for Gary Forystek, he took one of the most devastating hits I've seen in football. Luckily he wasn't seriously injured, and he ended up trying out for the 49ers a few years later.

But for me, it was being in the right spot at the right time and having the right things fall into place to be able to get into a game. The one thing I try to tell guys today is that if you're not starting, you've got to practice like you're starting because you may get thrown into a game, and if you're not prepared, you may only get one chance. That chance will blow by you quickly, and you won't get another chance if you're not ready.

I probably wasn't a very good practice player, especially when I was a freshman. I was overwhelmed once I got to Notre Dame, academically and on the football field. When I got here, there were 11 quarterbacks. There were two Parade All-Americans, and there were seven freshman quarterbacks. You start to think, "Oh my God, what did I get into!" Coupled with being away from home, as much as I wanted to be here, I really wasn't prepared those first years for what I was embarking on.

So that probably made me a bad practice player. Getting into Ara's offense was difficult for me to learn. I came from a pure numbering system into a pure word system. Some of that stuff is still Greek to me right now.

It was an ugly start. I started the same way in San Francisco. I keep telling my boys, "Don't feel bad, the first [pro] game I started was in Seattle, and I had two interceptions run back for touchdowns." One guy had the nerve to run me over on the second interception. So it was a shaky start on all ends and just a matter of settling down and getting comfortable with the system.

But I'll always be thankful for the opportunity I had to go to Notre Dame. Between Tom McGann's family and Mike DeCicco, whose son Nick was my roommate . . . Mike was the academic adviser to scholarship athletes, the fencing coach, and a professor. Between those two families, they took me under their wing and really kind of settled me down from being homesick and made sure I was doing the right things.

I always hoped that I would never see one of those, "Please report to Mr. DeCicco's office immediately, no excuses will be accepted" notes. Funny how I can remember that.

Of all the names whose mere mention inspires the glory of Notre Dame football, no one since the Golden Boy, 1956 Heisman Trophy winner Paul Hornung, has epitomized the Fighting Irish aura quite like Joe Montana from Monongahela, Pennsylvania.

Other quarterbacks recorded superior statistics, and others won more games at the helm of the Irish offense. But Montana's heroics, which inspired the nickname "the Comeback Kid," are at the forefront of Fighting Irish lore.

The 6'2", 190-pound Montana certainly wasn't blessed with great size and strength. But in leading the Irish back from deficits against Houston in the January 1, 1979, Cotton Bowl; North Carolina during the 1975 season; and Purdue in 1977, as well as directing 10 straight victories en route to the 1977 national championship, Montana etched his name among the greatest stories in college football history.

His stardom took full flight when he was a member of the San Francisco 49ers, leading his squads to four Super Bowl championships and winning three Super Bowl MVP Awards before concluding his career with the Kansas City Chiefs in 1994.

In 2000, Montana was inducted into the Pro Football Hall of Fame and now rightfully sits among the greatest who ever played the game.

VAGAS FERGUSON

1976–1979

M Y MOTHER PASSED AWAY WHEN I WAS EIGHT years old, and because my father was in the military, I didn't really see him much. My aunt also passed away at an early age. So my grandparents, Hattie and Joe Walker, took 10 of us in—7 children from my family and 3 from my aunt's. Here my grandmother was, after raising two sons and two daughters herself, taking in 10 more kids.

The way we were raised was to care for each other and to work together. We were taught that you reap what you sow. Now my grandmother is in her eighties, and even though she has had her setbacks, she's never alone and never lacking in love because of what she did for us. She is surrounded by grandchildren and great-grandchildren. It shows that if you do the right things for people, it comes back to you.

I'm noted for a lot of rushing records, but I didn't achieve anything by myself. From the assistant coaches to the practice players—which I was at one time—they all had a role in helping me get to where I did, so I've never looked at it as "my records." I don't even purchase the football media guides to look up my records. When I saw Julius Jones break my single-game rushing mark, I was proud of the young man, not because of that but because he came back to Notre Dame when he could have left and quit. That's what it's really about.

I didn't follow college football much until my sophomore year in high school, and I didn't know where Notre Dame was located, to be truthful.

Where I lived you heard more about Ohio State, Michigan, Purdue, and Indiana because it was Big 10 country in central Indiana.

After my junior year I was being contacted by all those schools as well as Notre Dame. The decision wasn't so much football-based. My guidance counselor and grandparents were pushing me toward an education and a degree. When I looked at schools, I listened to them from the standpoint of athletes graduating and academics. Lee Corso was the Indiana coach then, and he talked to me about being his star player and choosing my own number. But the hype and those kinds of things weren't important to me.

The final three schools were Ohio State, Michigan, and Notre Dame. Ohio State wanted to play me at defensive back. Most of the schools were kind of saying that, but I wanted to try running back because that's what I mainly was in high school. When Ohio State was emphasizing strictly defensive back, I kind of shied away from them. Even when I visited them I was kind of overwhelmed because it's such a big school.

Michigan was pretty much the same way: defensive back, but running back possibly. The thing I liked about Michigan was they talked about academics too. Notre Dame came in the door talking about how we want you as an athlete but we want you to be a student first and an athlete second. That impressed me.

199

My hosts were Luther Bradley and Ross Browner. That was in 1975, and they had just been reinstated after a suspension. One of the first things they said was, "If you're going to come to Notre Dame, you're going to be a student first. If you're not going to come to study and graduate, then don't come." That really hit me because everywhere I had been, it was about going out, showing me a good time, and encouraging me to come. But these two guys had been out and had gotten back in. It was impressive to hear that from players.

[Running back coach] Jim Gruden started recruiting me at Indiana University when he was the running backs coach for Corso. The first time I met him, I thought so much of him. I wanted to play for him, and then he ended up at Notre Dame after Hank Kuhlmann left. He taught me so much about the game, reading defenses, reading blocking schemes . . . it really led to my success. I couldn't believe the things I was able to do once he taught me. We became good friends long after I left the game. He was an inspiration to me, and a good friend.

His son, Jon, was just a kid running around all the time at practice with his brother. He's just like his dad all over again: a hard-working, determined guy. He worked us to death, but he loved us at the same time. Just watching his son, you could see he picked up some of those traits. It was nice to see Jon go back to Tampa, where his dad lives. I was really happy for Jim.

I never understood why most schools wanted me at defensive back. I guess I was physical and wasn't afraid to come up and hit people. They were looking at my physical ability and felt I could play at safety. I didn't think I was that fast and couldn't really outrun anybody. I was about 6', 190 coming in, so I wasn't that big.

I was moved to fullback because Jerome [Heavens] got hurt in the third game [of 1976] and was out for the year. Al [Hunter] was the starting tailback, and I didn't mind blocking and hitting people. The coaches saw that I could block, which is why they didn't have a problem putting me at fullback.

The week before the Alabama game, I had been playing sparingly, but never did I think I would start as a freshman. I kind of worked my way into fullback, and they told me midweek that I would start. But they brought me along the right way during the season. They didn't throw me into a lot of pressure situations early and kind of let me play my way in. So it wasn't really a big deal, other than the fact we were playing Alabama and Bear Bryant. When it came time to play, it was just basically doing the things you did in practice and learning some new assignments.

When Al got the 1,000 yards [in 1976] it wasn't a big deal for us. It wasn't about records for us, and I never understand why it is for other people today. When I look back, we didn't relish those kinds of things. We didn't talk about breaking records in the locker room. If it happened, you were recognized for it and you moved on. That's just the way we were.

We had good chemistry. We worked hard to make each other successful. If we had an assignment to block somebody, we made sure we got to that assignment. When we looked at film after games, we wanted to make sure we got our blocks to help that other back be successful. It wasn't about me getting the ball and running for 100 yards. We were there to complement each other.

Receiving the MVP Award in the Cotton Bowl wasn't nearly as important as the win itself. We were underdogs playing against Earl Campbell, the

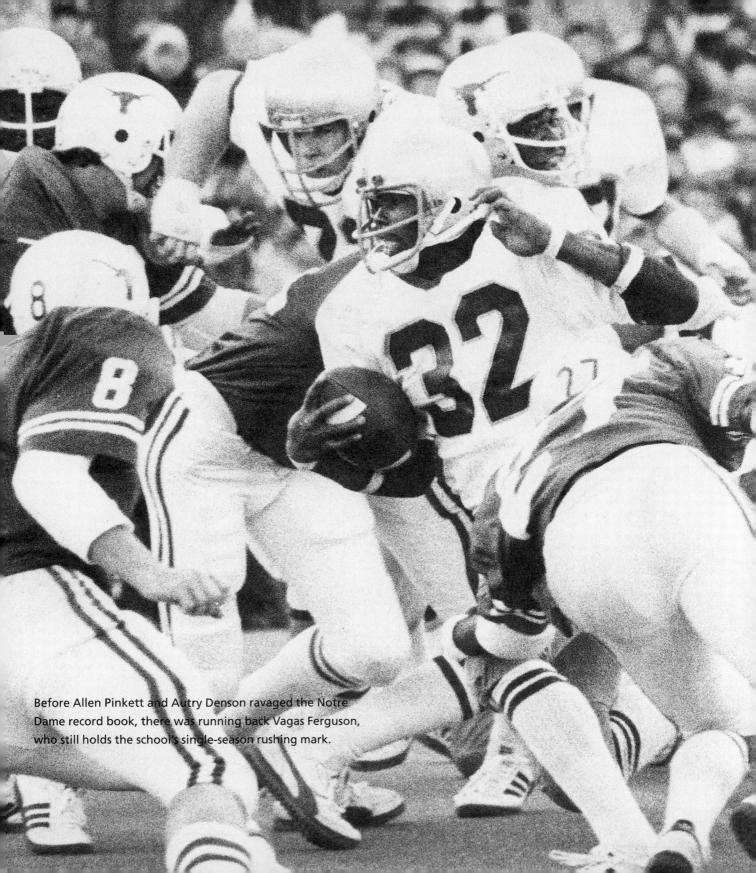

Before Allen Pinkett and Autry Denson ravaged the Notre Dame record book, there was running back Vagas Ferguson, who still holds the school's single-season rushing mark.

Heisman Trophy winner; Brad Shearer, the Outland winner; Johnny "Lam" Jones, the fastest guy in football; Russell Erxleben, the best kicker in football. . . . All we heard all week was how good they were, and it was unusual for us to be underdogs.

Like any successful coach, coach Devine was good about getting the best people around him. He let them do their thing, and he collectively kept everybody together. That's what it takes, because you can't coach every position. Even with Joe Montana, we didn't throw the ball that much. Devine just liked to pound the ball. It was about concentrating on assignments and hitting the spots you were supposed to hit.

When I think about Notre Dame, I don't think about the records as much as the people I played with and met. I always say that and truly mean it. I only look at the records when someone mentions it or it shows up across the TV screen. That's not what's important to me at this point. It's nice to know they're there, but I don't worry about them getting broken. I just hope the team does well, and I try to support the program as much as possible.

Upon Vagas Ferguson's enrollment, Notre Dame had never had a 1,000-yard runner. In Ferguson's freshman year, Al Hunter rushed for 1,058 yards. The next season, Jerome Heavens reached 1,000 yards before being thrown for lost yardage on his last carry of the season.

As a junior and senior, Ferguson rewrote the Irish record books. In 1978, he rushed for 1,192 yards, including 219 and 255 yards against Navy and Georgia Tech, respectively. It wasn't until 2003 that Julius Jones broke Ferguson's single-game standard. As a senior in 1979, the 6'1", 192-pounder from Richmond, Indiana, set single-season school records that still remain (301 carries for 1,437 yards).

In his first start (at fullback versus Alabama in 1976), Ferguson rushed for 107 yards. As a sophomore, he was named the Offensive MVP in the Cotton Bowl when he rushed for 100 yards and two touchdowns and made a 17-yard diving reception for a TD in the 38–10 victory over Texas to clinch the national title.

Ferguson spent three years with the New England Patriots and in 1983 played one game for the Houston Oilers and one for the Cleveland Browns.

The
EIGHTIES AND
NINETIES

MIKE GANN

1981–1984

WITHOUT POINTING FINGERS TOO MUCH, we had some great athletes whose talents were not fully maximized during my time at Notre Dame. Gerry Faust is a great human being and was a great recruiter. I just feel that we did not have the experience as an overall coaching staff in those years on the college level to make things happen.

I can't recall each game, but it seems to me we were ahead at halftime in a lot of those games. We were ahead of Michigan and some of those big teams. It just seemed like we could never hold the lead. I do know that we had the talent to be a major force in college football. But coaching obviously plays a big part of it.

Dan Devine did not recruit me because he had resigned. Gerry Faust had been hired, and Notre Dame came into the picture late. I had signed a Big 8 letter of intent with Oklahoma, and [Notre Dame offensive line] coach [Tom] Backhus began recruiting me.

Coach Faust was supposed to fly out to Denver to visit with me, but he was snowed in and couldn't make it. So I really didn't spend much time with him during the recruiting process. Coach Backhus, who was only there for a year, recruited me. In fact, he brought [tight end Mark] Bavaro in as well. So they began recruiting me late, but academically, Notre Dame was superior to all the other schools I looked at.

As a high school football player out of Colorado, I didn't know where I would stack up in the college arena. I had no idea. In fact, I was scared to death that first week of practice at Notre Dame. All these guys were my size

Defensive tackle Mike Gann was credited with 10 of Notre Dame's 15 sacks in 1984.
Photo courtesy of Gonzalo S. Reyes/Blue & Gold Illustrated.

or bigger, and in high school I had rarely played against guys my size. So that was quite a jump. But my parents were moving to Chicago, so I knew they were going to be close by, and I knew I would get a great education. I just felt like Notre Dame was the best thing for me. The other factor was that Notre Dame recruited me as a defensive end and OU recruited me as an offensive guard. Of course, I wanted to play defense.

I was a big Oklahoma fan growing up. I was born in Stillwater and my dad went to Oklahoma State. Buddy Ryan was a graduate assistant at Oklahoma State when my dad was playing, but I was a big OU fan growing up.

When I moved to Colorado, I was somewhat of an Air Force fan. I remember watching the Notre Dame highlights show that they ran every

Sunday morning, and I can remember not caring much for Notre Dame because they were always so good. They were always beating up on everybody, and one of my best friends in high school was always talking smack about Notre Dame. Ironically, we didn't have much success against Air Force after I got to Notre Dame.

The greatest impact Notre Dame had on me was that I met my future wife there. But the feel Notre Dame has . . . you know, you talk to other players from Notre Dame and players who went to other schools, and it has more of a family, close-knit atmosphere than other places. It wasn't an enormously big school, and it just had a good feel to it.

I had some great relationships at Notre Dame, and I liked the fact that you were treated as a student-athlete, not just an athlete. There were no dorms for athletes. So basically you were put into the mainstream of the college campus. I didn't know what to expect going in, but I think that was something that was a good experience for me. My roommates were not football players, and I liked that.

[Defensive line coach] Joe Yonto had just stopped coaching following the 1980 season and had moved into the athletic department. So unfortunately, I wasn't able to play for him. I had a lot of respect for him. I had Bill Meyers, Jay Robertson, and Greg Blache as defensive line coaches, and they were good coaches too, but I had hoped that I would play for coach Yonto.

206

It was a very special time in my life because of the overall atmosphere and tradition at Notre Dame. The tradition that is still there and has been there for a long time, you definitely felt that. The excitement of game day and running out of that tunnel is an experience I'll never forget.

How do I know it was such a special experience? Because I never heard that from guys with the Falcons as far as the college experience is concerned. It was fun and it was exciting, and it was an honor to wear the Notre Dame uniform, even though some of our records were subpar by Notre Dame standards.

When I think back to some of those games, the Liberty Bowl when we beat Boston College [19–18] and Doug Flutie in 1983 stands out. That was a big win for us. It was very cold that night, and I can actually remember looking up in the stands and some fans had built fires in the stands to stay warm. The field was as hard as cement. It was frozen. We were expected to go out there and chase down Doug Flutie on an icy, hard field. That seemed like an impossible task, so when we came out on top, that was a great win for us.

My senior year we beat USC [19–7] there, which was followed by my last game in a Notre Dame uniform against SMU in the Aloha Bowl in Hawaii [a 27–20 loss]. Beating Michigan at home [23–17] to start the 1982 season with the Musco Lighting Company providing the lights was a big win, and we beat Miami [16–14] a few games later, which was our only win against Miami during my time at Notre Dame.

I never regretted for a second choosing Notre Dame. If I had to do it over again, I guarantee you I would have made the same choice, even with the poor seasons, the poor records. It was a very positive experience that I wouldn't trade for anything.

Notre Dame's lack of success during the early eighties (25–20–1 from 1981 to 1984) probably prevented defensive tackle Mike Gann, a Lakewood, Colorado, native, from earning the accolades he deserved during his career with the Fighting Irish. Gann concluded his stint at Notre Dame ranked third all time in tackles behind the line of scrimmage (a statistic that the NCAA began tabulating in 1967). His 34 stops behind the line still rank seventh in school annals.

As a senior in 1984, while teaming up with future NFL defensive linemen Mike Golic and Robert Banks, the 6'5", 256-pounder recorded 10 of Notre Dame's 15 sacks and finished third on the squad in tackles with 60.

A second-round pick by Atlanta in 1985, Gann played nine years at defensive end with the Falcons.

MIKE GOLIC

1981–1984

QUITE HONESTLY, I REALLY NEVER CONSIDERED going anywhere other than Notre Dame. You grow up either loving or hating Notre Dame, and even before [my brother] Bob went there, we had always liked Notre Dame. When they came on TV, we just had to watch them! Certainly when Bob went there, my level of love and admiration for the place went up.

I was in a different position than most because I got to see Notre Dame from a couple of different perspectives. When Bob went there, I was 12 years old, so I was a little wide-eyed and had that "Wow, this is Notre Dame!" feeling about everything. I mean, here I am a 12-year-old kid, and I'm surrounded by Joe Montana, Ross Browner, Ken MacAfee, and Dan Devine.

Then when my brother Greg went there, since he and I were only a year apart, I would go up and see him, and now I got to see people who were closer to my own age. I wasn't the wide-eyed, admiring kid anymore. So I got to see it from a couple of different perspectives, and I think that helped.

When I was a kid and Bob was playing, I came to every home game and went to most of the away games that were pretty close to our home. My parents never missed a home game from Bob to Greg to me. We were always there. I was in the stands, I was hanging around outside the locker room, all the things kid brothers do.

I was incredibly proud of Bob. Here's a kid who comes in and starts as a 17-year-old freshman. Bob was an All-American high school football player and an All-American high school wrestler. It was a natural progression for him to go on and be successful at a top college. When I was offered a scholarship by Notre Dame, I wanted to go play and prove that I was that caliber of a player as well.

I had a lot of offers from different schools and some flat out said to me, "We'll really recruit you heavily if you're not considering Notre Dame." This was early in the process and I said, "I certainly like Notre Dame, but I'm willing to listen." But signing day was the first week of February, and Gerry Faust called me on Thanksgiving morning, and he offered me a scholarship.

In hindsight, I wondered if I should have said, "I'll think about it, Coach." But that was where I wanted to go, so I thanked him for the opportunity, took the offer, and never regretted it for a second.

I did try to take my other trips. I had trips set up to Michigan, UCLA, Tennessee, and Miami. I said, "Hey, Coach, I want to come [to Notre Dame]. But can we not say anything so I can go on these trips?" But that didn't work out too well. It kind of got out on the AP wire that I had committed to Notre Dame and everyone knew.

I would be lying if I said that when I went to Notre Dame all that mattered was the education and the experience. Quite frankly, not winning more seriously bummed me out. When you see your brother win a national title and the year before you get there, they're playing in the Sugar Bowl, and then you get there and my true freshman year, we win our first game and I'm getting some playing time for a team that is now ranked No. 1 in the country after beating LSU [27–9] . . . I had visions of grandeur dancing in my head about what these four years were going to be like.

209

Then the second week of the season we go to Michigan and get our butts handed to us [25–7]. We ended up going 5–6 that year, and during my time at Notre Dame, we were never better than 6–4–1. It was a letdown.

That said, all of those other things applied. I got to be at Notre Dame. That's where I wanted to be. I got the Notre Dame education. Anybody that knows the Golics knows that our parents stressed education, and getting a diploma was as important as being on the field. My parents passed that along to us. Notre Dame was just the place we loved.

Would I have loved to have won a national championship? Absolutely. I regret that somewhat, but in no way does it dampen my experience and love for Notre Dame.

Those were tough years because we had so many defensive line coaches during that time. I had Bill Meyers, Jay Robertson, and Bishop Harris. [Current Philadelphia Eagles coach] Jim Johnson was the defensive coordinator at one point. . . . It just didn't mesh.

Certainly there's enough blame to go around. I think one of the biggest mistakes Gerry Faust made, and I'm sure he would agree, was when he took the job—and who wouldn't take that job being in the position he was in?—he should have surrounded himself with experienced, talented coaches.

The thing was, it was all coaching talent that we already had. We had the George Kellys and the Joe Yontos of the world that [Faust] ended up putting behind desks instead of keeping them on the field. He brought in guys from high school, and I think that hurt. It stopped cohesiveness and it stopped continuity because we kept changing coaches.

With that said, I'll be honest with you—and this goes up to the pro ranks as well. Even if you have the most simplistic game plan in the world, at the end of the day players have to go out and they have to execute. For whatever reason, we didn't execute, and we did have talent. We had guys who went on to play in the NFL for many years, and we didn't execute.

210

Was some of it game plan? Absolutely. But we didn't get the job done on the field, either, so there's enough blame to go around, and I can't sit here and blame it on having three different position coaches and having high school coaches. That's not fair to those coaches who certainly tried. It was a combination of all of those things.

One of the first people I met when I started going to Notre Dame as a kid was the defensive line coach, Joe Yonto. Joe was such a big part of my family in initially getting Bob there, and then obviously when Bob was there, and then through Greg and me. He was and is such a nice man.

Probably the person we dealt with the most, God rest his soul, was George Kelly. I loved that man. When you talk about the Notre Dame experience and the Notre Dame man, the football player and the guys who were molded by coaches or teachers, George Kelly was the man who molded those guys. I could write a book on him alone.

When Bob first got there, George was Bob's position coach. We saw him the most and he always had the gatherings at his house with his wife Gloria. Their son Kevin [who ended up long-snapping for the Irish] and I were the same age, and we ended up rooming together our first year at Notre Dame.

At age 12, I had a buddy to hang out with. We were always over at the Kellys' house. They got to be our extended family. That's a relationship that extends beyond a quarter of a century. When I think of Notre Dame men, I think of George Kelly.

One other guy who scared the crap out of me when I got there was Mike DeCicco, who was the academic adviser for athletics and also the fencing coach. The fencing team was always fantastic.

I remember the freshmen scholarship athletes gathered in the auditorium with DeCicco. He comes into that meeting with us, and he has one of his swords in his hand! Here we are all scholarship athletes, the kings and queens of our high schools, or so we thought, and we're all obviously quite full of ourselves.

In comes DeCicco with this sword, and he begins to go into this thing about how he doesn't care if we get in for one play or play one minute, but we will graduate and we will get our diplomas. He talked about all the available help and what we needed to do, how you needed to budget your time. And he's saying this as he's drilling this sword into one of the desks! You want to talk about some cocky freshmen, sitting up straight with their eyes wide saying, "Who is this nutcase with the sword?"

But he got our attention and he let you know, "OK, you're the cream of the crop athletics-wise, which is one of the reasons you're here. But another reason you're here is because of your academic side and the person that you are. Don't forget that, and that's going to carry you farther than your participation in sports."

I still love seeing Mike today. I give him a big bear hug every time I see him because I appreciate what he was saying. Sometimes you don't appreciate things until after you leave. But I certainly look back at what he meant to that school. He was fantastic.

One of the highlights of my four years at Notre Dame was the first game I played in, against LSU in 1981 [a 27–9 victory]. A few teams ahead of us had lost, and we were elevated to No. 1 after that win.

No matter how you feel when you get there, and then you go through the preseason practices and you already feel pretty fortunate and special, there's nothing like running out of that tunnel for the first time. You're actually on the field playing for Notre Dame. That's about as vivid a memory of Notre Dame that I could have.

211

Another memorable game was the win against Pittsburgh my sophomore year [31–16 in 1982], when they were No. 1 in the country and we hammered them. Allen Pinkett had a great game [including a 76-yard touchdown run].

We're coming back from Pittsburgh, and the buses were coming down Notre Dame Avenue, and the streets were mobbed with people. The students were jumping into the buses and I remember thinking to myself, "I wish it were like this all the time. I hope it's like this all the time." As it turned out, we didn't have a moment like that again during my junior and senior years. So that Pittsburgh game was like a championship feeling.

And then certainly my last game in Notre Dame Stadium [a 44–7 victory over Penn State in 1984] is memorable. My brothers could only try to prepare me so much about how difficult your last game in a Notre Dame uniform is. I just saw myself wandering around, not wanting to leave the field, and looking for my parents to acknowledge them and thank them for coming to every home game for the past 10 years. At that moment, it all caught up with me.

My last game in a Notre Dame uniform was in the Aloha Bowl in Hawaii against SMU. I remember making a point of going to the juniors in the locker room and saying, "OK, guys, it's in your hands now. Things didn't go well my four years, and they're not going that well for you right now. But it's in your hands now. Take it." I did that with a lot of tears in my eyes.

I was named captain of the 1984 team at the December banquet in 1983 when I was also named defensive MVP. That was an incredible honor because when something like that is voted on by your peers and they think enough of you to select you as captain, it's remarkable. I started to think of the times when I was 12 coming to Notre Dame, watching my brother, who also was a captain, and then receiving that honor myself. To this day, I don't think brothers have ever been captains of the Notre Dame football team, other than Bob and myself.

Tyrone Willingham made a great move when he presented all the former captains with pins that signified they were captains of the Notre Dame football team. That meant a lot to us former captains.

One of the truest statements ever made to me, and now I tell other people the same thing, is this: you will be amazed at the response you get when you say you're a graduate of Notre Dame. Whether in business, in sports, or whatever, it brings an air of respect to some and it brings hatred to others. To some it brings jealousy because they're jealous they didn't go to Notre

Defensive end Mike Golic (left) was one of three from his family (along with All-American Bob and middle brother Greg) to choose Notre Dame. *Photo courtesy of the* Blue & Gold Illustrated.

Dame, and to others in brings admiration because they wanted to go to Notre Dame. It carries significance nationally.

I never played in an AFC or NFC championship game, and I never played in a Super Bowl. Had I done that, I might feel a little differently about this. But nothing in my sports world, even during my 10 years in the NFL, nothing emotionally compared to running out of the tunnel at Notre Dame.

Standing in that tunnel at Notre Dame, wearing that gold helmet and knowing what you're running out to, nothing compares to it. It's still one of the most amazing feats to me, and I feel very fortunate to have been able to do it.

You know, some people think us Notre Dame people are a cocky group, that we think we're better than everybody else. Well you know, Notre Dame doesn't take everybody. You have to be a special person to go there. It's hard not to be very proud of that.

My oldest son is a freshman in high school, and my kids love Notre Dame. They go to the football camps, the basketball camps, my daughter goes to the swimming camp. . . . They love Notre Dame, and they sure would love the opportunity to go there. We'll see what happens.

They're excellent athletes. They're better athletes than I ever was. They probably got a little bias from their parents because I went to Notre Dame and my wife went to St. Mary's College [across from Notre Dame]. But there's no lack of Notre Dame paraphernalia at the Golic house. And I've got a feeling it's going to be like that for a long, long time.

Mike Golic followed in the footsteps of his brother Bob, an All-American middle linebacker and captain of the 1978 Irish squad, as well as Greg, an offensive lineman who played with Notre Dame during Mike's tenure with the Irish.

As likable and affable then as he is today as a member of ESPN's TV and radio talent, Golic, from Willowick, Ohio, was one of several standouts along the Irish defensive line in the early eighties (including Mike Gann, Bob Clasby, and Eric Dorsey) who went on to play in the NFL.

The 6'5", 257-pound Golic was named tri-captain of the '84 squad (along with offensive guard Larry Williams and safety Joe Johnson). He and his brother Bob are the only siblings in Notre Dame history to captain the football team.

Golic was a 10th-round draft pick of the Houston Oilers in 1985, where he played for three seasons. He then spent six years in Philadelphia and one season in Miami.

LARRY WILLIAMS

1981–1984

L ET ME START FROM THE END OF MY STORY and work my way back because I think that will explain why I went to Notre Dame in the first place.

I was drafted by the Cleveland Browns, so I spent about five years in Cleveland where my wife and I started our family. My wife is from California too, but we found Cleveland and the Midwestern lifestyle the best place to raise children.

So when I finished my football career in San Diego, I was admitted to practice law in California, and I was going to accept this job in San Diego overlooking the San Diego Bay. But we reflected on it and thought, "Where's the best place to raise these kids?"

At the time we only had four and we made the decision to look back toward the Midwest and decided to invest the next however many years to raise these kids in an environment we had some comfort in. So lo and behold one thing led to another and I took a job from an Indianapolis-based law firm. And they said, "Oh, by the way, we have a South Bend office and since you went to Notre Dame, we're trying to expand our presence up there. Would you mind working out of our South Bend office?" That gave us reason to pause for a minute, but that's how we ended up back here.

I chose Notre Dame out of high school after being offered a number of opportunities to go elsewhere. For me, Notre Dame offered the perfect balance of academics and athletics in an environment that was based on spirituality. The other schools just didn't have the right balance for me. Stanford was one I considered and really liked, but it didn't show me the same commitment to the sport I loved, football, that Notre Dame did.

When I came here on my recruiting trip, it was during the season, the Miami game [1980]. It was a spectacular fall weekend, and I just got the sense that everybody in the whole community, the broader Notre Dame community, devoted the entire weekend to this event. How cool is that to a kid from Southern California, where you're used to showing up to a game in the middle of the first quarter and leaving in the latter part of the third quarter? It just seemed so neat that everybody paid so much attention to a game that I loved and offered an environment that I really felt comfortable in. The fact that the university is founded on the Catholic tradition was obviously something that appealed to me.

I don't really break out my experience at Notre Dame in terms of athletics or academics or spirituality. It's all sort of rolled into one, so I really couldn't tell you that my athletic experience was poor or great. My overall experience was very good.

216

True, I dearly wished we would have won more games, but it just wasn't meant to be. We just didn't have the right combination in a competitive environment that demands perfection. We just didn't have it, for whatever reason. Maybe we didn't have strong enough coaching, but you also have to put some of the blame at the feet of the players. Maybe we didn't have enough focus and the ability to learn and apply what we were taught.

There were some really good players. It was really amazing that we couldn't get that thing orchestrated to work. Everybody was performing sort of on a different page, and we couldn't get it all running together at the same time.

One time that we did put it together was at Pitt when they were No. 1 in the country [1982]. We played out there and Dan Marino was at quarterback and there was a glimpse of what we could do if we all got on the same page. Allen Pinkett went crazy, the defense played well, the coaching was great, a flea flicker worked, all kinds of things just sort of fell into place, and we won [31–16].

The Michigan game in 1982, which we won [23–17], was actually my first start, and it was the first night game in Notre Dame Stadium history. I remember going absolutely stir-crazy waiting for that late-night game. As a sophomore starter I'm bouncing off the walls, nervous as heck. Everything worked out really well. I got a great call [on TV] from [play-by-play

Offensive tackle/guard Larry Williams was a tri-captain on Notre Dame's 1984 squad. *Photo courtesy of the* Blue & Gold Illustrated.

announcer] Keith Jackson during the course of the game. He gave me one of his standard comments, and I still have that tape. I was on cloud nine.

Other games stand out on the negative side. We went out to Oregon in 1982 and played a bad Oregon team to a [13–13] tie. I say "we" and I should say "I" because I played terribly out there. For whatever reason, that one stands out too. I wish I had that back. That one sticks in my craw.

We played Boston College in the Liberty Bowl when it was amazingly cold in December of 1983 in Memphis [a 19–18 victory]. I have actually very little recollection of the game because I think my head was frozen. Weren't there fires in the stands, or is that just part of my imagination? My recollection is that people started these little bonfires in the stands. We thought, "Hey, we get to go to a bowl game in Memphis! Sunny, nice . . ." I didn't think it got that cold in Memphis.

But the following year we went to Hawaii to play in the Aloha Bowl. That was a neat one. We played an SMU team that had a lot of players on it. It was the latter part of their dynasty thing before they went on double-secret probation, and we lost, 27–20.

The USC series ranks high in my memory bank because I was from California and for so many years leading up to the time that I went to Notre Dame, USC had sort of dominated that series.

So it really did have some special meaning when we were able to beat them my junior year [27–6 in 1983]. We should have beaten them my sophomore year [a 17–13 loss], but they scored on a fumble that wasn't a touchdown. There were big pictures of it in the *L.A. Times* the next day. I felt bad for the seniors. But the following two years we beat them pretty good, or at least soundly. I don't know if we were better or if they were on the downslide.

My relationship with Gerry [Faust] was probably different than most folks'. It was much less coach and player and more friend and mentor. Gerry tried to help me out way beyond the football field. [Faust] was always thinking about the whole person and not just the player. And we came [to Notre Dame] in the same year, so we sort of had a bond. We were both trying to figure this thing out on the fly. He didn't have a lot of experience at the college level to rely on, and I didn't either. He had sort of a special bond with our class in that we all tried to learn together, and there were some pretty rough times.

Now I'm a young guy from Southern California, and I want to get on the football field and I'm going to do anything the coach asks me to do. So when Gerry said to me one day, "Hey, listen, I ran into this coed. She's from California; I know you're from California. Why don't you give her a call and see what happens?" I thought, "Holy smokes, am I being asked to do charity work? Whatever. I'm not sure how this whole thing works either, so I'll call her." It turned out my wife [former Irish tennis player Laura Lee] is a pretty good-looking gal, and it worked out great.

As I was leaving Notre Dame and preparing for a professional football career, Mike Golic and I worked out together. He and I had very similar paths. We were both late-round draft picks out of Notre Dame. We were

218

both counting on having a real good shot in the NFL, so we trained together and we both dated gals from school. We sort of went in sync.

It's great to get back together now at the Monogram outings and see some of the guys you haven't been able to stay in contact with because everybody is trying to raise a family and chart their own course in the world. So it's neat to get back in touch with them now and find that very little has changed in terms of everybody's emotional makeup.

I was very proud of being named a captain for the 1984 team. It may sound a little self-serving, but that was something that really meant a lot to me. I remember running back to my dorm room to call my dad and tell him, "Hey, you're not going to believe this, but I just got voted to be the captain at Notre Dame." He was proud, so that made me feel real good. It's not something I ever shy away from now. I put it on my résumé, and it's something I'm still proud of today.

No experience is ever 100 percent of what you thought it would be, but that's part of the beauty of it, and that's part of the value of it. The Notre Dame experience taught me things that I never expected to learn. So I value my time at Notre Dame very highly.

The early eighties were a frustrating period in Notre Dame history, not just because of the setbacks on the field but also because of the wealth of talent that dotted Notre Dame's rosters.

Tom Thayer, Phil Carter, Tony Hunter, Bob Crable, Stacey Toran, Dave Duerson, Mike Gann, Mark Bavaro, Steve Beuerlein, Mike Golic, Allen Pinkett, Wally Kleine, Robert Banks, and Larry Williams were just some of the quality players representing the Irish from 1981 to 1985. Yet the Irish managed just a 30–26–1 record during Gerry Faust's five-year reign.

Most of those players went on to successful professional football careers, including Williams. Fortunately for the 6'6", 276-pound tri-captain of the 1984 squad, his Notre Dame experience transcended the struggle of the Fighting Irish on the football field.

A Santa Ana, California, native and a three-year starter at tackle and guard, Williams quietly carved out a five-year NFL career with the Cleveland Browns, New Orleans Saints, and New England Patriots.

ALLEN PINKETT

1982–1985

CHOOSING A COLLEGE TO ATTEND WAS EASY because Notre Dame provided me the best opportunity to have success at the end of four years. There wasn't even another school that came close, and that was whether I played football or not.

I also wanted a school that had national recognition with regard to athletics, a chance to win a national championship, and a very sound academic program. Notre Dame, Notre Dame, Notre Dame!

I considered North Carolina and Penn State. I didn't want to stay in state. I guess my perspective was always broader than staying in Virginia. Coach [George] Welch came into Virginia the year I was a senior in high school, and he had turned that program around after coming in from Navy. But I just didn't believe they could win a national championship.

At Penn State, they sent you a letter offering you a scholarship, but Joe [Paterno] does not like that kind of formal stuff. He put a P.S. on the end of it and said how happy he was to do this. They were the first school to offer me a scholarship. I took several unofficial visits up there, and you knew he was a legend way back then. But to me it just didn't compare to Notre Dame.

Certainly Gerry Faust's enthusiasm was a factor, but I think you have to go to the school because of the school. Coaches come and go. [Defensive line coach] Greg Blache did most of the recruiting and then Faust took over. It felt like home, it felt like the place I wanted to be, and the campus was all that and more.

From the outset, I figured I would have to wait my turn. I just wanted to try to get to third string my first year. I came in and had a pretty good camp, but if Greg Bell had not been injured, shoot, I might not have touched the field.

After the success I had during camp, I knew I was going to get a shot at traveling [to road games]. But once you get a taste of starting, you don't ever want to come out of the lineup. I was fortunate to have such success so early.

You go through stages where you're happy to be on the team, and then you're happy to get in, and then you start to notice the crowd and that kind of stuff. When you become a full-time starter, you don't even see the crowd. Now it's a job; now you're going to work. Your focus is totally different. Once you get a taste of it being a job, you don't ever want to be on the sideline.

The Pitt game during my freshman year, no doubt, was a thrill. What a lot of people don't remember is that the week before the Pittsburgh game, I had gained more than 100 yards against Navy.

LSU in 1984 was sort of a similar situation to the Pitt game in 1982. Before that LSU game, we had lost three games in a row. LSU was undefeated at 6–0–1, ranked sixth in the country, and we were playing down at their place. We went down there and we thumped 'em [30–22]. That was the thing under coach Faust; we didn't win a lot of games, but we always found a way to win a big game.

The list of people who had a strong influence on my life at Notre Dame is long. One person was a secretary, Zorka DeFreeuw. I called her my South Bend mom. I would eat dinner at her house. It was just a place to escape, just a place to get away from the campus every now and then and relax. Life as a Notre Dame football player is a very public life. I guess that would be considered an NCAA violation today.

Now don't misunderstand, if I needed to go party somewhere, I knew where the party train was. I got my share of partying in, but it was life under a microscope, so if I were going to be drinking, I wouldn't wear my letterman's jacket. Everybody was always watching. But it was just good to have a place to go and get away from it all.

221

Allen Pinkett rewrote the Irish rushing record book when he strung together three straight 1,000-yard seasons in the eighties. *Photo courtesy of the* Blue & Gold Illustrated.

Dave Duerson was an excellent mentor on how to be a captain. He was my captain. The way he carried himself, the way he played . . . he was the epitome of a captain. Greg Bell was another guy like that, but in his own way. He made me a better player because he challenged me a lot.

Greg always made fun of my clothes. Some of my style I owe to Greg Bell. Leaving my dorm room, I always had to think, "OK, if Greg sees me, what's he going to say about what I'm wearing?"

I would have run through a wall for [running back coach] Mal Moore. I consider myself to be a student of the game and a quasi historian. I'm interested in what happened before I got to that place and what happened in football in general. To hear some of the stories that he told about being at

Alabama and coaching for Bear Bryant just made me feel like I was touching greatness. More than that, he was a great coach.

It was tough not winning more than we did, especially when the press usually came to me for an explanation. But my parents were never down about anything, and they always told me there was nothing I couldn't do. The word *can't* was never in my vocabulary. They were always supportive. Shoot, I didn't think there was anything I couldn't do.

I listen to coach Willingham at times and somebody asked him what type of player he likes and he said somebody who loves life and loves football. I know exactly what he's saying. He's saying that if you've got a chance to wear the Notre Dame uniform and you've got a chance to play against various competition, your team's record should never affect how you play. You've got to love to compete. So I was always that way.

I've had the pleasure to speak in front of the players there, and one of the things I've said is, "Look at it this way, guys. If you want to play in the pros, you've got 44 shots [games] to prove to somebody in the NFL that you're worthy."

So every single game was always so important to me, and I always approached it as if it was my last game. In my mind the worst thing that could happen was that I'd be sitting here 20 years later thinking about what I could have done or what I should have done. I did not want to have that experience whatsoever, so I put the extra time in the weight room, I put the extra time in the film sessions, and I left it all out on the field. For some folks, it's hard to get the football out of their system. Me, I'm done. I left it all out there. I don't need any flashbacks or opportunities because I did everything I wanted to do.

The coach plays a pivotal role because every guy that comes to Notre Dame wants the challenge of being on national television every week. But they're still 18- and 19-year-old knuckleheads. They still need some direction. I don't know why I had that type of maturity at that time, but I just did. Thinking back on it now and talking to some of the coaches, they said, "We knew we didn't have to worry about Allen Pinkett. We knew he was going to do what he had to do." But you don't have a team full of Allen Pinketts. Thank God for that.

It was nice to be able to leave a mark there. The only thing I wanted when I was there was a national championship. I did not try to run to become the leading ground-gainer. I knew I had a responsibility to play my hardest for the folks who had come through there before. I talked to coach Parseghian,

223

and I said, "I'm just trying to emulate the standard that you set." The tradition was important to me.

The time that it really hurt was my senior year after we had lost to Purdue [to fall to 1–2]. If you have one loss, you may have a shot at a national title. When you lose twice, you know it's over. But then I'd come back the next game and have 150 yards. You have to say to yourself, "We can't win the national championship, but we can still make the plays!"

It was hard on coach Faust. When I first came to that school he was kind of heavyset; his hair was brown. . . . When I left he had a nervous twitch, he looked kind of sickly, his hair was gray, and it looked to me like he was on the verge of a nervous breakdown.

People always wanted me to say something bad about coach Faust because we lost so often. But he's still the coach, he's still the leader, and how am I going to talk badly about a guy who gave me the ball 25 times a game? You won't find another guy who loved this school more or wanted to win more. He just didn't know how to do it.

Allen Pinkett burst onto the scene as a freshman in 1982 and became a true star in the making by his eighth game when his 76-yard touchdown run at Pittsburgh helped upset the No. 1–rated Panthers, 31–16. It was just the beginning.

Pinkett, a 5'9", 181-pounder, finished his four-year career at Notre Dame as the school's all-time leading rusher (4,131 yards) and became the first back in Irish history to rush for more than 1,000 yards in three separate seasons, including a high-water mark of 1,394 yards as a sophomore in 1983.

Autry Denson would later surpass Pinkett by fewer than 200 yards in his career, but the Sterling, Virginia, native still holds the school mark for touchdowns (49).

A third-round pick of Houston in 1986, Pinkett spent six years with the Oilers. He now does color commentary for Irish broadcasts on the Westwood One national radio network.

CHUCK LANZA

1984–1987

FOR ME AND MY FAMILY, [GOING TO NOTRE DAME] meant an awful lot. It was probably extra special for us because I, unlike a lot of other student-athletes at Notre Dame, didn't grow up a Notre Dame fan.

I grew up in Pittsburgh and I was a big Pitt fan, and then [we] relocated to Memphis because of my father's work. To have Notre Dame recruit me was very special when you're stuck down there in the land of SEC schools. My second choice was actually LSU, which at the time had a very strong program.

The first couple of years for us at Notre Dame were tough. With coach Faust, I think it didn't work mainly because the knowledge wasn't there to put together a winning program at that level. I think there was a huge under-estimation of what it would take to put together a program at that level and to be successful at a school like Notre Dame where you're under the micro-scope of the entire country. To Gerry's defense, without any prior Division I coaching experience or any coaching experience at the college level at all, that was a tremendous handicap.

When Lou showed up, I think he had 14 years of Division I head coaching experience, and that was evident from the day we met him. You could tell this was a guy who was extremely knowledgeable of the game and had a system in place, a system that had worked and had been very successful at other schools. We knew that we were in for a much different experience.

Do you know how many times I've told this story about coach Holtz yelling at me at that first meeting? [Editor's note: Holtz yelled at Lanza in his first team meeting when Lanza propped his feet up on the stage that Holtz

226

Center Chuck Lanza was one of the leaders of the eighties squads that turned Notre Dame's fortunes around under head coach Lou Holtz. *Photo courtesy of David Kusa*/Blue & Gold Illustrated.

was standing on.] When it first came out in coach Holtz's first few years on campus and the incident was reported in the paper, nobody ever mentioned who it was. It wasn't until later on that all of a sudden my name started being involved. I guess they thought it was OK to say my name after I graduated. Yeah, that was me. He got my attention, and he got everybody else's attention very quickly.

The 1987 season was a breakthrough for Notre Dame football under coach Holtz. I think it was a situation where we had so many changes implemented in the program and so much of the game is mental. You saw most of the players really starting to believe in coach Holtz's program.

The following year [1988]—and he mentioned this to me in years past— he had the majority of the players believing in what he was doing and what the program was about and what the system was about, and that's why it worked.

For us in 1987, things just started to gel. You become more familiar with the system and what he's trying to accomplish, and you really start to believe in what the coach is doing and what the system is doing. You can trace that to a lot of successful coaches in some of their turnaround experiences, not only in college but also in the professional ranks. I cite the Dallas Cowboys with Bill Parcells. So much of it is mental.

From a people perspective, what's so special about Notre Dame is that it's so far-reaching. No matter where you go, who you talk to, everyone certainly has an opinion about the school, albeit not a good one all the time. But for the Notre Dame family that is out there, I've never been turned away, I've never had a reception that wasn't very warm and welcoming, and that's what's special about it.

In terms of the games, the rivalries against Michigan, USC, and Penn State were always fun. The big win in our junior year at USC [38–37 in 1986] was the springboard of our success. It showed the resiliency of our team when we were able to come back in the second half.

A few things unfortunately didn't go our way late in the 1987 season. But for us to get to the Cotton Bowl [a 35–10 loss to Texas A&M] was a huge accomplishment. It was special to be a part of something successful for a change because there were so many struggles early on for a lot of us.

Tony Yelovich was my offensive line coach, and I stay in contact with him to this day. He was another important guy in my development. He made the experience very meaningful for me as well.

Teammate-wise, I stay in touch with Wes Pritchett and Frank Stams. I occasionally talk to Dave Butler and Steve Beuerlein. I try to get back for at least one game a year. This past year I went back for two games.

Obviously coach Holtz had a huge impact on me as a cocaptain my senior year. That was important to me, and a rewarding situation because [fellow cocaptain] Byron Spruell and I had to spend a lot of time with [Holtz], attending certain functions for the school and getting an opportunity to visit with him a lot one-on-one. That was important and meaningful to be involved with him as much as we were.

I think Tyrone Willingham will get it done if everything comes together from a university standpoint. I think as far as coaching skills and talent, he has all of that and more. I haven't met him and I don't know him. I just know what I read and hear. I think he's got a very challenging situation ahead of him.

After the 2003 season, it certainly gives you reason to pause and think, "Is the program really headed in the right direction?" At least with Lou, sure we had a losing season the first year. But we turned it around and what he was able to do beyond that is well documented. When we lost, we lost by a small margin. I really felt like we would win every time we took the field.

If anyone deserved to enjoy the fruits of his labors during the eighties, it was center Chuck Lanza, a true leader of the early Lou Holtz squads. As cocaptain of the 1987 squad, he was able to experience some success when the Irish won eight of their first nine games to rise to No. 7 in the country and eventually land a Cotton Bowl bid. But Notre Dame lost the final three games of the season, Lanza graduated, and the Irish went on to win the national title in 1988.

Irish lore has made Lanza somewhat infamous for being the player Holtz verbally lambasted for having his feet up on the stage when the new Irish head coach was introduced to the team in the Joyce Center auditorium. The 6'2", 270-pound cocaptain's impact, however, was much more profound for his leadership of the Irish squads that eventually transitioned into a national title winner.

FRANK STAMS

1984–1988

I**T NEVER REALLY WAS ONE THING FOR ME** when it came to selecting Notre Dame. It was a collection of three or four things. For me, it started at home with my parents. I remember my mom telling me, "Just about anybody . . ." I probably shouldn't even say this. I don't mean it in a bad way, but she used to say, "Just about anybody can go to Ohio State."

When I took my visit to Notre Dame, the person in charge of admissions said, "If you were to go out to football practice the first day and you broke your leg and never played football again, where would you want to be?" Plus, my dad was in high school in the late forties, and he'd always talk about the Notre Dame legends.

There was a guy here in town who was a good friend of my dad's and a good friend of Ara Parseghian's. His name was Eddie Niam, and he and Parseghian were high school buddies. They both went to South High School here in Akron. My dad was a teacher for 30-some years, and his high school was right across the street from this guy's little diner.

Eddie was around a lot when I was in high school, and there was that whole Notre Dame influence. Plus the fact that Notre Dame was a nationally recognized school and they weren't in a conference . . . You know, you're playing all over the country and wherever you went, it was like playing a home game.

It wasn't a Catholic thing. I remember some of the competing schools made reference to the Catholic institution. It wasn't about that for me, the religious aspect, but it was a handful of other things.

Who finished number two? That's a good question. In hindsight, if I hadn't gone to Notre Dame, I probably would have gone to Michigan because of Bo Schembechler. I had good feelings about him as a coach. But it wasn't about any one person. It was the whole thing.

It wasn't an easy adjustment for me at Notre Dame, even though there were so many factors involved in choosing Notre Dame. Maybe I saw *Animal House* one too many times. What a snow job they pulled on me! I went up there as a high school senior and [linebacker Tony] Furjanic, [center Ron] Plantz, and [guard Tim] Scannell took me to an off-campus party and we had a great time.

I'll never forget that spring watching the national news. I was in the other room and my parents said, "Frank, come on in here, you might want to see this." They were showing on the national news the Notre Dame student body protesting the new alcohol policy.

Notre Dame is a great school and I enjoyed my time there. But it was a little bit of a culture shock. I probably wouldn't have been able to go to Notre Dame if it wasn't for football. I'm not saying I didn't identify with the students there, but it was a little different from what I was accustomed to.

I broke my ankle there on Cartier Field in minus-20 degree weather in the spring of 1986. It was a bad break and it was a good break because that ultimately affected where I was going to play on the field. Had I not gotten hurt, I probably wouldn't have been around for 1988.

I never really expected to move from fullback, but you know, it was a change that I, at the time, welcomed. I wasn't a frustrated fullback or anything like that. I just didn't enjoy the whole offensive experience there, and I was much more suited for the defense.

I think it clicked better for me with a defensive mind-set. Foge Fazio was the coordinator, and then Barry Alvarez was brought in as the coordinator the next year, and it all really fell into place for the whole defense when Barry became the coordinator.

A big part of the success we had as a team was because of the groundwork that Foge laid, and then Barry was able to take the whole of that and take it one step further. The players really responded to him defensively. I think the coordinators' personalities brought out the best in the defensive players. The players just kind of fed off their attitude and their personalities.

Looking back, we were completely different—it was like night and day—between our offense and our defense. The personalities on defense were much different from the personalities on the offense. In fact, the only personalities on the defense that clicked together with the guys on the offense were Tony Brooks and Ricky Watters, and you know what happened to those guys the day before the SC game [in 1988, both were sent home for arriving late to a team meeting]. Those guys were a little bit too out of control sometimes. But they knew the limits and kept it together pretty good. They may have just been a little too immature at that stage of their careers to have it completely together.

Tony Rice would probably be another offensive player who was an exception in terms of sharing a defensive personality, but under Holtz playing offense, that was good for Tony. He was a better player at that position under a coach like Holtz.

There was a great mix between the young and the old on that team. To me, the personalities that were on that defense were so unique. Like Pritchett that one day when he took the cigar and went back out on the field. He was smoking it in his helmet. Barry looked at him like he was out of his mind, and then he cracked up laughing. It was that loose attitude, and it just seemed like the chemistry was really there defensively. The chemistry was there offensively, too; it was just a different mind-set.

231

I tell people with some seriousness that part of our motivation to be good as a defense was to keep Holtz off our side of the field during the week. If the defense had a bad game, there would be times when he would come down and coach the defense for a couple of days, and it was just miserable, miserable!

We were confident in the Fiesta Bowl against West Virginia, but give credit to Holtz. He always kept you on edge where the possibility of getting beat was always there. He didn't care who you were playing. It didn't matter whether you were playing Rice or Miami; he always kept you sharp. That was one real positive thing.

But part of my difficulty adjusting to Notre Dame was getting accustomed to playing for Holtz. I took a lot of the stuff he said and did personally, like when I broke my leg. I'm walking back from the practice field with a reporter. I was in a cast and [Holtz] was in that golf cart. He tells me, just to make himself look good at my expense, "You better go see one of those healers, an evangelist; that's the only way you'll get back on the field."

He's like a sugar high, but I have to admit, he does a great job with a team. I look at our team that we had, that 1988 team. . . . When I got there [1984],

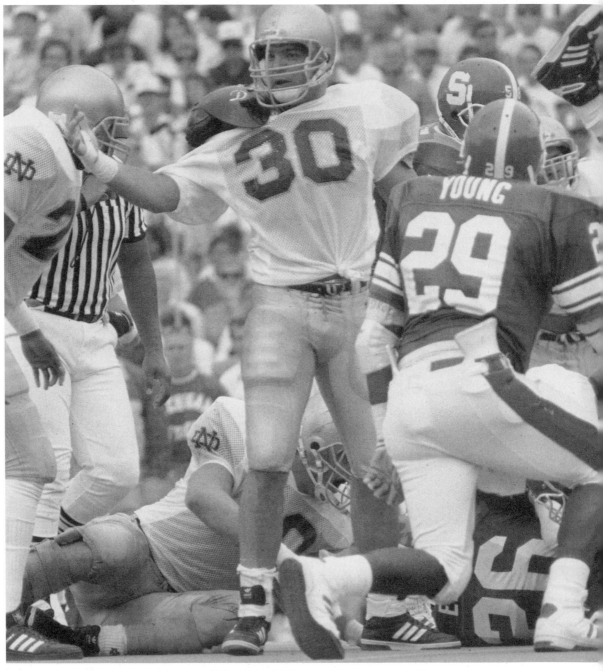

232

Frank Stams was a dominant force at defensive end during Notre Dame's 1988 national championship run. *Photo courtesy of David Kusa/*Blue & Gold Illustrated.

the players were more talented than the ones who went on to win a national title. Guys like Mark Bavaro and Mike Gann. I was like, "God, these guys are studs!" My senior year, it was just guys who played well together.

Another thing with Holtz was he had an offensive plan where he would score points. That Miami game, we caused some things to happen defensively, but we still gave up 30 points. And Holtz outscored them.

I tell you the guy who was a classic was [offensive line coach] Joe Moore. I liked Joe a lot. In the book that Holtz and [Notre Dame sports information director] John Heisler wrote after the season, I was credited with standing up and saying after Brooks and Watters were sent home, "I don't care if I'm the only guy out there or if we only have 10 guys out there, we'll do it!" That was because of Joe Moore. We had sat down with Joe Moore that day, or the night before, and those were the sentiments he expressed. I was basically repeating what he said.

My experience with [Moore] was limited because he wasn't my position coach, but it was really positive. I thought Joe was a genuine person, for one, and two, I thought he brought a lot of language to the game that made it easy to apply to your play. It wasn't anything fancy, but it was effective. I don't think there was anybody on that team who didn't respect Joe Moore.

233

When they talk about the personalities that epitomized the great 1988 Notre Dame team, no one was more prominent than the affable Frank Stams from Akron, Ohio. A fifth-year senior after breaking his ankle during the spring of 1986 while playing fullback, Stams made the transition to defense and became one of the impenetrable figures on Barry Alvarez's outstanding unit.

The 6'4", 237-pounder joined linebackers Wes Pritchett and Michael Stonebreaker to form a trio of quipsters known around Notre Dame as "the Three Amigos." Stams distinguished himself even more, however, as a dominant force at defensive end, where he was named a first-team All-American and MVP in Notre Dame's national title–winning performance against West Virginia in the Fiesta Bowl.

A second-round draft selection of the Los Angeles Rams in 1989, Stams spent three years on the West Coast before playing three years with the Cleveland Browns and part of 1995 with the Carolina Panthers and the other part with the Kansas City Chiefs.

MARK GREEN

1985–1988

I'M FROM SOUTHERN CALIFORNIA, but I was more of a UCLA fan than I was a USC fan. I visited Nebraska. I was just intrigued by Nebraska at the time because they had [1983 Heisman Trophy winner] Mike Rozier and Turner Gill and Irving Fryar. . . . It was just an exciting time for a young football player to be watching those guys. I went to the University of Washington for a visit. Don James was the head coach. And being in Southern California at that time, that was a primary target in recruiting for Washington.

But when I visited Notre Dame, it was the people that influenced me. The guys who were at Notre Dame were more like me. To put it in candid terms, they were the type of guys who would study and do the right things. You didn't feel threatened in any situation where you could potentially get into trouble.

Let me tell you, Nebraska had a bunch of hardheads. I looked at myself and said, "I could easily get into trouble around these guys." UCLA was kind of the same way. Good guys and good football players, but still I felt more comfortable with the people at Notre Dame . . . Steve Beuerlein, Tim Brown, Reggie Ward, guys like that.

It was Gerry Faust who convinced me to come to Notre Dame, but it was also the opportunity to come to Notre Dame. I'm very thankful that at 18 years old, I was wise enough to realize that here's a guy from the inner city of L.A. with an opportunity to go to a school like Notre Dame. I mean, you take advantage of that opportunity. You don't pass it up.

I had Don James recruiting me from Washington, Terry Donahue from UCLA, and Ted Tollner from USC. They came to my house and met my mom. It was a very small place, a two-bedroom house. Now in a black community like mine, when you see this white guy coming up to the door, it has to either be a recruiter or the police.

I remember those guys pulling up in front of my house, and they walked up to the door, knocked, and then shook my mom's hand. Very cordial.

When Gerry Faust came to my house, he knocked on the door, my mom opens the door, and coach Holtz reaches out and gives my mom a hug and a kiss. My mom looks back at me and says, "Boy, you're going with him!"

I can tell you why it didn't work under coach Faust without diminishing the name of Gerry Faust. One of the things that Lou Holtz brought in was a real diligence in paying attention to detail and really stressing specific components of the game that were essential in winning football games. Under coach Holtz, a running back fumbling was the worst sin in the world. For the defense, missing a tackle was an absolute no-no. So he really incorporated the fundamentals of football back into our games.

With Gerry Faust, it was more, "Catch it and run!" instead of really honing in to the fundamentals of football. That's what Holtz brought to it. There was a certain discipline that we had as well.

You know, people played hard for Gerry Faust. I felt I played hard for Gerry Faust. I wanted to win for him. But when coach Holtz came in, the attitude was, "We're not going to lose this game because of the details. If we lose, we're going to lose because the other team is better than us."

Coach Holtz used to say if you can't bench-press 400 pounds, you better be able to throw it and catch it. So we had guys working their asses off in the weight room.

He also talked about being seen rather than heard. That one stuck with me because it fit me the best. He said it's better to be seen than heard, meaning keep your damn mouth shut on the football field. Show people what you're capable of doing; don't tell them what you're capable of doing.

He used thunder as an example. All the loud roar and all the noise thunder makes, yet thunder on its own doesn't do a thing. It does absolutely nothing. And he said take the sun, the most powerful visible entity in the world. The sun doesn't make a sound, but look at the power that it has behind it. I liked those analogies. They applied to my approach to playing the game.

It was obvious from the start of coach Holtz's tenure that we were getting better. It was a project of continuous improvement. Once we got the fundamentals down, then we could begin to use that athleticism that we all were supposed to have as football players at Notre Dame.

It was a matter of learning how to win, and I think the real turning point was the last game of the season in 1986 when we beat USC in the Coliseum [38–37]. That was a real turning point because we came back when they were kicking the crap out of us. Tim Brown made a couple of big punt returns, Steve Beuerlein played well, and we got to the point where we said, "You know what? We can do this!" We took that momentum right into the next year and won eight of our first nine.

My junior year [1987], Ricky Watters and Tony Brooks arrived at Notre Dame. There's no question about their overall talent. Both of those guys were more talented than I was. But they had to learn the system. I don't think they were quite as disciplined as me, and I had my best year statistics-wise during my junior year. After that, they started to develop and understand what was expected.

But when we went back to the Los Angeles Coliseum to play USC in 1988, Watters and Brooks made a mistake. The coaches put it on the players and said to us, "What do we do?" The consensus at that time was, "Hey, look, we're here, we're abiding by the rules, and we're a team. Those guys don't have the respect for rules, the team, and each other." Everybody in that room agreed that the best thing to do would be to send those guys home.

Even with them going home, we still knew we were going to win the football game. We just didn't think anybody could beat us after we got by Miami [a 31–30 victory in the sixth game of the year]. After we got by Miami we knew we were going to win the national title.

We went through the practice sessions for West Virginia [in the Fiesta Bowl], and I remember this like it was yesterday. We put in five or six new plays for that game. Our coaches designed these plays, and we were running them in practice. Guys were open by 10 or 15 yards.

We were like, "Come on, man, we're not going to be this open! There's no way it's going to happen like this!" And our coaches were like, "I'm telling you, [West Virginia is] unsound on defense. It's going to work!" Sure enough, we had guys that wide open that game.

The people who had the greatest influence on me during my time at Notre Dame were the players: Corny Southall, D'Juan Francisco, George Streeter, and, interestingly enough, Ray Dumas. I don't know if you remember Ray Dumas. He was a wide receiver, and Ray was kind of a different breed. Ray was valuable to me because he was a demonstration of what not to do off the

Underrated Mark Green, tri-captain of the 1988 national championship squad, ranks 13th on Notre Dame's all-time rushing list. *Photo courtesy of the* Blue & Gold Illustrated.

field. Ray got into trouble all the time, which kept me on track because I knew I shouldn't do what he did.

Our running back coach, Jim Strong, was one of those guys who was in your face. A lot of guys didn't care for him. I liked him a lot. He was a great coach. I learned a ton from that guy. There were a lot of players he rubbed the wrong way. He and Brooks didn't get along too well. But I thought Jim Strong was a great coach.

He told me on many occasions, "Mark, the only reason you're starting is by default. We just don't have anybody else. Now get in there!"

The most significant part of being named a captain was that the players selected me, and nothing in the world is more valuable in my opinion than the respect of your peers.

When they voted, they voted for the guys who acted like leaders. My definition of leadership is going out and being able to display how things are supposed to be done. I used to tell the young kids, "If you want to do the right thing and make sure you're doing what you're supposed to do, do what I do. Watch me. Get in line, do what I do, and you'll do just fine."

I'm thankful for the opportunity I had at Notre Dame. I'm also thankful to my mother for making sure I went to Notre Dame and providing me with the maturity to recognize at an early age that Notre Dame was where I should be.

One of the unsung heroes of Notre Dame's national championship run in 1988, Mark Green wasn't very big and wasn't as fast as some of the other young backs on the roster. Yet he truly was one of the leaders of Lou Holtz's first squads and was appropriately honored by his teammates when he was elected a tri-captain (along with Andy Heck and Ned Bolcar) in 1988.

Listed at 6', 183 pounds as a sophomore, the Riverside, California, native paced Holtz's first Irish squad in 1986 with just 406 yards. He again led the Irish on the ground in 1987 with 861 yards and added another 646 yards in 1988.

Green stands 13th on Notre Dame's all-time rushing list with 1,977 yards and a sparkling 5.2-yard average per carry. Despite his lack of size, Green was a fifth-round draft choice of the Chicago Bears, where he played for four years.

WES PRITCHETT

1985–1988

Growing up in Atlanta, my dad had played football at Georgia, and Georgia had beaten Notre Dame in the Sugar Bowl following the 1980 regular season. Georgia tried to get me to commit early, before I went to Notre Dame for my visit, and I wouldn't do that because I'd always loved Notre Dame. My dad used to take me to the Notre Dame–Georgia Tech games.

After I went on my Notre Dame visit, I really wanted to go to Georgia. It just felt like it was the best fit for me. And then Georgia told me they didn't have a scholarship for me. They said if I wanted to come there, I could walk on, and if things worked out and a scholarship became available . . . I was like, "No, I don't think so! I'm going to Notre Dame!"

I wouldn't say I didn't want to go to Notre Dame, but it was always between Notre Dame and Georgia for me. My dad loved Notre Dame, and I loved Notre Dame growing up as a kid. But when I got back from my visit, where it was snowing, it was cold, and all my friends were going to the University of Georgia . . . I was torn. I wouldn't say Notre Dame won by default, but certainly what happened with Georgia made my decision a lot easier.

Another thing in Notre Dame's favor was that my dad was a homegrown Southern guy, as was my mother, and I was getting recruited by Mal Moore, who had been at Alabama his whole life before coming to Notre Dame.

Coach Moore was as Southern as Southern gets, and my parents and he got along wonderfully. They knew a lot of the same people, and he was roughly the same generation as my father. So that made my parents feel more comfortable and made me feel more comfortable. It was funny because when I got to Notre Dame, Rick Lantz, who was the defensive line coach, had been recruiting me to go to Georgia Tech.

I was right in the middle of the transition from Gerry Faust to Lou Holtz. In fact, I played a lot in the 58–7 loss to Miami to end the 1985 season in coach Faust's last game.

What was the difference between the Faust era and the Holtz era? I think it was really simple. Notre Dame, at the time, had a lot of talent when Gerry Faust was there. When I got to Notre Dame, there were players there like Mike Golic, Steve Beuerlein, Allen Pinkett, Larry Williams, Eric Dorsey, Mark Bavaro, Wally Kleine, Frank Stams, myself . . . there were a lot of good players there.

People go to Notre Dame to win. The guys who are recruited by Notre Dame are the kind of kids who are ultimately going to be successful. They just need to be motivated in the right direction or have a concerted effort that was heading in the right direction.

Gerry Faust was never that type of motivator. He didn't have an exact system. He didn't come in on day one and say, "These are the things we're going to do to be successful." He didn't have a formula. He was coaching by the seat of his pants from A to Z, and he never had a specific plan to do things.

You've probably heard the story of Holtz's first meeting with us, and as I look back on that, it's really amazing. Gerry said good-bye to us in the little meeting room there in the Joyce Center, and everybody slouched down. [Faust and Holtz] must have crossed each other in the hallway. Gerry is crying, "Good-bye, good-bye!" and within 30 seconds it was like, "Here's your new head coach, Lou Holtz."

All of a sudden it's, "Sit up straight in your chairs! You look at me straight in the eye! Things are going to change from this point forward!" Lou's going crazy. He said, "Things are going to be different. These are our four priorities: God, family, academics, and football." I think that was it. He put seven or eight things on the board. "These are going to be our priorities. We're going to do it this way. I'm not a patient man. You're going to do it my way or the highway." All of the clichés everybody came to know and love. And he never changed. He stuck to his guns every step of the way.

The first day, we were supposed to have a—quote, unquote—walk-through for the morning workouts at 6:00 A.M. Before it was over, the major-

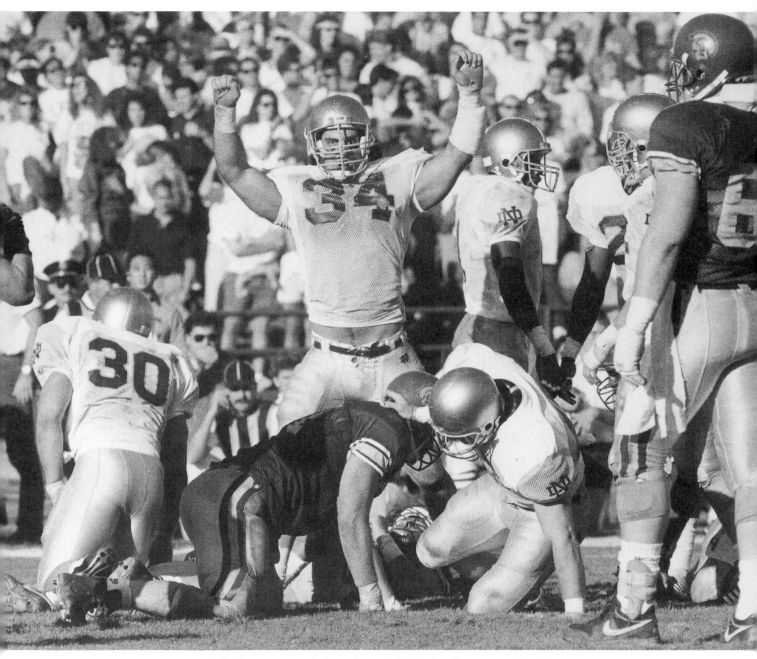

On a team full of stars, Wes Pritchett shone brightly for the 1988 national champions with a team-leading 112 tackles. *Photo courtesy of the* Blue & Gold Illustrated.

ity of the guys were throwing up. That was a wake-up call, myself being one of those people who were throwing up.

We just had never experienced anything like that. Everything had to do with discipline. Stand on the line! Do this! Break down! More than anything it was just discipline and trust in the coaches and working hard as a team.

Holtz always had you up emotionally for a game. We knew how to prepare. We made adjustments at halftime. Late in his career at Notre Dame, well after I left, everybody wanted to throw Lou under the bus. I kept saying, "You people are out of your minds! How can you do that?" Who wouldn't take Lou Holtz back now?

All the great coaches have down years. You don't know how kids are going to pan out. You're recruiting an 18-year-old. Let's face it, most kids that age are morons. Some kids are going to get kicked out of school, some are not going to be what you expect, some are going to develop, and some aren't.

The Faust years were tough. To see all that talent, and to feel what it was like to be booed off the field at Notre Dame after three straight losses, and to lose at Miami 58–7. . . . So when Lou came in, you realized this was a different way of looking at things and that this was a guy who was a proven winner.

242

[Defensive coordinator] Barry Alvarez absolutely had a lot to do with our success. Our assistant coaches were awesome. Barry was phenomenal. Barry was almost equally important to us winning the national championship as Lou Holtz, and I'll tell you why. Number one, Lou and Barry absolutely respected each other. Lou stayed out of the defense's hair. He let Barry do his own thing, and we had a unique group of guys on defense who had a phenomenal chemistry. Me, Frank, Stony, Zorich, Bolcar . . . there were a bunch of guys who just went out and played football and had fun. And that was all Alvarez.

Alvarez used to come in and say, "To work well you've got to have fun. To be successful, you've got to enjoy what you're doing." And that was the bottom line. It was a good-cop, bad-cop kind of thing between offense and defense because we were always a little looser than the offense and we kind of bumped things up a little bit. But everybody knew at the end of the day, if we needed to work harder or the going got tough, the whole team was going to buckle down. We just had a little more fun doing it on our side of the ball, and that was 100 percent Alvarez's personality.

A lot of things have to happen to win a national championship. You've got to get lucky, you've got to have the right players, the chemistry. . . . After we beat Miami, there was absolutely no doubt in anybody's mind that we were going to win the national championship. We knew we weren't going to lose.

Beating West Virginia [34–21] for the national title was great, but the [31–30] win over Miami was the pinnacle. There's no question about that for so many reasons. There was a lot of hatred between the two schools. That was the first year we had the fight in the tunnel. It was symbolic at the end of the day because of how far we had come since the 58–7 drubbing in Miami.

Miami was a team that hadn't lost in two years. Jimmy Johnson was at the peak of his career, and we beat 'em, and we really should have beaten them worse. They could argue about the breaks because they went back and forth. But at the line of scrimmage? We kicked their ass! Now, was their passing game tough to stop? There's no doubt. But I guarantee you, we kicked their ass up front.

Michigan, Southern Cal, and Miami, those were our three biggest games in 1988. We got in a fight with Miami before the game. We got done with our warm-ups and they came running through the middle of our drill. At the end of warm-ups, everybody would line up in the back of the end zone and we'd punt. They came running right through the middle of the drill and that set the tone because they realized that we weren't going to be intimidated.

If you go back and watch the Southern Cal game [a 27–10 victory], they moved the ball up and down the field. They were a damn good team. They had the biggest offensive line in the country. Their two tackles were like 340 pounds. I remember when they broke the huddle I was like, "Good Lord, look at the size of those guys!" They were huge, and their defense was in the top three or four in the country. It was No. 1 versus No. 2, 10–0 versus 10–0, Notre Dame versus Southern Cal in the last game of the season. How could it be any bigger than that?

I am absolutely happy I went to Notre Dame. It worked out. When I was making my decision on which school I would attend, one statement that my dad made to me was, "Go to Notre Dame, sacrifice for four years, and it will pay off for 40." And that's been extremely true because as my football career ended, I immediately had opportunities in a wide range of fields in a wide range of areas.

If I wanted to go live in L.A., I could have moved to Orange County. If I wanted to live in Miami, if I wanted to live in Atlanta, if I wanted to live in Chicago . . . I could go wherever I wanted.

When I decided I wanted to work on Wall Street, when I went to interview in New York, I had a letter of recommendation with my resume from Lou Holtz with that raised Golden Dome on the stationery. I was competing against all these MBAs from all these Ivy League schools. I got job offers from five different places, and in my training program, there were 37 people. Three did not have MBAs from Ivy League schools, and I was one of those three. Of the other two, one was a complete genius and the other was an Olympic discus thrower. So you tell me. That ain't happening in New York with a degree from the University of Georgia. That's the great thing about Notre Dame. It has so much notoriety, and it is such a national school.

Another great comment that my high school coach made to me was, "Wes, make sure you go to a school where if you get hurt the first day, you're going to be glad you went to school there." That was why Notre Dame was great for me. I went to a preparatory school down here. I actually thought about going to an Ivy League school, but Notre Dame was the best combination of football and academics where I could play big-time Division I-A football and I could get a great education. It was an unbelievable experience.

244

One of the more underrated members of the Notre Dame defense during its national title run, Wes Pritchett led the 1988 unit with 112 tackles—no small feat with teammate and fellow linebacker Michael Stonebreaker patrolling the middle with him.

Pritchett, an Atlanta native, helped usher in a new area of modern-day linebackers. At a time when the average weight of Notre Dame's starting offensive linemen was 264 pounds, Pritchett was a sturdy 6'6", 251 pounds.

A ferocious player on the field, Pritchett teamed with Stonebreaker and fellow fifth-year senior defensive end Frank Stams to keep Notre Dame's national championship team loose with their zest for living life to its fullest.

Pritchett was drafted in the sixth round by the Miami Dolphins in 1989, was a part of the Buffalo Bills organization for two years, and then finished his NFL stint with the hometown Atlanta Falcons.

NED BOLCAR

1986–1989

I GREW UP A NOTRE DAME FAN. My uncle Jim, a good Irish guy, Jim McFadden, which is probably more Scottish than Irish, loved Notre Dame. He used to come back from Notre Dame games back in the late seventies when I was a young kid and talk about the Fighting Irish. One of the first little jerseys I had said Notre Dame on it.

I remember him talking about the pep rallies and how exciting the game was. The fire station in downtown Phillipsburg, New Jersey, used to run trips to Notre Dame. In fact, they still do. Phillipsburg is basically a Notre Dame and Penn State town.

The first game I remember was the 1976 Notre Dame–Penn State Gator Bowl. I was nine years old, and I think Notre Dame won [20–9]. And then over the years I watched Notre Dame basketball with Kelly Tripucka and Digger Phelps, and then I watched Blair Kiel at quarterback and saw Harry Oliver kick the game-winning field goal against Michigan in 1980.

As time passed and I got older, I seemed to get more and more excited when they won and more and more upset when they lost. I can remember being miserable for a couple of days when the basketball team lost to Danny Ainge and BYU.

When it came down to making a choice of schools, Notre Dame wasn't a very good football team. Gerry Faust was there, and when I took my visits, in the back of my mind, I liked Notre Dame, but I realized that there were some beautiful schools out there with great programs, great educations, and great opportunities.

After I took my trip to Notre Dame, I went to Boston College, Stanford, Penn State, and Ohio State. Maybe now I would visit Florida State and Texas with all those pretty women down there in that warm weather.

My worst visit, by far, was Notre Dame. It was lousy weather, I didn't see any good-looking girls . . . I went to a basketball game and it took me until the second half to realize it wasn't an all-boys school. I was like, "You've got to be kidding me!" Then I ate one of those chili dogs by the old Bridget McGuire's and puked my guts out that night.

I thought there were a lot of cliques on the team, too. That just didn't feel right, and the program was struggling. I did a diary for *USA Today*, and I really didn't know who I was going to pick.

It came down to Boston College and Notre Dame. Penn State was a close third. Ohio State was in there, and Stanford was too far away. Plus, I didn't think they were ever going to be a big-time program, and I was right.

I figured at Boston College I would get a shot to start by my sophomore year. I got along well with [linebacker] Bill Romanowski, and they didn't have a lot of depth. They treated me like gold. I met with coach [Jack] Bicknell and he said, "You don't have to spend any time with us this weekend. Just go out and have a good time. Enjoy and make the best decision for you."

246

When I went to Ohio State, they put me with the third- or fourth-team quarterback. It took me about six hours before I realized that they must have thought I was a born-again Christian. Where that came from is beyond me, but the guy who was hosting me was a born-again Christian.

Finally, I had to drag him out to a bar on High Street. I finally said to him, "Can I have my 40 bucks? Thank you for your time. I'm going out." I started hanging out with Jeff Uhlenhake. D'Juan Francisco was hanging out with Cris Carter. Chris Spielman was there. I basically spent the rest of the weekend hanging out with guys like that.

I said to their assistant coach, Gary Blackney, "Why did you put me with a quarterback, number one, and number two, a guy who wants to sit and watch videos in my hotel room all night?" He stumbled and said, "Aren't you really religious? Isn't your mom a good Catholic?" I said, "Yeah, my mom's a good Catholic, but what does that have to do with me? I'm not a thug, but I want to go out and have a good time!"

The bottom line? I said to myself, "Where do you want to go?" And my heart told me Notre Dame. Notre Dame was a national school, an international school, and that's the biggest stage in the world for college football. I wanted to go compete against the best, play against the best, and if I proved to be the best, I would be at the very top of it.

I was one of seven freshmen to travel to all the games in 1985 except for the Miami game [a 58–7 loss], thank God. We played Ole Miss that year, and they were going to put me in when [linebacker coach] George Kelly said, "No, we're not going to burn up his year." Notre Dame sold itself on not redshirting, even back then, and I never considered redshirting. But it proved to be the correct decision.

I liked Gerry Faust as a person, but I was more than happy to see him go because Gerry wasn't a very good football coach. I remember the Michigan game in 1985 [a 20–12 loss], the first game of the year. I called home and talked to my mom and dad and said, "You know, I may have to transfer out of here. This school isn't for me."

I remember being so hyped up for my first game. I was a good player and a pretty good athlete, but I got more mileage out of my heart and playing on emotion than anything else. I knew I wasn't going to play in my first game, but hey, I was fired up and you never know, 20 guys might break their legs and suddenly I'm playing.

247

I remember coming into the locker room after pregame warm-ups, and I was jacked up. One of the players, I won't mention his name because I don't want to embarrass him, a big offensive lineman, says, "Hey, freshman, act like you've been here before. We don't act like that here." I thought to myself, "Maybe this is major college football, but it's not the same as it is at Phillipsburg High School where we used to get all jacked up in the locker room and basically tear each other's heads off and then we'd go out and win again."

So I go out for warm-ups and I was just hanging out, stretching. And then here comes Michigan, coming down that runway, jumping up and hitting that big blue Michigan sign and you could see the blood in their eyes, fire coming out of their noses and mouths, and their feet weren't touching the ground they were so jacked up.

I turned to George Streeter and said, "We're going to get the crap kicked out of us today," and sure enough, we did. I was so disgusted with what I saw on that team . . . I thought to myself, "Why did I ever come to this place? Ned Bolcar does not belong here!"

It got worse throughout my freshman year, and then Lou Holtz arrived. A good buddy of mine had been at Arkansas after Lou had been there and he told me, "Holy crap, Ned, we hear stories about Lou down here and he's tough!" And he was, but I thought, "Better that than what we have now." I wanted anything other than what we had the year before. I felt sorry for the guys who had been at Notre Dame four or five years before me because they had suffered through this, and I don't know how they made it.

I think Lou and I had a mutual respect for each other and a good working relationship today. He chose his all-decade team, and I was his starting middle linebacker. We've talked through the years, and if I ever asked him for a favor, I know he would do it for me, and vice versa.

I played for some great coaches, starting with Lou at the top: Foge Fazio, Barry Alvarez, John Palermo, George Kelly my freshman year, Joe Yonto . . . some of the best guys I could imagine playing for and playing with . . . Mark Green, Tony Rice, Chris Zorich, Jeff Alm, Mike Stonebreaker, Wes Pritchett . . . all those guys. I really enjoyed my experience with them.

248

We had a better team in 1989 than we had in 1988, I really believe that. Miami had a helluva team, and they were playing at home in 1989 [a 27–10 Notre Dame loss]. The week before we had played Penn State [a 34–23 victory], and the windchill was 20 below. So we go from State College in Pennsylvania to Miami, and you try to acclimate to the heat in two or three days.

Those Miami fans were the nastiest crowd I've ever played in front of in my life. I thought the one in Birmingham [Alabama in 1986] was bad. This was worse than any professional stadium I ever played in. I had friends in the stands that got hit. The wife of one of the team doctors was pushed up against the wall of the bathroom by another woman. We took a bus to the stadium and an old lady outside the bus—she must have been 70 years old—was flipping us the bird!

We walked onto the field two hours, an hour and a half before the game, and the stadium was three-quarters filled. We went out for pregame warmups and I'm standing five feet from Tony Rice as we were stretching, and I yelled to him and he yelled back and I couldn't hear a word.

Then I remember the defensive backs from Miami standing right in the middle of our passing drill. Three or four of them were wearing jerseys but not pads with headphones and their arms crossed. One of our coaches, Jay Hayes, and I think Pete Cordelli, told them to get out of the drill, and they

Linebacker Ned Bolcar is one of just 10 players since 1900 to serve as a Notre Dame captain for two years. *Photo courtesy of David Kusa / Blue & Gold Illustrated.*

basically told them to shut the hell up. Then Dennis Erickson came out and tried to chase them off and they said, "Screw you, this is our day. We're not moving."

Starting with the very first game against Michigan in 1986 when Lou came there, when a Michigan player came through our line and Tom Rehder stuck his tree limb–like arm out and clotheslined him, we had established that we wouldn't take it anymore. We weren't going to be intimidated, we weren't going to be pushed around, although I don't think we ever went looking for anything. We just wanted to show people we weren't going to take anything from anybody. We didn't start any of the fights, but we finished a lot of them.

So pregame is over and I'm exhausted because of the heat down there. No wonder they have such a home-field advantage! So we go out for the coin toss. Now Lou had been preaching to us that the school was concerned about our image, and he promised to resign if there were any more problems. Basically everybody was put on warning that that wouldn't be tolerated anymore.

250

I remember going out for the coin toss with Anthony Johnson and Tony Rice, and the whole Miami team had basically backed us up to our own sideline. I looked down our line of guys and I remember thinking, "We've got a lot of young guys playing in different roles, and this could be intimidating to them." I never felt like we had the edge on them the whole game.

There were two passes in the first half, one I should have picked off, the other one I reached out and just knocked down. I thought to myself, "I've got to come up with one of these!"

We had practiced against that play where the quarterback would roll out and they'd hit their tight end, I think it was Rob Chudzinski. We practiced it a few dozen times, and I remember on the bench before I went back out there I said to Demetrius DuBose, "I'm going to pick off the next one and run it for a touchdown!" I literally said that to him, and I never, ever said that in my life. Sure enough, a couple of plays later, here comes that play and I just stepped up, made the play, and jumped over [Miami quarterback] Craig Erickson, who made a feeble attempt at tackling me.

I've run into Erickson a couple of times since then, and he said, "I took more crap for that [attempted tackle]." I said, "You should have, you looked like a little girl diving on the ground!"

But our offense sputtered after that, Bernard Clark intercepted a ball, and then Stephen McGuire ran it in. The only time I was ever on the cover of

Sports Illustrated was Stephen McGuire's touchdown against us, and my hand is reaching out and it's right on his crotch.

Somebody called me that week and said, "You're on the cover of *Sports Illustrated!*" I thought it was for the touchdown I scored, but it was me with my hand on Stephen McGuire's crotch.

I said, "I'll show that to my grandkids someday." I'll say, "Yep, that's Grandpa grabbing the guy's crotch in the end zone."

One of the best games I ever playcd was against USC in 1987 [a 26–15 victory]. I had 19 tackles, a fumble recovery, and an interception. It was kind of a damp, cloudy day, and it was one of those days where I thought, "I'm going to make every tackle!" I just felt like wherever the ball went, I was going to make a play.

I loved the Michigan game in 1989 [a 24–19 victory] when Rocket [Raghib Ismail] ran back two touchdowns. I had a big game and landed on their quarterback, Michael Taylor, and separated his shoulder. Then Elvis Grbac came in, and that was a big mistake for us. Our offense wasn't moving the ball and I remember being on the sideline saying to the offensive players, "We'll play defense all day. Don't you worry about it. Just sit there and we'll handle it!" Whether or not it angered them, I didn't really care. I was trying to get our guys [the defense] jacked up.

251

The 1987 Michigan State game [a 31–8 victory] against Lorenzo White was another great one for us. Tim Brown had two punt returns for touchdowns and White had something like 21 yards when he left the game in the fourth quarter. We basically knocked him out of the game.

I don't watch old games, but I've seen some at Notre Dame gatherings. I said to Wes Pritchett one time, "Isn't it funny when you watch those games, we're never as good as we thought we were." The only guy who was better than I remember was Tony Rice. He was pretty damn good.

Lou was a godsend for Notre Dame. It took a guy like him to change that program around. The discipline he instilled . . . that first team meeting . . . Chuck Lanza had been voted team captain, and he had his feet up on the stage. I'm not even sure Holtz asked him his name. He said, "Son, how long have you been playing football?" Chuck said something like 14 years. And Lou said, "If your ass isn't pushed up against the back of that seat, your career will come to an end in two seconds!" And you heard 115 guys' rear ends hit the back of the seat.

I tell that story because it proves a point about leaders. In the next four years, I never saw anybody slouch in a meeting. If anybody ever fell asleep in a meeting, Lou was quick to send him out. Nobody let their eyes wander away from him or he would send them out of the meeting.

Lou was a leader by his discipline, and he knew how to organize a great coaching staff, he knew how to motivate the players, and he knew how to pull them together.

Those morning workouts . . . the only person you had to cling to was your teammate. They ran us to death and it was painful. But it was for a purpose: to bring the team together and to break down the barriers that were formed through dissension and years of losing.

I once heard the phrase, "Men want to be led . . . just not off a cliff." They want good leadership. If you have success with it, they'll gain confidence and do it harder. If you have somebody beating his head against the wall and there aren't any results, after a while he's going to say, "This is wrong," and then he's going to doubt everybody.

But give them a program that works, give them something where they can experience success and build some confidence, and that's what our coaches— led by Lou Holtz—did. All of a sudden a team that couldn't find itself became a great football team, and I was proud to be a part of it.

Only 10 Notre Dame football players since 1900 have served as captain of the Fighting Irish for two seasons. The most recent was Grant Irons (2000–2001). Ryan Leahy (1993–1994), the grandson of legendary Irish head coach Frank Leahy, and record-setting quarterback Ron Powlus (1996–1997), also were two-time captains in the nineties. Before them was linebacker Ned Bolcar (1988–1989), from Phillipsburg, New Jersey, and only Bolcar can claim he was captain of the Fighting Irish during their school-record 23-game winning streak.

Bolcar burst onto the scene in 1987, pacing the Irish in tackles with 106 (although Bolcar believes his actual total was much higher than that). He lost his starting job in 1988 to Michael Stonebreaker, but returned for a fifth year in 1989 and again led the Irish in tackles with 108.

Bolcar was drafted in the sixth round by the Seattle Seahawks, where he played for a year. He spent the next two seasons with the Miami Dolphins.

D'JUAN FRANCISCO

1986–1989

PEOPLE LIKE TO GO TO PROGRAMS with a history of winning. A couple of years before I got there, Notre Dame hadn't been winning, but they had that history of winning, and that was important to me.

My mother had been through the process with [my brother] Hiawatha because he was highly recruited. The places I visited had a good graduation rate, and if I didn't make it on the next level of football, there were people in place who could help me get my foot in the door. Notre Dame was one of those places.

Hiawatha didn't influence me one way or another, but we were a close-knit family. I look back now and I can't believe what a spoiled little kid I was. I didn't go to Michigan because they gave me a roommate when I visited. I thought, "You guys don't want me bad enough!"

At times I think I was fighting not following in my brother's footsteps. It's funny how God works. Hiawatha had a closer relationship with coach Faust than I did because he had him in high school. I didn't pay any attention to it when it was time for me to play high school because coach Faust wasn't around.

I visited North Carolina because at the time they had the most one thousand–yard rushers. I visited Ohio State, Michigan, Notre Dame, and I was supposed to go to Miami or Arizona, but I was tired of the recruiting thing, so I only took four visits.

You say all the right things in front of the camera like, "This is not just a four-year commitment, but a 40-year commitment." But then the second you're not getting any playing time, you're ready to get out of Dodge, and I was no different. It was frustrating for me not playing early in my college career.

So when things didn't work out for me early at running back, yeah, I was ready to leave. My friends still tease me about that. Coach Faust said, "You're a third-string tailback behind Allen Pinkett and Hiawatha, but I'm not going to play you your freshman year." I said, "That doesn't make any sense! I'm leaving!"

He said, "You're telling me that if the game is a blowout and we have an opportunity to play you, you want us to use up a year of eligibility?" I said, "Yeah, I want to play!" He said, "I'm not going to do that."

I think we were playing SMU my freshman year and we were winning big [Notre Dame beat SMU in 1986, 61–29]. I was stretching, preparing to be sent into the game. And I hear, "Corny Southall!" And Corny runs into the game. Everyone was playing. When I heard Corny Southall's name, I said, "I'm out of here!" I literally packed my stuff up after that game and prepared to leave . . . and then I missed my bus. I'm serious. I was ready to go to the airport. I have no idea where I was going. No one knew. Hiawatha didn't even know. But I was mad because I didn't play when I thought I was going to.

254

Coach Faust finally calmed me down and he eventually agreed to let me travel with the team. He said, "You'll get that experience of traveling and you'll be on the scout squad," and I began to understand my role. I reevaluated, sat down with Hiawatha and talked about it, and realized that it was probably in my best interest to stick around. Then coach Holtz came in and things changed.

I remember when we got smashed by Miami [58–7] in the last game of the [1985] season in coach Faust's last game. Our plane had mechanical problems. It was Monday morning, we had to go to class, it was warm when we left Miami, and we came back to snow. . . . Our plane landed and slid off the runway. We had to take a bus back.

I remember there was some bickering going on between the coaches and players on the sideline of that game. The season was over, and one of the coaches was like, "How in the world can you be having fun and laughing? We just got our asses kicked!" Another coach came over and said, "The season is over with; there's nothing they can do; let them be!"

So now the coaches are going at each other because they knew they were fired. That was just a long day, and then we came back and they announced Holtz as the next head coach.

I'll never forget the first meeting we had with coach Holtz. Chuck Lanza, a real leader on our team, had put his foot on the stage. He was just stretching out. As small as Holtz is, he picked on the biggest dude. He called out the biggest guy on the team. I mean, Chuck was a leader. He wasn't a troublemaker. He was a great guy. But coach Holtz screamed at Chuck to get his foot off the stage. After that we knew that [Holtz] would pick on anyone. So everyone sat up in his seat and that lackadaisical attitude was history.

Coach Holtz instituted those infamous 6:00 A.M. workouts. I remember one time I had pizza late the previous night, and boy did I feel it the next morning. So after that I didn't eat anything after 10:00. Guys were putting themselves on curfews. I mean, it was the off-season and we were used to having a good time. All of a sudden people were coming in on time, actually early because they wanted to be prepared. We would go over to the Joyce Center and the snowplows weren't even out yet. We were making trails in the snow to the Joyce Center.

255

We'd get over there and there were trash cans all over the place, not so we could throw away trash but so we could throw up in them. They didn't want us throwing up on the floor. People were sleeping in their workout clothes because no one wanted to be late.

Due in large part to those morning workouts, we became a close team. We all had something in common. That helped us bond. We lost some close games our first season, but we became more competitive. We lost like four games by 20 points, and then the following year we were 8–4 and lost the [Cotton] bowl game [35–10 to Texas A&M].

I think that a lot of guys got here and just wanted to stay eligible and graduate. Then coach Holtz arrived and your perspective changes. You want to win, you want to be able to wear your letterman's jacket with pride. All of a sudden you start to work hard and get upset when you lose because you expect to win.

A great example of the togetherness that we developed was following the 1987 season when we went 8–4. We were 3–0. We had opened the season with wins over Michigan, Michigan State, and Purdue, and we had a bye weekend. I don't remember how many of us there were, but it seemed like the whole team—black and white, freshmen and seniors—went to see . . . I think it was *Dirty Rotten Scoundrels*. We pretty much had the theater to ourselves. That was a great sign of the togetherness we had started to develop.

We started to police ourselves. You could see the team grow together; the chemistry started to form. Coaches can't be everywhere, and players start to develop a sense of responsibility for each other.

A converted running back, D'Juan Francisco helped spearhead the Irish secondaries in 1988 and 1989. *Photo courtesy of David Kusa/*Blue & Gold Illustrated.

I made the transition to defensive back in the spring of 1987, and I played a little running back on the scout team. [The coaches] always stroked my ego by saying, "We need speed out there on the scout squad." They'd talk about [Michigan State running back] Lorenzo White and [Penn State running back] D. J. Dozier, and how they needed someone to simulate those guys. I took pride in that.

At that point, you resign yourself to it and just do whatever the coaches ask you to do. I reached the point where I just trusted coach Holtz, and I realized that if you want to play, you do what the coach tells you or you're stacked behind people. Plus, once you start to win and you realize it's an opportunity to play, you just go with the program.

One of the most memorable games for me was the last game of the 1986 season when we went to USC [a 38–37 victory]. We came back after being down by like three touchdowns or something like that, and that was the turning point of the program. You sensed it. I was on the punt-return team, and I took pride in blocking for Timmy Brown. Special teams sparked that comeback.

We didn't know how to win under coach Faust. We were finding ways to lose. Now we were finding ways to win and we expected to win.

This may not sound very good, and I don't want people to misunderstand. But when I look back on some of those pregame fights with Southern Cal and Miami, it came to a point of personal pride. You want to make a contribution to the team, you want to be recognized and not criticized anymore. It simply reached a point where you couldn't take any crap from those teams anymore. You had to stand up for what you knew was right.

So when other teams started to walk through us while we were stretching during pregame, we had to stand up for our rights. We would never do that to an opponent. Then when we played Miami and they're walking over to our side of the field . . . we were running drills and had to start backpedaling because their linebackers kept coming into our drills.

I'm getting my helmet fixed, and all of a sudden I see [Irish strong safety] George Streeter and [cornerback] Todd Lyght in their faces. I grabbed my helmet; I had no pads in there because it was getting fixed. I strapped my chinstrap on, and the helmet was moving all around. I wanted a piece of the action because those were my boys, my brothers.

That's how the fight in the tunnel started. You have to protect the field. It takes the players to get that respect back. That's what those fights were about—respect—and we backed it up on the field.

Then coach Holtz said no more fighting, you've got to keep your composure. And then he said, "At the end of the game, save [Miami head coach] Jimmy Johnson for me!" He always knew how to say the right things.

Remember when coach Holtz would make reference to the Lady on the Dome? He always talked about the Lady on the Dome. I lived in Kavanaugh [Hall], and I switched my room so my last couple of years in Kavanaugh, my window faced the Lady on the Dome. Mind you, I'm not Catholic, but he kept talking about the Lady on the Dome, the Lady on the Dome, and I decided to switch my room.

I look back and think, "Man, this guy was definitely in my helmet." But you know, it all starts to make sense. You start playing for the school, you start playing for the coach, you start playing for your teammates, and you start to feel like you're part of something really special. That's why we didn't lose at home the last three years.

I was with the Redskins for a couple of years and had a couple of knee surgeries. I wrote a letter to coach Holtz to tell him about my experience here, and he read it to the team. Greg Davis, who was my backup in 1989, told me that Holtz had read the letter to the team. I didn't intend for it to happen that way. I just wanted to let coach Holtz know how he had impacted me. It was an amazing experience.

258

Following in the footsteps of his older brother, Hiawatha, who had played for Gerry Faust at Cincinnati Moeller High School before coming to Notre Dame, D'Juan Francisco was a highly touted running back like his sibling.

But it was at cornerback and then strong safety that the 5'11", 182-pound Francisco would make his mark with the Irish. He worked behind Stan Smagala at cornerback and served as an extra defensive back in passing downs during Notre Dame's national championship run in 1988, and then he took over for George Streeter at strong safety in 1989 amidst Notre Dame's 23-game winning streak. He joined Smagala, free safety Pat Terrell, and cornerback Todd Lyght in 1989 to form one of Notre Dame's more talented secondaries.

Although he was a 10th-round pick of the Washington Redskins, Francisco's professional career never got off the ground because of a knee injury suffered during his rookie year.

TONY RICE

1987–1989

RICKEY FOGGIE WAS FROM LAWRENCE, South Carolina, about 20 minutes away from me. We played against each other in high school, and I think he was the one who made the referral. He told coach Holtz about me when they were at Minnesota [Gophers] together.

Then [Notre Dame recruiting coordinator] Vinny Cerrato came to see me play in a couple of high school basketball games, and we spent a lot of time just talking about my involvement with Rickey and being a quarterback. [Cerrato] was the guy who really helped me understand about Notre Dame.

Finally coach Holtz came down and spoke with my grandmother, and he won her heart. I was like, "Wow, OK, I'll take a visit to Notre Dame!" Once I got up there, I fell in love with the place.

I took three visits, not five. Pittsburgh was one of them, and the North Carolina Tar Heels was the other. Notre Dame was my second visit, and I already knew I was going there. Being from a small town in South Carolina and never having traveled much, I went ahead and took my visit to Pittsburgh.

People always said that I was the perfect fit for coach Holtz's offense. But when I went to Notre Dame, I didn't really know coach Holtz's history and what type of offense he was looking for and what he was most comfortable running. I'd seen Rickey Foggie play, and he ran the option, so I was interested to see what type of scheme coach Holtz would want to run with me. He didn't really let me know at the time. He had [quarterbacks] Steve

Beuerlein and Terry Andrysiak there at the time, and those two guys were passing quarterbacks. When I came in I was more of a passer-runner.

I came to Notre Dame as a casualty of the Proposition 48 rule and was academically ineligible my freshman year, and some people made me feel uncomfortable. But I wouldn't really say it was my peers. It was more the fans. Coming in as a Proposition 48, I was labeled as the kid with bad grades who was allowed to get into Notre Dame. But most of the students on campus who didn't know me personally but knew my situation helped me along the way. I really appreciated that.

What was tough at first was having my roommate—offensive lineman Dean Brown—coming back to the dorm after practice. Dean was great. He made it easier for me. He was like another brother to me. He would come back from practice and downplay what was happening, just to make me feel good. He'd say, "Practice was so-so," just so I wouldn't feel like I was missing all the fun.

When I entered the lineup in place of Terry Andrysiak, who went down with an injury my sophomore year [1987], it was a difficult adjustment because I had missed the full year before and I hadn't taken a hit in live competition for two years.

People always ask me about how I got along with coach Holtz. My relationship with coach Holtz was wonderful. My first year, my sophomore year, I wasn't playing at the beginning of the season, but he didn't just coach one quarterback. He worked with all of us, and I think he made a concerted effort to spend more time with me, trying to get me focused, trying to make me ready for when it was my turn.

There was always this attitude that the practices were the hard part and that the games were the easy part. I thought [Holtz] did a great job doing that, and I've taken that into my life. When you're up against the wall, you take the attitude of, "Hey, I've been through worse things before." He was hard on me, hard as hell. But that just brings out the best in people. As an athlete, you want to improve each and every day, and coach Holtz provided plenty of motivation for me. He knew how to press the right buttons.

When I look back on that 23-game winning streak, it's still hard to believe. But while it's happening, you don't think about winning 18, 19, 20, 23 games in a row. I didn't realize what we accomplished until I graduated. We were on a roll, and you don't focus on what you're accomplishing as it's happen-

Quarterback Tony Rice truly was the straw that stirred the drink for Lou Holtz's offense during Notre Dame's 23-game winning streak in 1988–1989. *Photo courtesy of David Kusa/Blue & Gold Illustrated.*

ing. When it's all final and done with, it's like, "Man, we did have a great team!" I go back and look at the tapes and I still get excited, even though I know who won the game!

The 31–30 win over Miami [in 1988] was unbelievable. Coach Holtz worked us so hard that week. It was like, "Wow, when are we going to get to the game!" It was the "Catholics vs. Convicts" hype with the people on the campus. I remember it being so special because of the involvement of everybody on the campus.

Another game that stands out is the [27–10] victory at USC. Ricky Watters and Tony Brooks were sent home, and Mark Green stepped up like he had all season. Mark was a great runner. You realize at that moment that anyone can be replaced as long as someone steps up.

When [Holtz] sent [Watters and Brooks] home, I was surprised and I thought, "We're going to have to work extra hard or we don't have a chance!" But the captains made a decision to send them home, and whoever was there had to step up and fill the void.

One of the big plays in that game was my 65-yard touchdown run. I was shooting for one corner of the end zone. When I made the turn, I saw [USC defensive back] Mark Carrier cut across toward the pitch man, and I said to myself, "OK, that's it." Everybody else was accounted for, and the rest was easy at that point.

The national championship game against West Virginia in the Fiesta Bowl was interesting because they were playing man-to-man the entire time, and we had been practicing that in preparation for the game. For some reason, I was really on that day and it was like, "Tony, this is your time to shine!" I never lacked confidence in my ability to pass, but there sure were a lot of other people who didn't think I could.

We continued to win in 1989. In fact, we expected to keep winning. I never counted how many games we won or how many in a row we won. I just wanted to take care of my position and my responsibilities.

If we were playing at home, they were coming into our house, they wanted to take something away from us, and no matter what, we weren't going to let them do it. When we went to their house, we wanted to take it away from them. It sounds simplistic, but we had a way of maintaining our focus on what had to be done. We didn't complicate things by putting extra pressure on ourselves with the streak. It was a simple matter of doing what we had to do in order to win a football game, and we did that week after week.

They say that if we had beaten Miami that night, I would have won the Heisman. I don't know. I was disappointed like anyone else when you're up for an award and you don't win.

But it was fun going to New York. My mom, my grandmother, and the mayor of my town all went. Once I got there, you see all these people that you either played against or read about, and it was special to be able to sit down with them and talk about things in a way that you never could when you were playing in a game against them.

Despite all the great things that happened on the field, my graduation—getting my diploma from Notre Dame—was the greatest thrill, my greatest accomplishment. A lot of people doubted me, and a lot of people were backing me up, and I wanted to make them proud and make myself proud. My grandmother was the one who raised us, and she was so proud. She had wanted this for me, and I did what I said I was going to do for her.

His name is not prominently displayed in the Notre Dame record book for his individual statistical accomplishments. But there should be a list for "games won at quarterback." Tony Rice from Woodruff, South Carolina, would be among the best after helping lead Notre Dame to a 23-game winning streak from 1988 to 1989.

Rice, a lithe, solidly built 6'1", 200-pounder, commandeered the Fighting Irish to an undefeated season and the national championship in 1988 and then steered Notre Dame to 11 more victories in 1989 before finally falling in Miami.

Some think that had the Irish defeated the Hurricanes that night in Miami, Rice—who finished fourth in the voting—would have won the Heisman Trophy. In any event, Rice rightfully deserves to be considered one of Notre Dame's all-time great signal callers.

SCOTT KOWALKOWSKI

1987–1990

Y ES, NOTRE DAME WAS AN EASY CHOICE for me. I was looking for a smaller atmosphere with a larger name. I didn't even really know about Notre Dame until my junior year in high school. I followed Michigan and Michigan State. My dad went to Virginia.

Bo Schembechler and Gary Moeller were prominent at Michigan, and Jim Herrmann, who would go on to Michigan, coached me in high school. . . . Michigan was an attractive choice. But it wasn't for me. Notre Dame was close enough, although I visited UCLA, Colorado, Michigan State, and Virginia. Those were my choices, and it came down to the education first because my dad was a dean's list student at University of Virginia. And then the potential to play some great college football . . . once I learned about Notre Dame, the tradition and all that, I said, "Hey, man, that's for me!"

I remember Todd Lyght committed to Notre Dame and George Kelly, rest his soul, came to my house. He had just come from Todd's house to have me sign my letter of intent. I think it was February 11 of 1987. He said something to the effect that Todd Lyght sends his best. The funny thing was that I ended up playing with Todd again with the Lions in my last year.

I remember the day I decided I was going to Notre Dame. I was working out in my basement and my dad came down. It was getting close to national letter-of-intent day, and he made me go through the drill. You know, the process of writing down all the good things and bad, compare and contrast schools, and everything just pointed to Notre Dame for me.

So my dad came down and said, "Do you have any thoughts about this?" And I said, "Yeah, Dad, I think I want to go to Notre Dame." He said that would be a great choice, and the rest is history.

You talk about old school, my dad is old school. One of my favorite football stories was with my dad right before I went to Notre Dame. I was going to be a freshman in college, it was probably May [of 1987], and my dad said to me, "So you were recruited nationally, blah, blah, blah, blah, blah. You're pretty good. All right, let's see what you've got!" I guess he was in his early forties at that time.

So we went outside. He put on his old Lions gear, I put on my stuff, and we went one-on-one for about an hour and a half. How did I do? Not very well because the first play he jumped offside and head slapped me to the ground. He said, "This is what it's going to be like!"

So we went round and round, and he got into some teaching and some technique, but that's a true story. He wanted to see what I had; he wanted to test me and get me ready. He was a huge motivation. It was probably one of the more eye-opening experiences, and the tip of the iceberg of what I was going to get into.

Playing for coach Holtz was tough but good, and I think most people that I played with at Notre Dame would agree with me. He tried to make it as hard as possible in practice so that when it came game time it was easy. He's like that. Bill Parcells is like that. Bobby Ross was like that [with the Detroit Lions]. Old school. I liked playing for a guy like that because you always knew where you stood. There was no gray area.

265

The other reason I enjoyed playing for a coach like that was because I didn't know any differently. My high school program was like that, and my dad was that way.

When I think back about playing for coach Holtz, that guy was kind of amazing. He would will it to happen, and that rubs off on your players. I found myself to be that way. I was that way anyway because my dad was that way. So it was learned behavior. But that rubs off on a team. You usually take the personality of your coach, and I think that was the case with us.

We had to make a significant transition from 1989 to 1990. Barry Alvarez, our defensive coordinator, was gone, and Gary Darnell was brought in. He was our coordinator my senior year. Like everything else, as a player, you just have to roll with it. That's the nature of coaching. There's always going to be change. You have to be able to adapt to situations. You have to be able to learn on the run.

Barry Alvarez was a great coach and a great guy. One of the things he and Lou used to do my first few years in the NFL, once you made [an NFL] team, was send you a telegram congratulating you. That meant a lot to me. That was really nice.

Gary Darnell was a good guy too, but we struggled defensively in 1990. Remember, we lost some key guys from that 1989 defense such as Pat Terrell, D'Juan Francisco, and Stan Smagala in the secondary, Ned Bolcar at linebacker, and Jeff Alm on the line. We didn't transition well to that style of defense. We went from a bend-but-don't-break to more of an aggressive style of defense, and we just didn't adapt quickly enough.

My last game in a Notre Dame uniform was the 10–9 loss to Colorado in the Orange Bowl. Losing that bowl game was rough. Rocket Ismail returned about a 90-yard punt for a touchdown that would have given us the win, but Greg Davis was called for a controversial clip.

266

I personally don't think it was a penalty. I watched it. I saw it on replay. It was questionable. It was the referee's discretion. I felt really bad for Greg at the time. He felt the weight of the loss on his shoulders. Greg was a very quiet guy who just loved to play football. He didn't say much, he just did his job, and I felt bad for the guy. Not being vocal, I figured he would internalize it and suffer that much more.

We went 9–3 in 1990, which was a bad season on the heels of 1988–1989 [a combined 24–1]. But it wasn't like we had a bad football team. We were ranked No. 1 in the country two different times during that season, and we had good players. Rick Mirer was starting as a sophomore at quarterback. We had Rocket, Tony Brooks, Ricky Watters, Jerome Bettis. . . .

We had some great teams. The biggest thing that turned us around the national championship year in 1988 happened in August, right before the season started. We had a scrimmage and the coaches were pulling us back, kind of pulling back the reins because the hitting was so intense. That was kind of a turning point that year.

We had a good mix of young guys and older guys, good leaders, and that was what put us over the edge. It was our little moment of clarity where we realized, "Hey, we're pretty good!"

Offensively we had Andy Heck, Mike Brennan, Tim Grunhard—all strong personalities. Mark Green, Anthony Johnson . . . A.J. was one of my

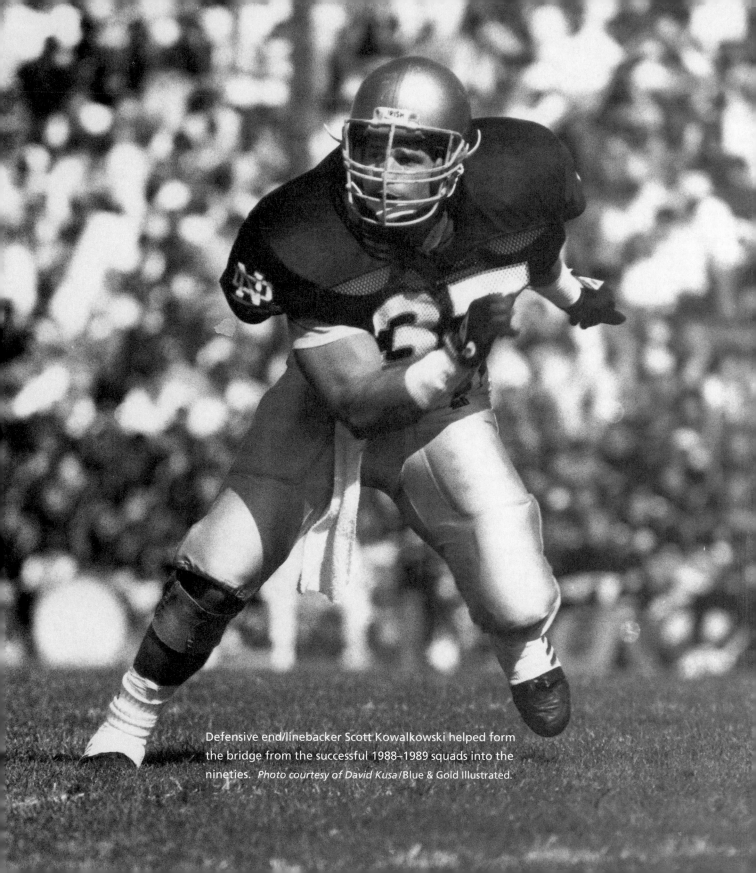

Defensive end/linebacker Scott Kowalkowski helped form the bridge from the successful 1988–1989 squads into the nineties. *Photo courtesy of David Kusa/Blue & Gold Illustrated.*

favorites. I used to hate going against that guy in practice. He was great. He did everything right all the time. I don't ever remember him messing up. Tim Ryan was my roommate, and he made the transition from linebacker to offensive guard.

I credit that to [offensive line coach] Joe Moore. He was a great coach. That guy was unbelievable. He's legendary in the pro ranks too. He was very colorful and will go down in history as one of the best ever. I was talking to these old-timers up there [in Detroit], and they said he's the best. He returned to his roots to end his coaching career by going back to high school.

The picture I have of him is us running sprints and Joe Moore standing off to the side smoking a cigarette. We'd be running sprints and he'd be smoking that cigarette and we were like, "Coach, man, can you put that out?" And he'd say, "Kolo, just shut up and run!" It was a typical answer for him. He was classic. He was the best.

As far as the Notre Dame experience, I loved it. I loved the school. I find myself watching it more and more as I get older, and now that I'm out of pro ball, I have more time. I'm getting into more Notre Dame club stuff in Detroit. I fully intend to come down to the spring game. It's such a close-knit, networking group of guys. That's what makes it special. We have a bond that can never be broken.

268

Simply put, Scott Kowalkowski loved playing football, and he proved it by turning a moderately successful major college football career with the Irish into a 12-year career in the NFL with the Philadelphia Eagles and the Detroit Lions. (Kowalkowski's father played for the Lions, and his mother still works for the organization.)

The Farmington Hills, Michigan, native helped form the bridge from Notre Dame's ultrasuccessful 1988 and 1989 seasons into the nineties, as Lou Holtz built his squad back up to a national title contender by the end of the 1992 season.

The 6'2", 230-pound Kowalkowski was not named one of the captains of the 1990 team. Mike Heldt, Todd Lyght, and Ricky Watters were. But anyone who played with Kowalkowski knew that he was one of the leaders of that squad, as well as one of the key pieces to the puzzle with the 1988–1989 squads that won 23 straight games.

RAGHIB ISMAIL

1988–1990

WHEN I FIRST MOVED TO WILKES-BARRE, Pennsylvania, from northern Jersey, I met a guy by the name of Brian Dwyer, who had just moved to Wilkes-Barre too. We both played football, and Brian and I struck up a friendship when we were like 12 years old.

I remember one weekend I stayed at his house and we stayed up all night playing this Spider-Man game. My next memory flowing into my consciousness was the voice of the Notre Dame band director saying, "The University of Notre Dame proudly presents . . ." and the Notre Dame fight song starts blaring, although I didn't know that's what it was. It scared me!

I woke up, and on the couch is Brian's dad, Wayne Dwyer, and this cat looks like he's straight out of Ireland. Red hair, glasses on, pipe, sitting in the rocking chair with this big grin . . . and he says to me, "Do you hear that, laddy? That's the greatest band in the land!" And the seed was planted.

From then on, it was all Notre Dame. All I thought about was playing football at Notre Dame. If I hadn't gone on to Notre Dame to play football, it would have been the biggest disappointment and letdown. At the time, "Wake Up the Echoes" was out and was really big. Mr. Dwyer pulls out the "Wake Up the Echoes" tape, and it was the best advertisement Notre Dame could have ever had with me.

I was a tiny guy. In eighth grade, when I was finally able to go out for freshman football, I was so small that I couldn't hold on to the ball. If I caught the ball five times a game, I fumbled it three times.

The summer between my sophomore and junior year in high school, something happened to me. I went from running like a 4.7 to 4.3. Syracuse University started to pursue me after I went to their football camp. I remember going up to the camp in the Carrier Dome, and they had all the guys lined up. I ran my 40, and the coaches looked at their watches, looked at each other, and said, "What did you get?" Then they asked me, "Could you run that again?" So I did, and the time was the same. From that point on, everything took off. Yet in my mind, it was Notre Dame or bust. They didn't have to send anybody to recruit me. If I qualified, I was going to Notre Dame.

I wore big shoulder pads and tried to look big, but I was probably 5'8", 160. By the end of my senior year, I think I weighed 166. Coach Paterno from Penn State came to the high school, then coach Holtz came to the high school, and when coach Holtz came . . . you know how you meet someone and you can tell when they're excited to meet you? Well, you also know when they're not excited to meet you, or they're disappointed. I could see in coach Holtz's face, even though he was smiling, that he was disappointed because I was so small. I felt like, "Oh, man, I just lost my chance to go to Notre Dame!" I was so afraid. I should have worn some lifts in my shoes. But my speed was such a factor that even though I was small, they had to take a chance on me.

We won every game my freshman year [1988] at Notre Dame, and then we won the first 11 games of 1989. Then we finally lost to Miami at the end of 1989, and then we lost a couple times in 1990. I really didn't know how to handle that after all the success.

When you win right off the bat, you don't have the character ingrained within you because you didn't earn it, per se. Experiencing it and not liking it, that's the key. I didn't understand that until my junior year.

I injured my thigh against Michigan State in 1990 [a 20–19 victory] and aggravated it against Purdue [a 37–11 victory]. Then we played Stanford, I didn't play, and we lost [36–31]. It was a home game and we had a whole bunch of turnovers. It wasn't until later in my pro career—I would say my third year with Carolina—before I realized how to push through an injury, and I regret not playing in that Stanford game.

I remember how disappointed coach Holtz was after we lost to Miami [27–10] in 1989. He called me into his office, and it was the first time I felt like he felt he didn't coach up to his potential. It was like he was going to cry.

He was watching the film of the loss to Miami, and he said, "Son, we should have given you the ball 10 more times." He was heartbroken, and he said, "I'm going to play you at tailback a lot in the [Orange] bowl game [against Colorado]."

I had a bunch of touches in that game [16 carries for 108 yards rushing] and scored on like a 35-yard run in the third quarter that stretched our lead [to 14–0]. That was the same play we ran earlier in the year against Pitt and Tennessee. I wish I remember how the blocking scheme was, but I know it was just so perfectly executed, I don't think I was touched. We went on to win [21–6] to cap what was another great season, but disappointing from the standpoint of losing to Miami.

My most memorable moment on the field at Notre Dame had nothing to do with any of the successes we had or what people would define as great moments. The most memorable moment was my very first game and the week leading up to it. It was Michigan at night in 1988 [a 19–17 victory].

I felt like I was having a surreal moment. They were thinking about putting me back there to return kicks. But I don't think I had caught one deep ball at receiver in three weeks. Coach Holtz was like, "I don't care if you catch it or not, I'm going to put you out there [at receiver] and put the fear of God in [Michigan]."

271

My mind was going 100 miles per hour the whole week. I remember coming out of the tunnel for pregame, and I felt like I was in the movie *What Dreams May Come* with Robin Williams and Cuba Gooding Jr. When they stepped into the afterlife, it was like walking into a painting, and that's how I felt when I came out of the tunnel. I felt like I was walking into a painting, and it felt like static electricity was in the air. It was a clean, brisk feeling, and everything was hypercolored. I remember my legs feeling so weak that I didn't know if I could walk. I was stumbling around in our pregame warm-up. I didn't catch a pass. I remember the Irish Guard seeming like they were eight feet tall. Every player for Michigan looked like he was as big as [6′8″] Greg Skrepenak, who was their big tackle.

During pregame coach Holtz told me he was going to put Mark Green back there for the opening kickoff, and I was so emotional that I started crying. But at the same time I was so relieved. I couldn't control my emotions. I started wishing my father was there, and he had died when I was 10 years old.

The first time I stepped on the field, I ran deep. Tony Rice called the play, and my heart was beating so fast. He looked at me and winked to try to relax me, but then when I lined up, here came the emotions again. The DB looked at me, and I remember running up on him and flying past him. I turned for the ball and I could feel the anticipation of the crowd. I looked up into the night sky and there was a small dot. All of a sudden I became so overwhelmed that [the football] hit me in the hands and I dropped it, and I literally felt the air in the stadium from the fans go out.

I came to the sideline and coach Holtz said, "Son, I told you I didn't care whether you caught the ball or not. You did exactly what I needed you to do." The next time he had me go in was the second half to return a kickoff, and I was determined to make up for that mistake to show coach Holtz I could do it. If I ran a 4.1 on my best day, I think I ran about a 3.9 on that return. Then I got hit so hard by a player from Michigan that I felt my organs smashing up against the front part of the inside of my body. It was like all of the air decompressed from my body, and my head hit the ground first. It was dead silent. I looked up at the sky and hundreds of white specks were flashing in front of my eyes. I got up, walked toward the sideline, and everybody looked at me like they had just seen me get hit by a car. I think they were afraid to talk to me.

Obviously, things got better from there, but by my junior year, with all the talk of the Heisman Trophy and all the interview requests, I started to panic under the pressure. It boggled my mind. I didn't understand what Notre Dame doing well meant to college football. Second, I didn't understand what it meant to be doing well at Notre Dame, while Notre Dame is doing well, and what that meant to college football. I was overwhelmed.

After games there would be hundreds of people outside the locker room, waiting for autographs. Mothers would come up to me and tell me something like, "My son doesn't listen to me. Could you please say something to him and tell him how important school is. . . ." I was totally overwhelmed!

I remember my junior year when they brought the team in and tried to help us learn how to conduct a good interview. That was the only training that I had for something like that. Other than that, there was nothing that was in place that showed me that I was perfectly equipped to handle what was coming my way. All you have to do is learn a couple of skills—time management, how to get all the requests in line, how to balance that with your class schedule—but I didn't know how to do it.

With the students it was fine. After a while, they got to know you and everything was cool. But on the football weekends, really from Wednesday to Sunday morning, I was walking around with a hood over my head trying to avoid contact with people. It was just a phase in my life that I was going through.

Of course now I recognize the needs and demands of the media. But at that time, the role the media played in sports was something I had no understanding of. I had no understanding of the dynamics of the relationship between an athlete and the media. My attitude was, "Report what I just did!" My role with the media, or my responsibility to the media, never entered my head.

[Notre Dame sports information director] John Heisler used to feel sorry for me. I started bartering with him. By my junior year the requests for interviews were huge. And then we had that media day and I told John, "I'm feeling sick! I think I'm going to hurl!" Man, I just couldn't deal with it.

Some people have heard the story about the time I rode in the laundry basket from the stadium to the ACC to avoid the crowd. It's true. It might have been after the Miami game in 1990 [a 29–20 victory], one of those games that if you watched the game, you felt like you played in the game. So if you played in the game, you were physically and emotionally spent.

273

Now I used to try to sneak out the back. Back then the guts of the stadium would allow you to walk all the way around to the other end zone, cross the street, walk behind the ACC, and I could mingle in and then go back to my dorm at Grace Hall. The later it got in the year, the darker it got.

But word got out that I was leaving that way, and it reached the point where there were as many people back there as there had been at the other exit. So I remember thinking, "I've got to find a way to get out of here!"

I talked to one of the equipment managers—you become close to those guys. So one day, I was like, "Hey, man, where is that basket going?" Well, they were taking the laundry back over to the ACC, and that's where our lockers were. I was like, "Hey, let me get in there, you guys push me across the street, and when we get to the front door, I'll get out, and I'll be home free." It was the best ride I ever had. But one of the guys must have said something like, "Guess what Rocket did today!" Before you knew it, it became public. But that's how that happened.

I had the fullest intention of coming back for my senior year [in 1991]. I hadn't made my decision when we came back from the Orange Bowl [a 10–9

274

There has never been a more explosive offensive threat at Notre Dame than the incomparable Raghib "Rocket" Ismail. *Photo courtesy of David Kusa/*Blue & Gold Illustrated.

loss to Colorado], and Rodney Culver [who would captain the 1991 squad] and myself, and I think Derek Brown, were talking about what good captains we were going to be.

That night I had a dream that my brother woke me up and that the mother of one of my teammates had died. At least I think it was a dream. The next thing I know my brother is coming into my room waking me up and saying, "Chris Zorich's mom died." That changed my perspective on everything.

Your whole life you've been thinking about how your skills and abilities will be able to get your mom a new house. That's when it hit me. You don't know what's going to happen tomorrow. If I would have gone through what Chris did, I would have been devastated because I didn't have the opportunity to do for my mom what I had wanted to do since I was a little boy. I think it was right then that I made up my mind that I had to turn pro, even though I had no idea what I was getting into, even though I had no idea about the drama that was going to intensify.

When I looked back on Notre Dame, I was really sheltered and had a protection mechanism in place, even though it was a pretty intense magnifying glass. But the death of Chris' mom is what provoked the decision. All the money stuff came after.

275

Some of the NFL teams were talking about $8 million over four years, and [Toronto Argonauts owner] Bruce McNall came into the picture and said, "I'll give you $16 million over four years." That made it a pretty easy decision at that point.

One day I woke up and I had a $4 million balance; I was 21 years old, and I had an ATM card. But I couldn't remember the code. I was in California somewhere, and I couldn't get any money out. I'm like, "I got $4 million and I can't get to it!"

What is cool about my Notre Dame experience is that after all the drama that I went through, I feel tremendously equipped to impart to people on a level that can better prepare them to face any kind of challenge, great or small.

The best time I ever had at Notre Dame as a student was the two spring semesters that I came back after leaving after my junior year. In Canada, everything was from June to November, so I came back to Notre Dame two springs in a row and that was the best time ever. I was a student and I could enjoy the campus. I didn't have to worry about going to practice, I didn't have to worry about people hunting me down. I got my degree in April of 1994.

That was my best Notre Dame experience. I was able to get into the college experience, the college environment. I would get into conversations at The Huddle with people. . . . It was a completely different perspective.

My mother and grandmother were there for my graduation. They were all emotional. It gave me such a feeling of finishing what I started and that enduring quality. That was the first cog of the process of becoming an adult. I owe that to Notre Dame.

> When people talk about the quickness of a football player and use the term "Rocket Speed," they are referring to the incomparable Raghib "Rocket" Ismail from Wilkes-Barre, Pennsylvania. Of course, there's never been a player at Notre Dame with the speed of the 5'10", 175-pounder.
>
> Ismail was a one-of-a-kind talent, a true triple threat running the football, catching it, and returning it. A two-time first-team All-American, Ismail finished second in the 1990 Heisman Trophy voting behind Brigham Young's Ty Detmer and won the Walter Camp Player of the Year Award.
>
> The gregarious Ismail holds Notre Dame records for yards per catch in a career (22.0 on 71 receptions), kickoff returns for a touchdown in a game (two versus Rice in 1988 and two versus Michigan in 1989), and kick return yards per attempt (27.6 on 46 attempts). Ismail returned five kickoffs for touchdowns at Notre Dame, also a school record.
>
> Lured by the Toronto Argonauts of the Canadian Football League, Ismail left Notre Dame after his junior year but eventually fulfilled the wish of his mother and grandmother by returning to earn his undergraduate degree. Ismail was a fourth-round selection of the Los Angeles Raiders in 1991, where he played from 1993 to 1995. He concluded his professional career with stints with the Carolina Panthers (1996–1998) and Dallas Cowboys (1999–2002).

RICK MIRER

1989–1992

M Y DAD WAS A FOOTBALL COACH, although I didn't play for him in high
school. So when I was young I was around his practices, the guys he
coached, and the guys he taught in school. We didn't spend hours and hours
studying the game like it sometimes happens with a player whose father is a
coach. But I got to witness how to practice, how to work out, how to prepare, and all the lingo.

I went into high school understanding what two-a-days were going to be
like, while some guys didn't have any idea what they were getting into. Both
my parents taught school too, so I took that seriously and did well. I was well
prepared for what I was getting into in high school, as well as at Notre
Dame—maybe more than other guys.

I had visited Michigan and had a good feel for the people there, but with
Notre Dame coming off the national championship [1988] and the guys that
were there, Notre Dame seemed like the right choice. I couldn't make a bad
decision between those two.

I never gave much thought to the type of offense coach Holtz was running with Tony Rice at quarterback. Looking back at it, I've heard and seen
people who were in my position who made decisions because of the type of
offense a school runs. But I didn't really look at it like that. I wasn't trying to
get ready for the next level, the NFL, at that point in my life. I was just trying to pick the best school and the best group of guys and the best chance to
win, and I was told we were going to open it up a little more, and we did.
But it wasn't going to be like Miami, and I knew that. Being a part of an

Rick Mirer was the quarterback for what some believe was the best team in the nation down the stretch of the 1992 season. *Photo courtesy of the* Blue & Gold Illustrated.

offense like Miami's or Florida State's wasn't what I was comfortable with anyway.

I visited UCLA and Indiana. I wouldn't say I strongly considered anywhere else. I had a visit set up for Florida State but didn't go because the position coach, Mark Richt, left to go to East Carolina. I considered Stanford briefly.

My first year at Notre Dame [1989], to be behind a quarterback who had already won a national championship made it so easy to just go in and inherit a good team. By the first game of my second year [a 28–24 victory over Michigan in 1990], we were ranked No. 1 in the country and I was on the cover of *Sports Illustrated* [with the headline "Golden Boy"]. It was pretty overwhelming. You never expect that to happen. I thought we'd have a good season, but you could never anticipate something like that so fast.

The win over Michigan was a close game, and then we went to Michigan State and won by a point [20–19]. . . . It was kind of hard to imagine it all started out so smoothly. I was in good company, and we knew we were going to be a good team, and to be the quarterback . . . let's just say it's nice being surrounded by players of that caliber. I just tried to hold up my end of it.

You get a little more nerves at first when it becomes your job and your team. You just want to get off to a good start. Things went along pretty well that first year [9–3]. The bowl game [a 10–9 loss to Colorado] was kind of a downer, but to be the guy the whole year was fun. I wasn't worried too much about how much we threw it; I was just trying to win games.

The game that stands out for me my junior year [1991] was the Tennessee game [a 35–34 loss]. I think we were winning 31–7 at halftime. Our biggest problem on offense sometimes was that we would get conservative when we would get ahead. That bothered me that we would seem to let teams slide back into the action.

When [Notre Dame] won a championship in 1988, it was more of a defensive-heavy team, and my first year, we played great defense. Then it kind of went the other way and the defense struggled a little bit. The blame didn't land on me that much because our offense had so many good football players.

Coach Holtz had a very disciplined, very professional way, an old-school kind of way of treating the team. I think the guys who were part of his programs during that time period grew up a little faster than maybe some other guys who went to other places where it was a little looser. Because of that, it wasn't fun and games every day. It was very serious, and sometimes we didn't get to enjoy our victories a whole lot. Every time we would win, we would seem to downplay it.

Coach Holtz recruited guys who he knew could handle that, and therefore he was coaching a pretty mature group of people. It wasn't flashy, we didn't get caught up in our successes, and his attitude kind of filtered into everybody else's quotes in the paper. We just kind of kept our mouths shut and played. I've been around a lot of coaches since, and [Holtz] commanded your attention and respect.

I remember we were ranked 18th and Florida was ranked 3rd for the Sugar Bowl [a 39–28 victory on January 1, 1992]. They were playing closer to home than we were, and it seemed like the stadium crowd was lopsided in their favor, which was weird for us because it wasn't normally like that.

I seem to remember some of the stuff our defense did in that game more than our offense. We would rush two guys once in a while. Our defense just kept coming up with huge plays, and they never expected that kind of defense. Offensively, we just kept hammering away with Jerome [Bettis] making a couple of huge runs. That was a real memorable game because of the anticipation of the bowl game, Steve Spurrier . . . that was very rewarding. We came out in green [trim on white jerseys]. That might have been the last time we won wearing the green.

By the end of the 1992 season [10–1–1], we were clicking really well. Stanford had beaten us [33–16] and Bill Walsh was the head coach. I was sick that we didn't win a national title when I was playing because our teams were good enough to do it. It was one game here and one game there that knocked us out of it. We had good teams, teams that were good enough to be national champions. I was lucky as hell to be playing at a time when you'd hand the ball to Reggie Brooks and he'd go 80 yards for a touchdown.

Being named a captain at Notre Dame was special, but it didn't have the significance at the time because I had already played a couple of years. I already felt like I was a captain. Being a captain is a bigger deal than you realize at the time. Then you look back and realize all the guys who were captains, all the tradition . . .

I was cocaptain with Demetrius [DuBose], and when he died [DuBose was shot and killed by the San Diego police a few years later], it was awful. And Demetrius wasn't the only captain who had died [1991 captain Rodney Culver was killed in a plane crash]. It was awful.

[Former linebacker coach and Notre Dame associate athletic administrator] George Kelly was a guy I really respected. [Former assistant athletic director] Brian Boulac was another guy who was very kind to us, and someone we could count on for any kind of advice. Coach Holtz obviously was special. You don't get the personal relationship with him as you're playing for him, but you sure get a lot of other lessons along the way.

My first year I was in [university president Reverend Edward A.] Monk Malloy's literature class, so he knew me and we spent quite a bit of time together. That felt good, and it was very rewarding. He was nice enough to make sure his door was always open, so that was neat.

[Former team chaplain] Father [James] Riehle and [former executive vice president] Father [E. William] Beauchamp both lived in Alumni Hall, and Father Beauchamp ended up marrying my wife and me a couple of years after I left Notre Dame.

You have to remember that Notre Dame was my Catholic experience, and the guy who made that so interesting for me was Father Riehle. The masses with him, his way of praying in the locker room . . . he made the whole experience of becoming Catholic very cool. We had guys from all kinds of different faiths, and Father Riehle made it like we were family in one day.

As they always say, college is the best time of your life. I probably didn't know that at the time, but I had a ton of fun and we won a lot. The friends I rely upon today more than anybody else are the guys I met during that time: Todd Norman, George Poorman, Derek Brown, Aaron Taylor, Bryant Young, Nick Smith.

I remember thinking when I was there that you never saw Joe Montana. But he was still playing. I think that was when he was 11 years out of Notre Dame, and now I'm 11 years removed from Notre Dame. For the first time I'm starting to look ahead and imagine going to a game one of these next couple of seasons. Five years ago, I never thought about that. Now I look forward to going back and seeing some people again. I've just been busy in the fall.

I'd like to be more involved with Notre Dame. When I'm done, I'll probably go to spring practice. I can imagine taking my kids there every year and going to play in a tournament or just going to see the guys. I look forward to that. Other schools kind of have that, but I think our school's tradition runs a little deeper than anybody else's.

281

As great a college quarterback as Rick Mirer was, he probably didn't get the credit he deserves. The Irish won 29 games during the three years (1990–1992) that the Goshen, Indiana, native served as the starter, including an upset victory over Florida in the January 1, 1992, Sugar Bowl and a 28–3 whitewashing of Texas A&M in the January 1, 1993, Cotton Bowl.

Had Notre Dame's defenses in 1990–1992 been of the caliber of the ones in 1988–1989, Mirer's star would have been a little brighter. As it was, the Irish were among the nation's top 17 in total offense in each of Mirer's three years as the starter, including 1992 when Notre Dame ranked third in the land with a 470.4-yard total offense average. Mirer is third on Notre Dame's all-time passing yardage list (behind Ron Powlus and Steve Beuerlein) with 5,997 yards and 41 touchdown passes (second to Powlus' 52).

The second overall pick in the NFL draft by Seattle, the 6'2", 217-pound cocaptain of the 1992 Irish squad had a brilliant rookie season, but began moving around after four years with the Seahawks. Mirer has had stints with the Chicago Bears, Green Bay Packers, New York Jets, San Francisco 49ers, and Oakland Raiders.

KEVIN McDOUGAL

1990–1993

THE REASON I CHOSE NOTRE DAME was it had prestige in everything. They had just won a national title [in 1988] and barely missed another [No. 2 in 1989]. Pretty much everyone thought we would win three more titles during my four years. Another big thing was they had just gotten the NBC-TV contract. And of course, there was the graduation rate, which was about 99 percent for athletes. It was hard not to choose Notre Dame. Everybody around me wanted me to go there too.

I visited Notre Dame, Michigan, Syracuse, West Virginia, and Penn State. The Florida schools recruited me, but I wanted to get away from home and experience something different. The Florida schools also didn't have a good graduation rate at the time.

[Notre Dame recruiting coordinator] Vinny Cerrato was really good. They sent letters every day. I got more letters from them than anybody. West Virginia had just lost to Notre Dame for the national title, and they were losing Major Harris. Syracuse came up because I wanted to play both football and basketball, and they were good in both. That was before I knew all that was involved in playing two sports. I liked Penn State because of Joe Paterno . . . all the schools I liked were up north.

When you're a young kid and you know you're good, you don't think about other quarterbacks who have come in. You think you can beat them out. Plus, the coaches don't talk about the other quarterbacks as highly when they recruit you. I knew Tony Rice was graduating, and they made it seem like I could come in and play. If I had known Rick [Mirer] was going to start for three years and go in the first round, maybe my mind would have changed. But Rick and Jake [Kelchner] were freshmen [in 1989], so they probably weren't playing as well while adjusting to school and coach Holtz's coaching style. That's probably why the coaches didn't talk about them much. They had me feeling like I could start two or three years.

After B. J. [Hawkins] and Jake left and Paul [Failla] moved ahead of me, I talked to the coaches about why I wasn't moving up. The answer always was about me needing to be a better leader, be more vocal. My stats in scrimmages would be better than Rick's or Paul's, but the coaches kept saying I wasn't vocal. I'm still not, and that seemed to hurt me.

I didn't try to be vocal because that wasn't me. If you try to go against who you are, the players would know that. I can see coaches getting on you for that if you're not producing. Then you need to say, "Hey, get these guys on track!" But I've never been in a situation where I wasn't producing—except the preseason scrimmages of my senior year.

Transferring goes through your mind, but as soon as I would call home my parents would tell me to hang in there. They reminded me I was there for my education first because anything can happen in football, whether you get hurt or not. Stay in school, get your education, believe in your skills, and keep plugging.

283

After Rick's senior year [1992], I definitely felt I was next in line because of the success I had experienced as a backup. In the spring and summer before my senior season, every magazine said it was going to be a down year for Notre Dame. We had lost Rick, Jerome [Bettis], and Reggie [Brooks] in the backfield, and everyone was saying Ron Powlus would be the starting quarterback. But I was very confident because we had a good spring against our defense—a defense that had almost everybody play in the NFL. On the inside, we knew we had a good offense with Lake Dawson, Derrick Mayes, and Clint Johnson catching the ball. Aaron Taylor and Tim Ruddy were leaders along the line. I was doing well, as were Ray Zellars and Lee Becton.

I got flustered a little in the preseason, not because I could see Ron was taking the quarterback position, but how it was being taken. If you looked at his stats, he was throwing screens and slants for touchdowns that weren't occurring against the first-team defense. He never went against the first team. I was going against the first defense and getting killed. I was like, what's going on? Why can't they see this? I felt I had no control, no matter how well I did.

Doubted by skeptics—including head coach Lou Holtz—quarterback Kevin McDougal was brilliant in leading Notre Dame to 10 straight victories in 1993.

Photo courtesy of Professional Photographic Services, Inc.

I don't want to say it was a conspiracy, but I think there was a prejudgment of wanting Ron to be the starting quarterback. That way, maybe in their minds, if a mistake was made, they could say it was a freshman that made it and he's got three more years. When Ron made mistakes, the coaches didn't think about it as much because people already were thinking we were rebuilding. With me, it was another example of, "that shows we don't need him."

As well as I played in the spring, I was still listed as 1-A and Paul was 1-B. Once the coaches did that, I felt they set it up for Ron to be the starter in the fall. Ron had high school stats that were out of this world, everyone thought he was going to win three Heismans, he could have gone to the pros out of high school . . . people were getting fed with this and buying it.

The week before the opener, Ron got hurt in a freak accident during a scrimmage. The whole team rallied around me and said, "We've got to keep going. Ron was a good quarterback, but you've shown what you can do throughout the years." I think a lot of the seniors figured I didn't do anything to lose my position. They knew it was tough on me and I had been fighting for so long to start. They just wanted the coaches to get off my back and everyone just said, "Hey, let him play!"

Coach Holtz and I had a conversation afterward that had nothing to do with Ron. My talk with him was strictly about me. Nothing against Ron, but I felt coach Holtz knew I could do the job, yet the media and hype might have turned him toward Ron. I basically told him, "If you want to win a national championship, you need me to play. I will bring you your national title." That was point-blank. I had nothing to lose because my back was against the wall. He had already said I wasn't going to start. There was nothing left for me to do but state to him how I really felt and what direction this team needed to go in order to achieve our goals.

It's almost like it went in one ear and out the other because he already felt Ron was his guy. His stats from the preseason were good, but I told people they were deceiving. I knew the difference between scrimmages and when you step out into those games.

That first game against Northwestern [a 27–12 victory] was really nerve-racking for me because of all that had gone on. I fumbled, we fell behind in the second half, but we came back to win. Once I got past that first half of the opener, it was like I had it all out of my system and now it was time to play. Heading into the Michigan game, I'll never forget the conversation I had with my parents. They told me, "There is nothing for you to do but to do what you do best." That really hit home. It's almost like I exhaled and said, "Let's do it!" I got my wake-up call and let go of all my anxieties.

Every time I look at that game at Michigan [Notre Dame entered as a 9-point underdog and won, 27–23], I get chills because it was like everything was going in slow motion for me and I knew exactly what to do. All the pieces came together for us, and we were so pumped and focused. Coach Holtz was mind-boggled after that game. He told me he had never seen anything like that before where his quarterback just dominated the game against such a good team and looked so confident. [McDougal passed for 208 yards and added touchdown runs of 43 and 11 yards.] That Michigan game set the tone for the rest of the year.

I separated my throwing shoulder on a fluke play against BYU [in the seventh game, a 45–20 victory]. I got hit from behind and I fell on my shoulder. I took some painkillers and it went away from me enough to make it through the game, but I was done for the next week against USC. I cried all the way home on the plane.

286

I could throw by game time, but not well enough to risk my team losing. I did think Paul was a good quarterback and could definitely guide us to a championship. I knew in college football if you lost, that was it as far as winning a national title. I didn't want to let the guys down by being out there knowing I was hurt and messing it up for them. A part of me said, "Man, I want to play, I want to play!" But coach Holtz said, "No, we can win against USC. Let's get through this. If we need you, we'll bring you in." It was at that point that I realized he had gained confidence in me. [Notre Dame defeated USC, 31–13, without McDougal.]

While Ron was healing, we were unbeaten and having a great season, but word came out that he was going to start against [No. 1] Florida State [on November 13]. I was like, "What's going on? How can I not start now with the season I've had?" Then I realized there was nothing I could do about it. I told myself, "Just keep on doing your thing. I don't have time to worry about that anymore. I'm trying to graduate, I'm trying to help us win." When I went out to practice on [October 17], I hadn't gotten taped yet but I heard a yell. Ron had broken [his collarbone] again while practicing throwing.

I've never seen anything like the hype for the Florida State game. You had the Heisman Trophy winner [Florida State quarterback Charlie Ward] in the game, Aaron Taylor won the Lombardi Award . . . probably every major award winner was in that game between No. 1 and No. 2. Once we won [31–24] against that caliber of opponent—probably one of the greatest teams ever assembled—we felt we were on our way. We were 10–0 and No. 1.

There was a little letdown after that, but we were on such an emotional roller coaster all year. . . . Boston College was the better team that day, and no way did we play up to our standards. Boston College was clicking. [Quarterback] Glenn Foley was great, [tight end] Pete Mitchell had 13 catches, 10 for first downs . . . that happens in sports. That's why it's unbelievable when a team goes undefeated, because you figure one team is going to be so hot on a given day that it's tough to overcome.

We were down 38–17 with about 11 minutes left, but coach Holtz wasn't just a good motivator—he was a great one. All during the week and in everyday life, his teachings kept coming back to us. He groomed you into thinking you could always come back.

I actually called the fourth-down touchdown play to Lake Dawson that put us ahead. Lee Becton brushed a linebacker's leg, and the linebacker barely missed me on the pass rush. That gave me just enough time to find Lake. It was my last pass in Notre Dame Stadium, but then Boston College drove down and kicked the field goal.

287

I'll never forget when we were getting ready to play in the Cotton Bowl, coach Holtz walked up to me and said in front of the whole team, "Kevin McDougal, I will never lose you a lead again!" That's when it hit me: he had finally realized what I achieved and what kind of player I was. We had gone through so much during the season. Words were exchanged back and forth. It was like his acceptance of me.

After we won the Cotton Bowl [24–21 over Texas A&M], we got back to the hotel, and when we saw Florida State barely made it past Nebraska, we definitely thought we would be cochampions. Everybody was saying it. Even coach Holtz was saying, "We'll at least be cochamps!"

We were heading back to the airport the next day when they announced on the radio that Florida State was No. 1 and we were No. 2. That was probably the lowest I'd been, even worse than losing to Boston College. I just felt like the voters didn't do the right thing.

I could accept that Boston College beat us [41–39] on the field fair and square, and we had done everything we could. But how were you going to give the national title to somebody we had beaten? If anything, don't give it to either of us. But it was between two teams that had each lost—and we beat them.

My degree was the icing on the cake because that's what my parents ultimately wanted me to do. I would have never thought that our 1993 team would be the last one in the past 10 years to finish in the top 10. That's a long time ago. It really means so much to me now when people remember me and our accomplishments in 1993. It makes you appreciate how all the hard work and patience were worthwhile.

When he enrolled in 1990, Kevin McDougal was the "other" quarterback in his class, while classmate B. J. Hawkins received the fanfare. Plus, Rick Mirer, the number two pick of the 1993 NFL draft, was just a sophomore, and classmate Jake Kelchner also was highly touted.

Hawkins and Kelchner transferred to Virginia and West Virginia respectively, yet in 1991, freshman Paul Failla leapfrogged McDougal to number two, behind Mirer. McDougal plugged along and then moved into the number two slot in 1992. As the backup, McDougal led Notre Dame to 10 touchdowns in 14 drives.

After Mirer graduated, the 6'2", 195-pound senior from Pompano Beach, Florida, was the heir apparent—until Ron Powlus, the most publicized recruit in Notre Dame history, signed with the Irish. Despite a stellar spring, McDougal was not anointed number one, and Powlus actually seized the starting role in the preseason until he broke his collarbone the week before the opener. McDougal then took command and had one of the greatest seasons ever by an Irish quarterback.

AARON TAYLOR

1990–1993

GOING TO NOTRE DAME was probably the best decision I ever made in my life, and if I could replay time and I had to make the decision again, I would do it. It was absolutely a positive experience.

Notre Dame was as advertised. That was the first trip I had taken, and I came in on the banquet weekend. Something like 80 to 90 percent of the guys that ended up signing with Notre Dame that year came in that weekend. We all talked and decided there was a fairly good chance we were going to go to Notre Dame. It was interesting because after we left that weekend, we already had a pretty good idea amongst ourselves that we were going to be there. So we knew who our teammates were going to be.

When my plane landed in South Bend for my visit and I was heading to the campus from the airport, I was in a car with Dean Lytle, and I remember seeing the Golden Dome for the first time lit up at night. Something about that triggered a visceral response in my body that let me know that this was right. Literally, the moment I arrived on campus, my gut, my instincts, the bells, all that stuff was going off. I knew this was a special place and this was where I wanted to be.

My athletic director in high school was a Notre Dame alum, so the sell job was very easy because every day I got a different story about Notre Dame, what the experience was like for him, what it could mean for me. He was by far Notre Dame's best PR agent.

He had a little key chain that played the Notre Dame fight song. He'd call me into his office before practice and he'd play the fight song for me. So I was kind of brainwashed a little toward Notre Dame.

Notre Dame was the first of five trips I had scheduled. The others were South Carolina the very next week, and UCLA, Washington, and Cal were up in the air: all West Coast and Notre Dame. I committed to coach Holtz the Friday afternoon they brought us in for that banquet. My decision was made, but I ended up taking the trip to South Carolina as per their request. I was looking at it like I just wanted to have fun. I had a buddy who ended up going there.

Coach Holtz was an incredible speaker, witty, kind of an intense guy in the sense that he meant business. I was in awe of him. He was a legend. I had heard so many different stories about who he was, what he was about, he was this, he was that . . . to finally meet the man, as a 17-year-old snot-nosed kid, was an experience.

And when you're talking about Joe Moore, oh, my gosh, one of the best. Of course, the Joe Moore I met on the recruiting weekend was different from the Joe Moore who ended up coaching me. That was the biggest sucker job. He wasn't chain-smoking, he wasn't calling me bad words, he wasn't throwing dirt on me, and he wasn't running us until we were puking and our guts were coming out. And he wasn't holding us before and after practice to make sure we got some extra work. I didn't meet that part of Joe Moore until probably about the first 30 seconds of my first practice.

But despite all that, the one thing you came away realizing about Joe Moore was that he cared. He really cared. And as much as we all despised him and hated him, as much as we would be pissed off at him for what he put us through, we always respected him, and we knew without a doubt that he cared. He was part of our unit. He worked us hard because he wanted us to succeed. Even when we didn't get that on a conscious level, it was always there.

Anybody who has been as successful as coach Moore was will approach the game passionately. But with that passion comes compassion. When he was kicking our asses and beating us down, that wasn't the compassionate part. He cared about us as football players too. He very much wanted us to succeed, but if he had the choice, I'm sure he would have much rather had us be fine people.

Guard/tackle Aaron Taylor (left), with center Tim Ruddy, was the emotional and physical leader of Notre Dame's powerful 1993 offensive unit. *Photo courtesy of Hans Scott/Blue & Gold Illustrated.*

As a freshman, my tactic was out of sight, out of mind, because pretty much nothing I was going to do was going to be right with coach Moore, and we were going to work over and over and over on certain things until they were right.

We would do one-on-one drills against live people, never a blocking dummy. I don't think I hit a blocking dummy at Notre Dame once. We always used the second-team offensive linemen or the scout defensive linemen because that was more realistic. We used real, live bodies, and they were instructed to not just sit there and let us push them back. If we blocked them, they would have to "crab [walk]" and do some sort of physical punishment. So they would give us a pretty good look.

The story that personified Joe Moore was one day after practice. He just ran us into the ground, and it was myself and Tim Ruddy and Todd Norman, I believe. It was just brutal. Probably as physically tired as I've ever been on a football field.

Afterward, we were talking and he said, "Remember how I told you we were going to go for another half hour and you thought there was absolutely no way that you could do any more reps? And then we'd do another 50? That's what I want you to remember on game day. When you're tired and it's fourth-and-1 and you think you can't run downfield or move that guy out of the hole, always know that you've got a little bit more."

There's no doubt in my mind that I wouldn't have been the ballplayer I was without Joe Moore. Maybe not even drafted. What Joe Moore gave me, which allowed me to stay in the [NFL] after I got hurt, was that he was an absolute fundamental technician.

I was shocked when I got to the NFL and saw how bad and how fundamentally unsound the players were. How did these guys even make it to the NFL with the bad technique they had? Common sense, basic fundamental football: keeping your hands inside, staying low, bending your knees, keeping a good base . . . those things were beat into you over and over by coach Moore, which is why it came naturally when I went to the NFL.

For me, when I got hurt [in the NFL], I couldn't physically dominate people anymore. I had to position block and outsmart them and know where they were going, cut them off, and give them one angle. I was able to hang around as long as I did because I had good fundamentals.

Before the start of the 1993 season, I think there were a lot of questions surrounding Kevin McDougal following the departure of Rick Mirer. What a job Kevin did! I still, to this day, do not know how he didn't make it in the NFL and did not get drafted. He was unbelievable—not only what he did physically throwing the ball and running the ball and making the plays, but that guy was a winner and he was a leader. We believed in Kevin and we would bust our asses for him, and he would lead us down the field and make plays. We looked at him as our guy.

The loss to Boston College that year was devastating. It was an absolute 180-degree, seven-day period from November 13 against Florida State [a 31–24 victory] to the Boston College loss [41–39] on November 20. I have never been as emotionally high and then so emotionally low.

We didn't sense a letdown against Boston College, but the coaches sure did. We certainly talked about it as players, that we couldn't have a letdown and that we needed to do certain things. But I didn't think we would go out there and play that poorly against Boston College, and the opportunities for us to win that ballgame were so numerous it's ridiculous.

I have never been in a quarter of football like that fourth quarter when we scored those three touchdowns to take the lead. I knew that God loved Notre Dame when I saw Derrick Mayes make that catch. It was a shame that we let it slip away.

The Florida State game, with us ranked No. 2 and them No. 1, was by far the biggest game any of us ever played in. They arrived in South Bend and certainly didn't show us any respect. But that comes with the territory with those guys—the cocky swagger they have. . . . Whether or not they respected us more than any team in their lives, I think they still would have acted that way. That was the makeup of what those Florida teams were about.

I think the message they were trying to pass on, not knowing Bobby Bowden, but I think it was all about, "We're not going to be in awe of what you guys have done." They were coming into Notre Dame and this is South Bend and this is the house that Rockne built, but they weren't going to be in awe.

293

We knew coming in they were talking and they were cocky. Joe Moore said up front that these guys were very good on defense. He said, "They run around and they fly to the ball and they are by far faster than any defense we've faced, and we will probably not be able to run outside on these guys, which is OK because we're going to run it right up their ass!"

When we didn't get a rematch with them in the bowl game after we lost to Boston College, we felt slighted, and that was probably one of the first big issues of the bowls and polls and all this pre-BCS stuff. We beat them in head-to-head competition, yet at the end of the day, they were national champions.

There was a lot of talk about how [the media] had picked Bowden over Holtz for the national title. I don't think there's any question we were the best team in the country that year. Florida State was damn good, and if we had played them again, you could flip a coin. But we knew we deserved to be called national champions.

[Florida State quarterback] Charlie Ward was a special talent, an incredible athlete. That was a helluva ball game, and when it came down to it, we won head-to-head and we played better than they did that day. All of us felt we should have won the national championship. But you know, we had an opportunity and we didn't do it, so we don't have anybody to blame but ourselves.

Then we went to the Cotton Bowl to play Texas A&M [a 24–21 victory], and let me tell you, those guys brought it. I struggled in the first half. I had turf toe and they had a guy who took it to me. I was a senior and Joe Moore just smiled at me, put his arm around me, and said, "Let's go play football." I ended up playing very well the second half.

Another guy at Notre Dame during that time that meant a lot to me was George Kelly. He was a father figure to me in a lot of ways, and he was somebody associated with the coaching staff that I could talk to like a friend and that I knew I could trust. He was more interested in me as Aaron Taylor the person than as No. 75 the left guard and tackle, and he treated me as such. He was just a special, terrific person who totally embodied what the spirit of Notre Dame is all about. I will forever associate my experience there with him. The three times I was back, he was a person I made sure I saw each of those times.

I was leaving for South America and I had a chance to talk to him in February of 2003. Both he and Joe Moore. I knew when I hung up that phone with George that there was a very good probability that that was the last time I was going to talk to him. I prayed for him every day. He was a warrior and he was very much a father figure for me, somebody that you could count on that would be in your corner and was with you whether the chips were up or down.

With coach Moore, we talked about his smoking habit in our last conversation. And I remember him saying, "People can say what they want about me, Taylor, but we had fun, didn't we?" He reminisced a lot and it was sweet, if I can use that word. It was sad. But when I look back on those days, all of us old offensive linemen laugh so hard talking about coach Moore.

I've bumped into Todd Norman several times and Tim Ruddy. All those guys, whenever we bump into each other, Joe Moore stories come up all the time. There are an endless number of stories about him. We always end up laughing about something he did or said.

[Receiver coach] Skip Holtz was another guy who had a great impact on me. A conversation we had my senior year sticks out. There was a question after my junior year about whether I was going to come out [for the NFL draft], and I didn't think I was ready for the next level physically or mentally. So I came back my senior year and I was a preseason all-everything. We had our first game against Northwestern [a 27–12 victory to open the 1993 season], and I played like crap. I mean, terrible! I couldn't block a paper sack. The pressure had gotten to me. I was trying to do too much. I was trying to be perfect and do too much. Joe called me in and was like, "Who is this guy? I want Aaron back." I had gone into the tank.

I remember bumping into Skip the Sunday or Monday after the Northwestern game. My confidence was down, and I was in the tank—I was in a funk. He took me aside and was talking to me like a buddy. He said, "I want you to think about walking. Put your right foot in front of your left and swing your left arm back and your right arm forward and then alternate with your left foot forward" . . . and as I was doing this, it was all herky-jerky.

And Skip said, "Aaron, that's what you're doing when you're playing. You're thinking too much." He said, "You know how to walk; you've done it a million times. You know how to block; you've done it over and over and over. Just go play!" And it was like everything became clear again. I had a great week of practice and I won the Lombardi Award that year. That guy from Northwestern had to feel pretty good because he kicked the Lombardi Award winner's ass.

295

I didn't get the significance of [the Lombardi Award] at the time, especially being up against [Florida State's] Derrick Brooks, who was the NFL defensive player of the year a couple of years ago, and [Texas A&M's] Sam Adams, who is still in the league. And all the other terrific linemen that came out that year, including one of Notre Dame's great defensive linemen, Bryant Young.

It's much more meaningful now than it was then. It's an interesting dynamic in football with the "never let them see you sweat, never rest on your laurels, never be satisfied" mentality. Built into that, awards and things kind of go by the wayside, especially at the end of your senior year when you have to turn the page and go to the next level where the Lombardi Award doesn't mean anything.

So I was able to enjoy it as much as the football dynamic allowed, which at the time was probably not nearly as much as I do now. It was a very special thing, and I'm proud to have won that. It probably didn't hurt that I was on national TV every week.

I had always recognized that football was temporary for me, and it was a matter of when—not if—the game would end. I got hurt so early that that was always on the forefront of my mind and my body. By the time it was all said and done, I was so tired of pills and anti–inflammatories, and Vicodin before the game, and one at halftime, and shots here and cortisone there, and the pressure of having to go out and play to a certain level with a body that was only capable of doing certain things . . . I wasn't having fun. I didn't enjoy the game.

The only thing that remained for me was the money, and at that point, it wasn't enough anymore. That was the decision maker.

I left about $4 million on the table. To put that in perspective, I could have toughed it out in year three. Year four, I wouldn't have been physically good enough, and they would have had to cut me or reduce my salary.

But don't feel sorry for me. I went to Notre Dame. I ain't no dummy. If I left $4 million on the table, it wasn't because I was broke on the other end.

Of all the great offensive linemen developed by coach Joe Moore at Pittsburgh and Notre Dame, Aaron Taylor takes a backseat to no one. Taylor helped form one of the great offensive lines in Notre Dame history in 1993, which also featured center Tim Ruddy as well as Ryan Leahy, the grandson of legendary Irish head coach Frank Leahy.

Reporters could always count on Taylor's honest and frequently colorful analysis of Notre Dame football. But the 6'4", 299-pound quad-captain (along with Jeff Burris, Ruddy, and Bryant Young) played an even better game than he talked, helping pave the way for the sixth-ranked rushing offense in the country in 1993.

A first-round draft choice of the Green Bay Packers, the Concord, California, product won an NFL championship and appeared in two Super Bowls during his four-year run in Green Bay before a two-year stint with the San Diego Chargers. Taylor retired following the 1999 season due to a serious knee injury.

PETE CHRYPLEWICZ

1992–1996

THE ONLY SEASON THAT WE REALLY STRUGGLED during my time at Notre Dame was in 1994 when we ended up 6–5–1 after the bowl game. That was a rough year. We were accustomed to winning, so that was a very mediocre year for us. But otherwise, we were pretty good during my time at Notre Dame.

Playing for coach Holtz, to sum it up in one word, was exhilarating, both in a positive and negative way. He was a very demanding coach. He expected excellence, expected the best from his players on and off the field. He put so much pressure on you during the week of practice that Saturday seemed like a scrimmage.

He felt that if he could count on you Monday through Friday in practice, under his scrutiny and watchful eye, he knew he could count on you on Saturday in third-and-1 and fourth-and-1 situations with the ball game on the line.

For a lot of guys, that was a very difficult situation to understand and comprehend. The physical labors as well as the mental part of it were difficult. More than anything, it was a mental challenge every day. But at the end of the day, after you've weeded through everything, you know who you can count on and who's going to be out there on Saturday.

He wasn't just a football coach. He was a mentor in life as well. He had so many good stories and teachings—philosophies on life that to this day hold true. He didn't just produce football players; he produced young men who

Pete Chryplewicz continued the long line of quality tight ends at Notre Dame under head coach Lou Holtz. *Photo courtesy of Michael Murray*/Blue & Gold Illustrated.

were ready to go out into the real world if you listened and understood what he was saying.

At the same time there were plenty of times that I cursed him in Polish behind his back in practice when things were tough.

When I think about my teammates, to this day, the one senior that pulled me aside during my freshman year to offer some advice was Irv Smith. He was a senior tight end, he was having a great year, and he was bound for the NFL. He pulled me aside when I was struggling one week, probably the whole year, but he finally decided he had seen enough, and he pulled me off to the side and had a one-on-one conversation with me.

He told me, "Just remember, Lou Holtz will test you; he'll try to break you, and then break you again. Don't ever quit. Whenever he tells you to get off his team or get off his field or transfer, just take a break, go get some water, then come right back in the huddle the next play."

That became reality my sophomore year [1993]. I was starting against USC, and they were ranked highly. They had a guy by the name of Willie McGinest playing right across from me. He was the fourth pick in the first round that year [1994], and he's still in the NFL [with the two-time world champion New England Patriots].

So here I am 18 years old starting against Willie McGinest, and coach Holtz put an unbelievable amount of pressure on me that week of practice. He beat me up. He rotated four guys over me throughout the practices for the entire week, telling them to tee off on me. Hit him, hit him again, and when he gets up, hit him down again.

So it was a long, hard week for me, and on Thursday I get a message from his secretary saying that coach Holtz wanted to see me. I walk into his office thinking that he was going to say, "You endured a lot this week, I put you under pressure, congratulations, you made it through boot camp." He ended up telling me to transfer.

You can just imagine me sitting there, two days before I'm ready to start against USC and Willie McGinest at home, and he tells me, "You know what, son? You're a great person, you're a great athlete, you're going to be a great player, but not here at Notre Dame. You're not cut out for Notre Dame. So don't bother coming to practice today. Come back tomorrow morning; tell me what school you want to go to; I'll write a letter of recommendation; I'll call the AD and the head coach and give you my blessing."

299

And then he said, "Excuse me, I've got to prepare for practice." Then he put his head down and started working.

You can imagine . . . I was just floored! Your heart drops, your stomach aches, there are no words to describe it. I took a couple of steps out of his office and remembered what Irv Smith had told me. "He's going to push you, he's going to test you, he's going to push you to the limit!"

So I turned around, went back into his office, and said, "I'm staying. I'm not transferring. I'm going to start for you this Saturday, and I'm going to be the best tight end you ever coached." The rest is history, I guess you would say.

Back then, coach Holtz's assistants didn't hang around that long. If they were good, they moved on. Position coaches went to coordinating jobs, and coordinators went to head coaching jobs. There were a lot of them.

Obviously, Joe Moore was an inspiration from the blocking aspect. I'm sure there are a lot of offensive linemen in this country who will tell you that he's one of the best as far as technique goes. He harped on it and he made you perfect in practice so that game days were cake.

Joe Moore was tough. You hated him, but he demanded excellence, and if you did what he said, the technique didn't fail unless the guy across from you was Godzilla, and then he understood you did your best.

But he was tough. One-on-ones seemed to last forever. His meetings were fun. Very animated. He'd start talking about your hand being outside instead of inside, and the next thing you know he's calling you a liberal and you're the reason this country is going down the drain. Those meetings . . . when you get together with the guys who played for him, those are some of the things we talk about, those meetings.

He'd smoke half a cigarette, put it out on his watch, put it in his pocket, go yell at you, and then walk back and light up the cigarette he had put in his pocket. He was a classic, an out-of-this-world classic.

Skip Holtz was fun to work with. He was offensive coordinator and receivers coach. He was all into the passing game when Lou was into the running game. That was interesting at times.

A great benefit to me was when Bob Chmiel came over from Michigan. He had recruited me to go to Michigan, and then he became Notre Dame's recruiting coordinator and tight ends coach. That was great because our relationship just grew. He was more of a friend and a father figure than a coach.

Why Notre Dame? Anybody that has been to Notre Dame as a fan, as a tourist, they'll tell you it's a special place. It's unique. I honest to God feel that there isn't a better place in the country to get an education in an atmosphere that compels you to strive both on and off the field. It's a great environment. You're close with your student body. It's just one of those campuses that gives you a good feeling about yourself and what you're doing. To this day I tell everybody it was the best decision I ever made for myself, especially now on the outside looking back in.

When you're there, you piss and moan about the little things, the insignificant things like having an 8:00 class in the morning instead of a 10:50, or I can't believe I'm going to practice again, or study hall. . . . But now with the alumni network as strong as it is, you just appreciate the value of the Notre Dame education. I feel fortunate to have experienced it.

Dave Casper and Ken MacAfee, who played at Notre Dame during the seventies, generally are considered the two best tight ends ever to wear an Irish uniform. But during the Lou Holtz era, the Irish produced a steady stream of quality tight ends, starting with Andy Heck, who would convert to tackle in 1988, and followed by Derek Brown, Frank Jacobs, Irv Smith, and Oscar McBride. Pete Chryplewicz was next, followed by steady Leon Wallace and even a walk-on of note, Kevin Carretta.

In 1996, Chryplewicz, from Sterling Heights, Michigan, became the first Irish tight end to lead the squad in receptions since Mark Bavaro snagged a team-leading 32 in 1984. No Irish tight end has led the squad in catches since that season.

The 6'5", 267-pounder was a fifth-round draft choice of the Detroit Lions, where he played for four years before a one-year stint in Oakland.

DERRICK MAYES

1992–1995

T HEY CERTAINLY WEREN'T THROWING THE BALL that much at Notre Dame, so obviously that wasn't the reason I chose to go to school there. When it came time to make a decision on what institution I wanted to go to, we—my parents and myself—thought the priority needed to be not as much on the Xs and Os but where I wanted to spend the next four years of growth into becoming a self-sufficient young man. That overrode any offense, any style of play. That meant coming to a place where you knew you were going to get the best bang for your buck, a place where you could grow and your peer group was going to be able to help in that ascension.

Michigan, Ohio State, Miami, and Penn State were the other schools I considered. Outside of Miami, they were all in the Midwest, which probably had something to do with my Midwestern values that attracted me to those colleges. Penn State wasn't throwing any more than Notre Dame. But again, I don't think my decision really came down to Xs and Os. It was more about how I could put myself in the best position to walk away as a successful human being.

Certainly for me to have learned under Lou and Skip Holtz, having Skip as my personal coach and having coach Holtz as my head coach, I couldn't have asked for anything better. And I'm talking beyond the Xs and Os. The genuine affection that we had for each other went beyond coach-player relationships. That's something I'll take with me to the grave. I'll always be indebted to the Holtz family because of that relationship.

Wide receiver Derrick Mayes ranks fourth all time on Notre Dame's reception chart, with 129 catches.

Photo courtesy of Professional Photographic Services, Inc.

When we went through the recruiting process, I knew if my home-away-from-home were to be with Coach and Skip, I couldn't go wrong. You can't say that about all institutions. If Skip and coach Holtz hadn't been here then, I've got to believe I would have gone to Notre Dame anyway because of what the university represented. But having those two guys was one helluva bonus.

Of course, [Lou and Skip] were always fighting over the offense. Always! They still go at it in South Carolina. Skip reflects so much the new regime of college sports, and coach Holtz represented the traditional regime, which is why they complement each other so well. A lot of [Lou's] success has to do with the two of them working together. Obviously it's a father-son relationship as well, so that takes on its own course.

I worked hard on my receiving skills at Notre Dame and had some of the best teachers. I remember my freshman and sophomore year when Lake [Dawson] and I would work on catching the ball at its peak. To have a big-brother figure like Lake around, and to have Skip there as your receiver coach to emphasize the specifics really helped. He would say, "Catch the ball at its highest point. Derrick, you know you can jump higher than that. You time that thing up so either you catch it or nobody catches it!"

304

Geographically speaking, it wasn't a culture shock [going to Notre Dame] being from Indy. In my high school, it was 70/30, where the blacks were a minority. With sports at Notre Dame, more than most places, you're able to transcend race and social status and intellectual status. The students really embrace each other.

The great thing about Notre Dame is that the athletes are truly students. To be in the dorm room and stay with your dorm mate, the fact that they have nothing to do with what you do on the football field gives you a more well-rounded experience. What you have as a common thread is that you're Notre Dame men and you're going to these classes and you're spending the necessary hours to get the papers done and to get the work done. That's where the true growth for me came.

Physically, by the time you're 18, you're going to grow and get as big as you're going to get or work as hard as you're going to work. But intellectually, spiritually, and emotionally, I was able to grow and have a very awesome cast of peers.

The competition level was the same off the field as it was on. When you're in the classroom, you're competing to be the best. Not to be better than your classmate, but to be the best as an individual. Those lessons that were learned hopefully will carry on for a lifetime for me.

This place has allowed us to flourish beyond the time spent here on campus. The first thing that I do in any particular business venture, I get on my Notre Dame website and look up someone that might be in my region or might be in that same profession to ask them for their opinion, for some guidance. The network that we have here is like no other. I think that's why the ascension continues.

My most memorable moment in a Notre Dame uniform? I had some pretty good games. But I've got to say the last salute to our student body on our way out after the Navy game [a 35–17 victory in 1995] stands out the most. I had a helluva game that night, but it couldn't compare to the emotions that were running through me the last time I was able to raise that helmet in front of the student body. I'll never forget that feeling.

The first three times Derrick Mayes caught a pass in a Notre Dame uniform (1992, his freshman year), he scored a touchdown. It was a trend that would take him to the top of the school's all-time touchdown chart by a receiver (22) and place him fourth all time on the Notre Dame reception chart (129 catches) behind Tom Gatewood (157), Jim Seymour (138), and Tim Brown (137). To put Mayes' effectiveness into perspective even further, he scored once every six times he caught a pass at Notre Dame.

Mayes, an Indianapolis, Indiana, native, was one of five captains on the 1995 team (along with Paul Grasmanis, Ryan Leahy, Shawn Wooden, and Dusty Zeigler) that finished 9–3, narrowly falling to Florida State (31–26) in the Orange Bowl in Miami. The 6'1", 208-pounder scored two touchdowns against the Seminoles, as he had the previous year against Colorado in the Fiesta Bowl.

His 47 receptions (with 11 touchdown receptions) as a junior in 1994 were the most by an Irish player since Ken MacAfee in 1977. Mayes came back as a senior and finished with 48 catches and six TDs.

Mayes was a second-round pick of the Green Bay Packers, where he played in two Super Bowls (winning one). After three years in Green Bay, Mayes spent two seasons in Seattle and one year in Kansas City.

MARC EDWARDS

1993–1996

NOTRE DAME WAS A PRETTY EASY CHOICE for me. Basically, if Notre Dame offered me [a scholarship], I was going there. I took other visits just to make sure [Notre Dame] was what I was looking for. But overall, the academics were second to none as far as I was concerned.

People always ask me if I grew up a Notre Dame fan, and I've got to say, when Notre Dame was in the middle of that 23-game winning streak in the late eighties, I really didn't pull for them that much. They won all the time, and I actually found a folder from my freshman year in high school and I had written on it, "Notre Dame sucks."

So it wasn't until later that I really cared for Notre Dame. I was rooting for Miami to beat them to end their winning streak [in 1989], and then lo and behold, Notre Dame started calling me. When it came time to make a decision about which school I would attend, I thought, "This is a pretty good place to go."

The fact that coach Holtz emphasized the fullback so much was most definitely a factor in my decision to attend Notre Dame. I saw what Jerome [Bettis] was doing and Rodney Culver, Anthony Johnson, and some of those guys, and [Holtz] had a great reputation for utilizing the fullback. So yeah, that was one of the major reasons I looked so strongly at Notre Dame.

Actually, there were a bunch of reasons: the academics, how the fullback was used in the offense, how close it was to home, every game I played was on national TV . . . all those factors, plus the alumni connections, which you don't fully realize until after you leave. Also, the fact that everybody graduates from Notre Dame.

My freshman year [1993], I didn't think I would lose a game the way we started off [10–0]. We struggled a little bit the first game against Northwestern [a 27–12 victory], and then went up and had a big win at Michigan [27–23]. Then we started running the table; we beat Florida State [31–24], and then we were upset by Boston College [41–39].

The transition into 1994 [a 6–5–1 season] was difficult. I think it was the loss of talent. We had lost two first-round picks a year early the previous year [Bettis and Tommy Carter], and three first-round picks [Bryant Young, Aaron Taylor, and Jeff Burris] and a second-round pick [Tim Ruddy] after the 1993 season. We lost a lot of great players. We lost Jim Flanigan, Pete Bercich, John Covington, Lake Dawson . . . there was just so much talent on that 1993 team, and by the next year, we just didn't have that.

The only thing that was really tough for me as far as the overall Notre Dame experience was that first semester of my freshman year. Coming in and playing against guys who were three and four years older than me, to compete physically on the field, learning all this new stuff, being away from home, and competing in the classroom as well . . . my first semester was by far my worst as far as my grade point average. But once I got over that, I started to figure out what was going on, and the learning curve was gone. I improved from there, and after that, I really took off and just enjoyed every aspect of it.

307

The great thing about Notre Dame is that there are some people from the general student body that I still keep in touch with today. My sophomore year I started in the Big Brothers program, and I still keep in touch with the guy I met when he was nine years old. He's a senior in high school now. When I played at Detroit with the Patriots [in 2002], he and his family came to the game.

Playing for coach Holtz was hard. When you're a player, especially a young player, it's very, very frustrating to be a player under him. His coaching methods . . . you think, "Why is this guy still screaming and hollering?"

My freshman year there were times when I dreaded going to practice just because I knew he was going to chew my ass. I can remember walking over to practice and I felt like I had 10-pound shoes on my feet because I knew he was going to find something wrong with what I did.

Marc Edwards continued the succession of top-notch fullbacks during the Lou Holtz era at Notre Dame. *Photo courtesy of John Gentry/Blue & Gold Illustrated.*

If I made a step that was only within an inch or two of where he wanted it to be, he would chew my ass because I was a young player who had to play. He wanted to put a lot of pressure on me in practice so I wouldn't have as much pressure in a game. But even if you realize that, it still doesn't make it any easier.

It's embarrassing to be sent down to the scout team, and I got sent down there a lot. The scout team is the loneliest job in the world. I was coming off my first start against Navy, and I think I had like 98 yards rushing and a couple touchdowns. I was feeling pretty good about myself.

We had a bye week and then it was Florida State week in 1993. We ran a play on Wednesday, and somebody messed up and he said try it again. We ran the exact same play and the linebacker takes off in the direction where I can't get to him because he already knows the play. Holtz screams at me, sends me down to the scout team . . . when things like that happen you think, "Man, I got it right the first time; the guy read the play; he knew what we were running; what am I supposed to do?"

So then I come back from the scout squad and I do something else, make the wrong step or something like that, and he sends me down to the scout team again. And then I come back up and I mess up again. I think I went down there three times. It was a humiliating time.

309

I was named captain at the banquet after my junior year, before we went to the Orange Bowl to play Florida State. They announced the MVP, and I was a little disappointed that I didn't get MVP because I had a pretty solid season [717 yards rushing]. Then they announced the captains for the following year, and that was much more meaningful to me than any MVP award could have been. I was extremely proud of that.

We were disappointed with the last two years. My senior year we were 8–3, we lost the Ohio State game [29–16], and they beat us up pretty good. We were right in it at the end when that punt got called back that would have put us within a few points.

At Ohio State [in 1995, a 45–26 loss], we were beating them at halftime, we got the ball, went down and scored a field goal, and we were up by a touchdown or so. Then they were three and out, they punted, but we fumbled the ball, and they just rolled from that point on.

One of the most awesome experiences was our trip to Ireland to play Navy in 1996 [a 54–27 victory]. I think we left on a Tuesday, got there on Wednesday, and didn't leave until Monday. The culture was great, and obviously we dabbled in the pubs a little bit. That was during the time when Holtz had a no-drinking policy in place, but he bent it a little bit in Ireland. He said you could have one Guinness . . . if you were 21. I think we indulged in more than just one Guinness one night.

Coach Holtz's last home game was special, but unfortunately, I was in a knee brace at the time. The last home game was a rout of Rutgers [62–0], and the fans' appreciation of coach Holtz was just great. Remember how they used to do that little "Lou! Lou! Lou!" thing at the beginning of the fourth quarter? This time they did it the entire quarter. It was the coolest thing ever, and we kept looking around at the wave. That was something special.

Coach Holtz was a little emotional with us, but most of it happened out there on the field. We stayed out on the field a little longer than we normally did and talked to everybody. It was definitely a surreal moment.

Going to Notre Dame was a 100 percent right decision for me. I have absolutely no regrets whatsoever, other than Florida State stealing a national championship from us in 1993. Everybody felt bad for Bobby Bowden, but we should have won the national title.

Marc Edwards followed in the long line of talented, productive fullbacks at Notre Dame during the Lou Holtz era. He emerged as a contributor as a freshman behind Ray Zellars during Notre Dame's national championship run in 1993 and then quickly became a mainstay in the Irish backfield over the next three seasons.

The 6', 237-pounder from Cincinnati, Ohio, rushed for 1,591 yards and 27 touchdowns with the Irish and served as tri-captain of the 1996 squad, along with linebacker Lyron Cobbins and quarterback Ron Powlus.

To this day, no former Irish player is a more ardent follower of Irish fortunes on the field than Edwards, who was a second-round draft pick of the San Francisco 49ers, where he played two years. After two years in Cleveland, he went to New England, where he won a Super Bowl ring. He spent the 2003 season in Jacksonville and is on their 2004 roster.

MELVIN DANSBY

1993–1994, 1996–1997

My first introduction to Notre Dame came in 1992 when they played Penn State [a 17–16 victory]. It was one of those magical games with the snow, and you could feel the electricity inside the stadium. You could sense the never-say-die attitude from that team. When one of the coaches came to talk to me, it wasn't a hard decision to make Notre Dame my only trip outside the South.

When I was ready to take my Notre Dame visit, I was coming off a trip to Tennessee where it was 70 degrees and beautiful in January. All of a sudden I'm going up to South Bend, and by the time we hit Indianapolis we ran into a snowstorm. We kept hearing about how it was the worst storm in 20 years. We kept on driving and then realized that we didn't know where we were going. We could only see about two feet in front of us, and my mom and I were really freaking out. It sounds corny, but at the end we could see this glow and realized we were just half a mile away from Notre Dame.

Sitting down in one of the football meetings with Lou Holtz helped make up my mind for me. It was the postseason wrap-up, and all the seniors walked in, Lou gave his speech, and then the seniors walked out. Then the juniors moved down, and it was a kind of a changing of the guard. By the end of the meeting I was fired up and ready to go. I was like, "Pad me up, Coach!" What made Notre Dame a magical place for me was the school itself, but you can't leave out Lou Holtz. He was part of a special time in Notre Dame football.

You sit down and listen to the other coaches that would come into your home. Gene Stallings [Alabama], Pat Dye [Auburn], Terry Bowden [Auburn] . . . they'd give their pitch about what they were going to do and what you could do for their program and that's it. When Lou came down, it was school first. He talked about being a student-athlete first, then talked about how football came second. That's how he sold Notre Dame. He took all the pressure off the decision being about who you'd play football for. He made the choice a lifetime decision, not selecting a four-year institution.

But when you come from the South and especially Birmingham, Alabama, it's almost blasphemy to go outside of the state. It's the Crimson Tide or Auburn, otherwise you almost get run out of town. I had people calling my house wondering what I was doing with all those Yankee Catholics. They'd tell me they'd pray to Bear Bryant to forgive me. Down here it's Alabama country. I walked into one guy's office who was the president of the college my mom was attending at the time, and he wanted to persuade me to go to Alabama. I looked up on the wall and he had a picture of Bear Bryant walking on water and another picture on the other wall of Bear Bryant on top of Mount Sinai holding the Ten Commandments. It was that deep.

Once you arrived you saw Lou as the general. You knew that you were the grunts in the army and we were out protecting the general. He was a tyrant, and nobody was going to talk back to him. It was his word and that was the last word. You accepted it. Here's this guy who was barely 5′5″, and he could just break you down with a stare. It got to a point where you'd hear someone coming down a hallway and if you even *thought* it was Lou Holtz, you'd go the opposite way. You avoided him during the season because he was so intense. Then in the off-season he was the nicest person you'd ever want to meet.

As much as my freshman season [1993] might have been a magical fall, nobody really had high expectations that year. That's amazing to me. The year before we lost some really good players, most notably when Jerome Bettis decided to leave, and you were without a core of the offense. Everyone started to doubt each other. Then when Ron Powlus, who was supposed to be "the man," goes down before taking one snap, it was all she wrote right there. It's amazing to see how a group of juniors and seniors banded together to make it happen. In some ways we didn't have any pressure because we were always the underdogs that year. The next thing you know you're 10–0 heading into Boston College.

Lou did what any other coach would do with Ron. He had him running with the number one team but then switched gears and put Ron with the number two group to see how he'd react to actual pressure. The second-team offense was still pretty good, but look at that defensive line with Bryant Young, Jim Flanigan, and Oliver Gibson. All of a sudden you see Ron Powlus with 500 pounds on top of him, and it's not a good formula for success.

Being a freshman at that time, I was alienated. You'd think you had leprosy. Those older guys hated freshmen. My class tried to change that outlook, but some of the older guys had some bad experiences with freshmen costing the team games, so they treated you like crap. Flanigan didn't speak to me until my third game when I got in and he was trying to give me advice. Before that, I thought he was a mute. We had some soft-spoken guys on the line in the older classes that year, and I thought either something was wrong with them or something was wrong with me. As the year went on they warmed up when they found out I could play.

I can't help but remember Boston College the most from that season. It's not how you start; it's how you finish. Florida State was a good high point, but it only lasted a week. We came that close then put it all in the hands of the voters, and they didn't vote for us. I guess they wanted good ole Bobby [Bowden] to win it more.

313

I remember every pregame pep talk that year, Lou would make us feel like crap, telling us that we weren't a good football team and that we really had to work hard to get results. He said that every game, then we'd go out and kick everybody's tail. Line them up; we'd knock them down. Then all of a sudden before Boston College, Lou tells us, "You know what men? We're a good football team." We all looked at each other. You had that feeling going in that something was off, but being a freshman I sat back and just watched everybody.

By the 11th game everybody had their pregame rituals, but everything was different before Boston College. Different people spoke. The locker room was loud. It was like, "Are you guys ready for this game or what?" But I was a freshman, so I didn't say anything.

You saw what the score was in the first half. We were awful. We fought back and it came down to a field goal, but the rest was history.

Moving into 1994, we lost guys to graduation, transfers, or injuries. We just didn't have the depth that I thought we were going to have. Ron came back, but he wasn't as mobile as the season prior. As a freshman I really thought he was the second coming of Joe Montana, throwing bombs, showing pinpoint

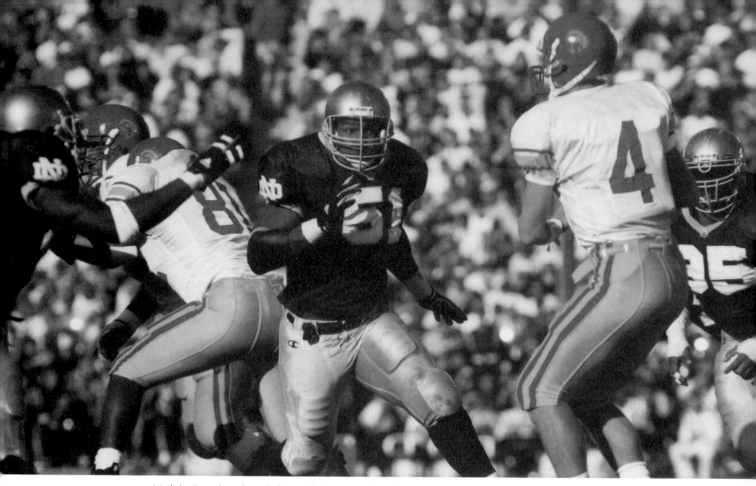

Melvin Dansby played through knee and neck injuries to become Notre Dame's most productive performer along the defensive line during the late nineties.
Photo courtesy of John Gentry/ Blue & Gold Illustrated.

accuracy, and threading balls between two defenders. As a sophomore you thought something was wrong. He gained weight and didn't have that spark after the [collarbone] injury.

As a team we relied a little bit too much on Ron and his reputation. We thought we were going to get some breaks along the way and we didn't. Lou was right, we had to work for what we wanted. Everybody was gunning for us, and if a team beat us and went 1–10, that would make their season.

The most embarrassing thing about [1994] was being invited to the Fiesta Bowl. When you win time flies by. When you're losing, the season seems six months long. You're happy to go to an Alliance Bowl, but you know you didn't deserve to be there. Going in and getting our tails whipped by Colorado [41–24 to finish 6–5–1] wasn't a good feeling.

The season renewed everyone's commitment to come back and work harder in the weight room and get on the same page. In 1994 you had a lot of so-called vocal leaders who didn't go out there and perform the way you thought they could. They got weeded out, our class started coming of age, and we started playing ball.

During the spring of 1995 I was having the best spring of my life and won the spring MVP. But during the third scrimmage I was running to the football and got hit. The next thing I know I'm lying on my back looking at the clouds. I was thinking about getting up but couldn't. Then I started feeling a tingling, thank goodness. Then I walked to the sideline, and a few minutes later the coaches were yelling at me to get back in. So I started looking for my helmet and one of the trainers had hid it in a drainpipe or something, thank goodness. If I had gone out there for one more play I could have been dead.

I had done serious damage to my neck and herniated a disk that knocked me out for the year [1995]. At that time those injuries were not well known. The only guy I could think of who had something similar was Sterling Sharpe, and he was done. In the end I had three choices: get operated on and never play again, get operated on and [maybe] play again, or not get operated on and never play.

I didn't have that many choices that I liked, so I took a shot at it and went to a doctor in Chicago who did the procedure. Everything held together, although that first hit was the hardest coming back. You can be in drills and that's not that bad, but getting into a scrimmage and getting that live contact, that's when the shell shock wears off. I worked hard that entire year to get back after dropping from 267 to 230. I bulked back up over eight months to 280 and was right back at it.

When you're injured you try to hang around, but you're pretty much a cheerleader. You'd like to think that you're old enough to be a resident assistant coach, but I was still a young guy. At the same time, I was able to get a regular student's experience, walking around before the games and soaking up the atmosphere. At least I can say I got a full experience.

I have mixed emotions about 1996 [8–3] because I thought I was going to be the next Bryant Young and then all of a sudden I get rolled in the knee against Texas, so I go into the Ohio State game against Orlando Pace at less than 100 percent. Not good.

We had high aspirations that year as a team, and that loss against Ohio State [29–16] really started a tumble. Even though our other two losses were in overtime [20–17 to Air Force and 27–20 to USC], at Notre Dame you always expect to come out on top. But nothing panned out.

Honestly, we felt like we let Lou Holtz down that year because he was only a few wins away from Knute Rockne's record. I think that last game against USC was the real decider for him, and had we won that last game instead of it ending in an overtime loss, I think he would have stayed another year. That was the most embarrassing thing—losing to USC after we had this 13-game unbeaten streak over them.

When Bob Davie took over he was one of the coaches I was close to, but things changed when he became head coach. We started hearing the rumors about how he stabbed coach Holtz in the back, and we didn't know how to feel about that. That said, we were really optimistic with a young coach coming on the scene with some fresh blood.

But we still had mixed emotions. He was a great assistant coach and defensive coordinator because he was one of the guys. But when he became the boss it alienated us. He changed a lot and ended up trying to be another Lou Holtz, and that looked fake.

There were all these things Davie used to mention he'd do if he were the head coach, and then he became the head coach and those things weren't the case. He used to think it was so crazy for us to go through live-contact practices, and he thought they were too long. He always talked about how crazy that was, saying, "Half the team is going to be injured by the middle of the season." Then he becomes the head coach and the practices were longer, and we'd hit four days a week, and we *were* injured.

If things went well during games Davie would be happy to step up and take all the credit, whereas if things didn't go all that well it seemed like he sold a team member out, like, "I don't know what that guy was thinking!" Lou Holtz was always like, "Well, I guess I didn't get my boys ready enough to play today. We'll work on it next week." Lou wouldn't hang us out there to dry.

I've always been a lead-by-example type of guy who let other people take note. That's all you can do. We had a lot of young people on the team, and we had to fight through a lot of adversity in 1997 [7–6]. We thought we'd have a Randy Moss-type player. We thought we'd have some really good wide receivers. And we had some depth deficits that really hurt us that year.

We had some undersized defensive linemen. The guy next to me, Corey Bennett, only weighed like 255 playing nose guard. We were not dipping very deeply into the talent pool that year. Guys who had transferred in earlier years had really come back to haunt us that season too.

My career at Notre Dame inspires mixed memories. Some of the best moments were with Lou Holtz as the head coach. I think he's the epitome of Notre Dame. He even looks like a little leprechaun. The most special people I met along the way were the people in my class.

People ask me if I had a kid, would I encourage him to go to Notre Dame. Absolutely. It's a great school. Everybody was right when they said it's not just a 4-year decision, it's a 40-year decision. I met a lot of great people while I was there and since I graduated. Like all families, we had our ups and downs. But it's a big family, and one that's really tight.

When people tell you stories about Notre Dame, you think they're just spouting BS. Then you experience it, and you realize it's true. It really is a Notre Dame family.

Birmingham, Alabama, product Melvin Dansby overcame neck and knee injuries during his five-year stay at Notre Dame to become one of the school's most productive defensive linemen ever. His 103 tackles in 1997 were the most by a down lineman since the incomparable Ross Browner (104) in 1977 and the talented but injury-plagued Steve Niehaus (113) in 1975.

The 6'4", 276-pounder joined Ron Powlus and Allen Rossum as captains of the 1997 squad—Bob Davie's first Notre Dame team. Dansby moved into the starting lineup in 1996, teaming with future NFL performers Renaldo Wynn (the 21st overall pick by Jacksonville in 1997) and Bert Berry, as well as productive nose guard Alton Maiden.

A serious knee injury kept Dansby from what appeared to be a promising professional career.

RON POWLUS

1994–1997

B EFORE MY SENIOR YEAR OF HIGH SCHOOL, I was very fortunate to have the experience of traveling around to a number of schools throughout the Midwest and the East with my father and my high school coach. We had a chance to see a number of different programs in the spring, which is more of a true picture of what really goes on. On a recruiting weekend, a school can make you see whatever they want you to see. So it was nice for us to get out and see a true picture of what was going on.

So during my junior year of high school, the standard was pretty much set, and it was set by Notre Dame. In my 17-year-old mind, when I walked onto the campus and had a chance to meet some of the people, Notre Dame was the picture of what college should be. Combine that with the outstanding football and academic tradition and it was a pretty easy decision. As I went into the recruiting process and when it was time to choose a school, no one could offer more to me than Notre Dame.

Of course I looked at Penn State because it was close to home and had a great reputation. I visited Pitt, Miami, Stanford, and Florida State too. As I told all those schools when I made my decision, there really wasn't anything wrong with them. They didn't do anything wrong recruiting me. It wasn't anything bad about those schools. It was just a matter of nobody meeting my expectations to beat out Notre Dame.

The thing I tell young kids now when they ask for counsel on recruiting is you have to evaluate schools based on this fact: the first day of practice, your football career could be over. Someday, your football career is going to be over. Where do you want a degree from? For me, it was an easy question to answer.

When I was choosing a school, there was a guy by the name of Rick Mirer who was the quarterback at Notre Dame. He was contending for national championships and ended up being the second pick in the NFL draft. He had a great career at Notre Dame, and Rick and I had similar styles. Throughout my high school career I rushed for 60 touchdowns and 1,700 yards. I didn't mind running the football at all. So you sprinkle in a little option and that was just fine with me.

So it wasn't a matter of me saying, "Does this style fit me?" When I evaluated it, Notre Dame was a place where I could go with a chance to win a lot of games under coach Holtz.

Getting injured my freshman year [a broken collarbone in 1993] was a rude awakening, especially coming off the high school experience I had, which was marvelous. It was a script that couldn't be written any better coming from [my hometown] Berwick [Pennsylvania]. When I got injured, it was like, "Wow, I'm human! I guess I can get hurt!" Those kinds of things had never really entered my mind. So it wasn't pleasant, but it gave me a chance to experience a whole different side of Notre Dame. For a year I was as normal as I could be, just going to school at Notre Dame.

When I was injured during the preseason scrimmage of my freshman year, I think there was a number 1, a 1-A, and a 1-B quarterback. Going into that scrimmage, coach Holtz told me that with a good scrimmage, there was a good chance I would be named the starter.

He said, "I don't want to put any more pressure on you, but I want to know where you stand. So we'll rotate the quarterbacks with the first-team offense and rotate you in versus the first-team defense." The way it worked out, I ran against the first-team defense first by running the scout team, and that's when I suffered the injury.

It was disappointing to be out, but that was a great group of guys and it was fun to cheer for a guy like [quarterback] Kevin McDougal. He was a great story and he did an outstanding job. So it was easy to root for that team as an observer. I didn't spend much time thinking about what could have been. I've never lived my life like that, and I didn't that year.

When I did finally get the chance to play in 1994, I started to develop a great relationship on the field with [wide receiver] Derrick Mayes. Derrick's talents speak for themselves. He was a great receiver and a good guy, and just through working and practicing together, we started to develop a pretty good chemistry.

The more balls you throw to somebody and the more you practice with them, the more you get on the same page. I can remember a fourth down against Florida State [a 23–16 loss] when we were playing them in the Citrus Bowl toward the end of the [1994] regular season, and [Mayes] ran the same play we had been running all year long. [Florida State] covered it, but I just knew where he was going and he just knew where I was going to throw it. It was that kind of thing that developed, and the more time you work with somebody, the easier it is to form that chemistry.

Being the quarterback at Notre Dame with the expectations that came with it was very demanding, but I don't think I ever let that overshadow all the positives that came with being at Notre Dame. You've got to remember that where I went to high school, I was used to a good deal of publicity. Obviously it was nothing like Notre Dame, but on the high school level, I was dealing with the high school version of the Notre Dame publicity. Now multiply that a hundredfold, and that's Notre Dame.

320

But it started before I got there, and because of that, it was my life and my lifestyle. I didn't have a choice. I didn't go from being an unknown entity to all of a sudden being Ron Powlus, the quarterback at Notre Dame. It started before I walked on campus. It wasn't always the easiest experience with people questioning everything I did. But at the same time that was being the Notre Dame quarterback during that era.

I had tremendous expectations for myself. Maybe the difference was that my expectations weren't quite as specific as other people's expectations. I wanted to go to Notre Dame, and I wanted to represent myself, my family, the school, and the fans in the best way possible by working hard, putting forth great effort, and hopefully winning some football games along the way. So from that standpoint, I feel like I lived up to those expectations. I believe strongly that I set a good example and represented Notre Dame well, on and off the football field.

To be elected a two-time captain by your teammates at Notre Dame is something that is very special to me. It is a reward for the lifestyle that I lived, the way I led the team, the way I tried to set an example for everybody by doing what was right. It obviously was seen by my teammates and rewarded by being voted as a captain for a second year. There's no question that was

Ron Powlus holds numerous Irish passing records, including career pass attempts, pass completions, passing yardage, and touchdown passes. *Photo courtesy of Matt Cashore* / Blue & Gold Illustrated.

something special and a great memory that I take from my Notre Dame football days.

When I suffered my second injury [a broken left humerus in the November 4, 1995, Navy game], the only good thing about that was that it was toward the end of the season and I didn't miss many games. The real unfortunate thing was that we went to the Orange Bowl that year and I didn't get to play [versus Florida State, a 31–26 loss]. But it was great to see Thomas Krug get a chance to get on the field. He was a good guy and a good QB. But as a competitive guy myself, you wish you were the one out there. I'm sure Thomas felt that way every game that I played. But it was tough not being part of the team that was trying to win that last [regular-season] game [versus Air Force, a 44–14 victory] and then the Orange Bowl.

I played high school football for a demanding coach, and I played college football for a demanding coach, so I appreciated coach Holtz's style and the type of coach he was.

I had a great relationship with coach Holtz. I think there were times when the media wanted to create issues between coach Holtz and myself. But I really never felt that way about him. I respected coach Holtz, and I still respect him for the kind of coach he is and what he did and the way he achieved at Notre Dame and wherever he's been. I really have nothing but good things to say about coach Holtz.

I did say that I wouldn't have returned for a fifth year [in 1997] had coach Holtz remained at Notre Dame, and as I look back that was my feeling at the time and that is still my feeling. I answered the question very honestly and truthfully.

But the simple reason I wouldn't have come back had nothing to do with any rift or any problems that I had with coach Holtz. I just felt like coach Holtz and I, as far as succeeding together, had run its course. I didn't think there was a lot left for coach Holtz and I to do together on the football field. We had some good times, we did some things well together, we had a fine relationship, but I felt like our football relationship was maxed out.

At the time, my comment that I wouldn't have returned in 1997 if he had come back got a lot of play and quite frankly, rightfully so. But it wasn't a matter of me not liking coach Holtz or being sick of him or anything like that.

Coach Davie certainly had a different coaching style from coach Holtz, and it was clearly different with him than it had been. But I don't know that you're going to go to Notre Dame and lighten things up too much. It's not the environment to create that kind of atmosphere. Because of the attention, because of the scrutiny, and because of the type of program it's been throughout history, everything is too important for things to "lighten up." I don't say that negatively; it was just a tall order for coach Davie to remove the pressure and expectations that come with being at Notre Dame.

As far as people outside of football, Father Al D'Alonzo was my academic adviser, and he was a great person to have around. He was a great listener. He would listen to problems, he would listen to concerns, and he was a great source of strength. Of course, there was [football team chaplain] Father [Jim] Riehle, who was always with the team, and a guy like [associate athletic director] John Heisler was always a good friend who helped me out.

Sometimes with the injuries and other things, it was tough. But I love Notre Dame and I enjoyed my experience there. I'll always feel that way about Notre Dame.

One could make an argument that no player in the history of Notre Dame football arrived with greater expectations than those placed on Berwick, Pennsylvania, quarterback Ron Powlus. In most instances, Powlus lived up to those expectations.

Powlus owns numerous Notre Dame single-season and career passing records. He ranks first in the Irish record book in pass attempts (969), completions (558), passing yardage (7,602), and touchdown passes (52). His 19 touchdown passes in 1994 is a Notre Dame single-season record, and his 4 touchdown passes in a game, which he accomplished on three occasions, is tied for the Notre Dame record.

Undrafted following the 1997 season, the 6'2", 220-pound two-time captain of the Fighting Irish spent two years (2000–2001) as a member of the Philadelphia Eagles organization.

BOBBY BROWN

1996–1999

Living in Florida and growing up a Miami fan, it was a tough decision to go to Notre Dame. But Dennis Erickson had left Miami and Butch Davis was coming in, and I didn't know who Butch Davis was. To show you how the world works, he ended up coaching me in Cleveland.

Coach Holtz was just an unbelievable recruiter, and he made my mother comfortable. That was a major thing. With my mother being in education, she wanted me to be where she would be sure that I was surrounded by other people going to class. Notre Dame's graduation rate at the time, and it's probably the same or even higher now, was second to none. That helped me make the decision, and coach Holtz was the person who sealed the deal.

The thing about coach Holtz was that he personalized everything. He came to my basketball games and people mobbed him. They were all around his car trying to get autographs, and at that point, I realized how big Notre Dame and how big coach Holtz being the head coach at Notre Dame was to a lot of people. That was amazing to me, how people gravitated around him.

To this day he knows all of my siblings' names and he knows my parents' professions. He personalized it and wanted to know how Notre Dame would fit into the characteristics of my family. By doing that, he sold all of us, all the way down to my sister's boyfriend at the time. Because of him, we all believed Notre Dame would be a good option for me.

The reality was [Notre Dame] wasn't far from the way [Holtz] described it would be. Every coach is going to stretch it a bit. It was cold, a lot colder than I imagined it would be. And as a freshman I wasn't ready to play.

Wide receiver Bobby Brown remains one of Notre Dame's most underrated pass catchers, with 96 career grabs for 1,521 yards. *Photo courtesy of Matt Cashore/Blue & Gold Illustrated.*

We flirted with the idea of me playing that year. We were blowing someone out and they didn't put me in. When I realized I wasn't going to play my freshman year and that I would have to go to practice all the time and keep up with a demanding schedule that Notre Dame requires with the academics, it was tough.

But the one thing that remained very consistent was that coach Holtz, even though we were peon freshmen, made sure we were all OK emotionally. In between yelling at us, he'd say something that carried over for two weeks. Then he'd yell at you for two more weeks, and then he would say something else that would make you think, "Yeah, this is the place I need to be."

Coach Holtz was smart. He knew he could push you to the point where he thought you'd collapse, and then he'd say something like, "You're going to be a good player," or "I'm seeing some great things of you on film and with the scout team." Just some things that would make you think, "I'm making my presence known here, and he realizes how hard I'm working!"

I think it all clicked for me on the field the spring before I started [as a sophomore in 1997]. I came into the spring, at best, third on the depth chart at my position. Everyone around me had big-play capabilities. Shannon Stephens moved from defense to offense, Raki Nelson was over there, and there was talk of Joey Getherall coming in that fall.

I just got to the point where I wasn't going to allow the coaches to have any room to take me off the field. I'm one of those people who is very determined and motivated. We sometimes have a problem with authority, and I went through all of that. At the same time, I realized that being a team player and cutting down on "the looks" at the coach are part of the sacrifice to get on the field.

I went into the spring thinking that way, and three days into it, I realized the positive attitude was working. It became the normal way for me to play, and that was a new feeling for me on that level.

Coach Holtz's last home game at Notre Dame against Rutgers [1996] was big. The emotion that surrounded it . . . I can remember vividly him calling us up as a class and telling us what his next step was and the emotions surrounding it that were pretty profound. I'll never forget all of the 6′4″, 300-pound football players reduced to tears because we had come to Notre Dame, and we had come to believe in a coach, and he wouldn't be there when we came to the finish line. It was emotional and I'll always remember that.

The place was the same and the atmosphere was the same under coach Davie. I think he's capable of being a great head coach. I just don't think he was ready for that position at that time. He and I, we argued and we hugged about every other day. Our relationship was up and down. It never got to the point where I didn't respect him as a coach. I thought he had a great football mind. I just don't think it was the right time and the right place.

One of the most memorable moments wasn't a very good one for me. It was 1999 and I scored to put us up late, but I was called for excessive celebration, and we were penalized on the kickoff. Michigan came down and scored and won the game.

I didn't believe I had done anything wrong. The sign made was very positive and meaningful to me as an Omega Psi Phi. I just wanted my point to be understood and, at the time, there was still a game going on. I thought coach Davie panicked when he confronted me on the sideline.

That's where coach Davie and coach Holtz differed. Holtz would walk up and down the sideline during the most adverse situation and say, "We're still going to win this game," and that's what I had become accustomed to.

As for going to Notre Dame, I would do it all over again, even if I knew coach Holtz was going to leave and coach Davie would be coming in and we would struggle. I met some of the most amazing people in the world, some of my best friends, people who are good people, not just good football players, that you would take with you onto the battlefield of life. A lot of people can't say that.

Bobby Brown, from Lauderhill, Florida, arrived at Notre Dame in 1996 without much national acclaim. He eventually emerged, however, as the go-to receiver for Ron Powlus in 1997 and Jarious Jackson in 1999.

Brown paced the Irish in receiving in 1997 with 45 catches (6 for touchdowns) for 543 yards, which is tied for 10th on Notre Dame's all-time single-season reception chart. Malcolm Johnson led the Irish in receptions (43) in 1998, while Brown was limited to just 13 catches. But those 13 receptions averaged 22.0 yards. Brown became Jackson's top weapon in 1999, with 36 catches for 608 yards and five touchdowns. The 6'3", 194-pounder totaled 96 receptions for 1,521 yards and 12 touchdowns in his career.

Brown went undrafted following the 1999 season and signed as a free agent with the Cleveland Browns in 2000.

JARIOUS JACKSON

1996–1999

COMING FROM A SINGLE-PARENT HOME as an only child and coming from Mississippi, I thought I was Tennessee bound. I had attended football camps at the University of Tennessee, and I was stuck on Tennessee.

At the last minute, I decided to take my visit to Notre Dame. I'd seen snow before, but it had been a long time. It may have been when I was 12 years old. Well, once I got to Notre Dame for my visit, I saw the snow and just the emotions that I was feeling . . . I don't think I had even met a coach or a player yet. The only guy I had met was Bob Chmiel, who was the recruiting coordinator at the time, and he dropped me off at my hotel room. Come to think of it, [quarterbacks coach] Tom Clements had come with Bob Chmiel to pick me up at the airport. But it was more the emotions I was feeling than any one individual.

I checked into the hotel, called my mom right away, and said, "I'm going to Notre Dame!" It was just something about being there, the atmosphere, just the whole environment. My mom can vouch for that. I knew right away that I wanted to come to Notre Dame.

I think I came in on December 9 for my visit. There were probably 10 inches of snow on the ground, and it was overcast. It was cold as all get out. I had the warmest coat I owned, and it was too thin. But it all seemed right.

I had been on the phone with coach Chmiel a lot of times, and I think I had been on the phone with coach Clements once. To this day, coach Chmiel is like my second dad.

So I get home that Sunday night and there's a Tennessee assistant coach sitting in my living room at 12:30, 1:00 in the morning. My mom was like, "He's been here all day once he found out you were taking the visit to Notre Dame." He sat with my mom for like 12, 13 hours.

At that point, I was 100 percent sure I was going to Notre Dame. But I didn't tell him that night what I was going to do. I wanted to wait and announce it later, just to be sure, but I knew I was going to Notre Dame.

Coming from Mississippi, everything about Notre Dame seemed glamorous to me. I had been to Mississippi State and Ole Miss, and those are great places, but I knew I wanted to get out of Mississippi. For me, Notre Dame was more than I expected from the student perspective and as a football player. I knew the class work would be hard.

Notre Dame is not the biggest social scene if you want to compare it to Miami and USC or places like that. But you're going for school and to play football, so I honestly didn't take [the social life] into account. If I had, I would have gone to a place like the University of Miami. I just wanted to go to a great school and get a great education, and coach Holtz definitely was one of the major factors in going to Notre Dame.

329

With coach Holtz, it was just his whole reputation. He had been there 8, 10 years before I got there, and you had watched him pace up and down the sideline. I hadn't always been the biggest Notre Dame fan growing up. I would watch their games every now and then, but even though Notre Dame is such a prestigious school and is always on TV every Saturday, you tend to watch the teams in your area, and a majority of the SEC schools are what I paid attention to and watched.

I can remember thinking in the 10th and 11th grade that I was definitely going to go to an SEC school. But when it all came down to it, I started paying more attention to Notre Dame and some other schools that were out there. When you're young, you think strictly in terms of football. But when the time comes, that's when you start to analyze things.

Coach Holtz was there for my first two years. Then he resigned, and the last three years were under coach Davie. I enjoyed my time with coach Holtz, and I enjoyed learning from him.

One of the few times I played under coach Holtz was the last couple of series against Purdue [a 35–0 victory in 1996]. I remember I had a pretty decent run, but I fumbled the ball. Coach Holtz grabbed me by my esophagus, and I didn't think he was going to let it go. We had a meeting on Monday and he said the NAACP and a bunch of different organizations were calling him because he had grabbed me around the neck and it was on TV.

If you know coach Holtz, you know that's the type of coach he was. He literally was a hands-on type of coach, a hands-on person. Every time you were on the practice field, you were trying to smell that pipe so you knew where he was.

Waiting my turn behind Ron [Powlus] was very tough. The first couple of years it wasn't a big deal because I was here, I was learning, I was getting adjusted to the speed of the college game, I was learning the terminology . . . but after a while, I felt like I was ready to compete. I was definitely ready to get more playing time than I was getting, so at that particular time it was tough.

Then I moved into the starting lineup in 1998. We had the No. 1–rated recruiting class in the nation in 1995, and most of the guys that were playing that year were from that recruiting class. We beat Michigan [36–20] in the first game, Michigan State kicked our butts [45–23] in the next game, and then we won eight straight games before I got hurt against LSU [a 39–36 victory]. We were 9–1 going into the USC game, but I hurt my knee right at the end of the LSU game.

To this day, that bothers me. To this day that was the worst injury I've had as a football player—a torn MCL. There were nine seconds on the clock, and the idea was to drop back in the end zone, waste as much time as I could running around, and then get out of the end zone. That's what the plan was.

Jamie Spencer was my right up back, Autry Denson was my left up back, and the receivers were out wide. When I dropped back, Jamie was facing to his right, but instead of Autry facing to the left, he was facing to his right as well. I dropped straight back and then to my right, and I was looking right. I had a blind spot on my left side, and Autry was supposed to be protecting the backside, but he wasn't.

So when I hit my last step at the back of the end zone, I was going to try to turn left and run toward the corner of the end zone in the opposite direction to try to waste as much time as I could. But as soon as I turned, that's when the guy hit me up high and my right knee crashed down inside and that's when it tore.

I really can't blame anybody. If it was meant to be it was going to happen. I don't blame anyone. It was just such a sick feeling to know that one more

Quarterback Jarious Jackson shattered the Notre Dame single-season marks for
pass attempts, passes completed, and passing yards. *Photo courtesy of Matt Cashore/*
Blue & Gold Illustrated.

game and we could have easily beaten USC if I would have been healthy. I think that year we could have easily run through USC, and that was the difference between being in a BCS bowl and the Gator Bowl. Instead, we had two guys behind me who hadn't played a down all season, and we lost [10–0].

As much as I appreciated the opportunity to come in under coach Holtz, I thought it would be a great situation for me when coach Davie became the head coach. But as it turned out, it wasn't so great because that was the year [1997] that I thought I would be able to get in. If you remember, coach Davie flew out to Pennsylvania and talked to Ron and his family to come back for his fifth year. So there I was sitting on the bench for another year.

I don't have any complaints about playing for coach Davie. I don't know if he was ready for the job, but at the same time he was more of a defensive-minded coach. He let his coaches on the offensive side of the ball coach. Every now and then he would come over and try to put his two cents in, but for the most part he let his offensive coordinator do the work. I was under three different coordinators while I was at Notre Dame. For me it was totally different because coach Holtz was totally hands-on with the offense, whereas coach Davie was more of a defensive coach.

I'm the type of person who respects people regardless of who you are or what your position is. But coach Holtz leaving and coach Davie stepping in, those are big shoes to fill no matter who you are. Some things started to slide a little because when coach Holtz walked through that door, you could expect guys to sit up at attention. Of course, coach Davie was always on time, but guys were slouching in their chairs, guys would still be mumbling to someone. . . . When coach Holtz walked through the door, you could hear a pin drop. That was just how his demeanor was so different from coach Davie's, and that carried over into other areas.

I was the first solo captain since Rodney Culver [1991], may he rest in peace. That was definitely a huge honor for me. I totally couldn't believe it. When people bring it to my attention today, I still feel a tingle in my body. I was a solo captain at Notre Dame! That is such a prestigious honor and something nobody can ever take away from me.

The Notre Dame experience was definitely a stepping-stone in my life and a great decision. If I had it to do over again, I would. To get a degree from Notre Dame, how I've learned to deal with different things, how to deal with the media under the microscope, learning discipline from coach Holtz . . .

Notre Dame will teach you how to become a man, and I'm sure that's something a lot of other schools don't offer. Notre Dame definitely made my life.

I'm not knocking any other schools because I'm sure there are some schools out there that do the same thing Notre Dame does, but I know that at least 90 percent of them don't. You run into guys from other schools and you can relate to their experience because of the time commitment to football, but our experiences in college really were quite different.

At Notre Dame, you have to compete in the classroom, and while the other students are running around and playing, it's 9:00 at night, you're worn out from practice, and you have to go study now. The next morning, you have to go compete against them in the classroom. Some guys [from other schools] went through that, yet some guys talk about how they hired somebody to do their papers and other work. That didn't happen at Notre Dame, and we're all better people because of it.

333

Jarious Jackson from Tupelo, Mississippi, never expected to end up at Notre Dame. But the sturdy 6'1", 235-pounder not only would fit in with the Irish, but also would emerge as Notre Dame's first solo captain (1999) since Rodney Culver headed up the 1991 Fighting Irish.

Jackson played sparingly in his first three years in the program but became the successor to Ron Powlus in 1998. After helping knock off No. 5 Michigan to open the campaign, the Irish lost to Michigan State before stringing together eight straight victories. Jackson would finish with 1,740 yards passing and 13 TD passes in 1998, followed by a record-setting 1999 campaign in which he broke school records for passes attempted (316), passes completed (184), and passing yards (2,753) while throwing 17 TD passes.

Selected in the seventh round in the spring of 2000—the only Irish player chosen in the draft—Jackson has been a member of the Denver Broncos organization since his departure from Notre Dame.

The
NEW MILLENNIUM

JOEY GETHERALL

1997–2000

MY DAD WENT TO USC, and growing up I was always a USC fan. Then I started getting my own opinion and my own views. Then when I started to get recruited by the USCs and the UCLAs, I started to determine who I liked the best.

Notre Dame came into the picture, and I was like, "Wow, my dad always despised Notre Dame!" I think that was one of the reasons I started liking Notre Dame, just to have a little rivalry in the house. Then when USC stopped recruiting me, I think I was even more determined to go to Notre Dame. Maybe I was trying to get a little payback to USC, showing them what they missed out on since USC was Notre Dame's biggest rival.

Growing up I was always a USC fan, so I never really was into the Notre Dame tradition. Once you go there you learn about it. I think it's that way with a lot of players. They learn about the Notre Dame tradition when they get there, unless they grow up with a family member who went there or grow up as a big fan. I wasn't a very big fan until I got there.

It was a little strange because that was the year [1997] of the coaching transition from Holtz to Davie. The person who recruited me from Notre Dame was [defensive back] coach Tom McMahon, who has passed away since. He was recruiting me my whole senior year, and I remember in about November he called me and said he didn't know what was going to happen but that they would probably be going through a coaching change and that I was probably going to stop receiving calls until they knew what was going on.

336

So I started thinking about maybe having to look at some other colleges. They said they weren't going to do anything right now because [the assistant coaches] weren't sure whether they were going to keep their jobs. So I started looking around the Pac-10, places like Washington, Washington State, and Oregon.

A few weeks later, they decided on coach Davie. They called and set up a recruiting trip, and I enjoyed it. It was one of the few warm weekends in December. It was 60 degrees and sunny, and I guess the next weekend there was a blizzard.

I went to [Davie's] house, and I met with him in his office at the stadium. He talked about the opportunity I would have at Notre Dame and offered me on the spot, and I committed right then and there. He said he didn't think I seemed too excited about the offer, but the reason I didn't seem too excited was because I was in shock, I was in awe. I couldn't believe I was getting offered right there. I told him I wouldn't disappoint him.

As a freshman, you feel comfortable around your classmates. But that first day you're sitting in the lunchroom and all the sophomores, juniors, and seniors walk in, and they're huge. You start to wonder if you can compete against these guys.

I mean, these guys were mean looking. The Lamont Bryants, Kory Minors, and Mike Rosenthals . . . all that was going through my head was, "Protect yourself against these guys!"

But in high school, I had a lot of Division I guys as teammates, like Kory Minor, Daylon McCutcheon [USC], Ralph Brown [Nebraska] . . . guys who were great players. And I was somewhat reassured by that because if these guys could compete on that level, why couldn't I?

I wasn't really in shock of the stadiums or the amount of people who were there. Coming from a high school where there were fifteen thousand people, I was pretty well prepared for college. That helped, as well as playing against the guys I mentioned.

The first day we were with the varsity, they put me up against [cornerback] Allen Rossum. I remember beating him on the post, and after that, he wanted to go against me every time so we could compete against one another.

I don't think I was ever in awe of my situation. I might get butterflies before a game, but once the whistle blew I was ready. I never worried about being smaller than everybody else or getting injured. That's just not my nature, especially being a wide receiver going against defensive backs.

Joey Getherall, the spunky wideout, was a fan favorite with his pass-catching and punt-return skills during the Bob Davie era. *Photo courtesy of John Gentry*/Blue & Gold Illustrated.

When I look back at my career at Notre Dame, I think of games like the one against Oklahoma my junior year [a 34–30 victory]. We were down at halftime against Oklahoma, and I had some big catches and had more than 100 yards receiving. Also in my senior year, even though we lost the game, I had that long punt return against Nebraska to tie the game. I thought after that we had the game in the bag, but we lost [27–24] in overtime.

I was watching the Utah–Air Force game [during the 2003 season], and I saw coach [Urban] Meyer coaching Utah. He was my receiver coach at Notre Dame, and they went into overtime against Air Force and won. Well, my senior year we went into overtime against Air Force and won, and I scored the winning touchdown. I think I had three touchdowns that game as well as the game winner.

We were on the sideline during a timeout, and coach Meyer told me that the reverse is going to me but he didn't want to look at me on the sideline because he didn't want everyone to know the ball was coming to me. So he talked to me while kind of looking in the other direction. That was one of our bread-and-butter plays that year, and that secured our spot in a BCS game in the Fiesta Bowl against Oregon State.

There's so much to being a part of Notre Dame, including the friends you make. At Notre Dame it's different from other colleges. You don't have fraternities. You meet a lot of guys in your dorm. You meet people from all over the place. It's not like if you go to a state school and you're mainly with people from that state. I knew people from Florida, Pennsylvania, Texas, everywhere. I still talk to people like Mike Gandy [from Garland, Texas], J. W. Jordan [Brooklyn, New York], Malcolm Johnson [Washington, D.C.], Bobby Brown [Lauderhill, Florida] . . .

The person who probably had the greatest influence on me was coach Meyer. I think coach Meyer is one of the best coaches in the game. The job he did at Bowling Green and now at Utah is incredible.

Everyone always says you're playing with the previous coach's players, he needs time to bring in his own players. I think that is a lot of BS. I mean, who wants to go to Bowling Green when you're 1–10? But coach Meyer finished 8–3 and beat teams affiliated with the BCS. Another great example is a guy like Bob Stoops. The second year he was at Oklahoma they won the national championship.

I don't understand how people can say Notre Dame doesn't have enough talent when they're in the top 10 in recruiting virtually every year. They've got players who are Parade All-Americans. I think there are a lot of people who are making a lot of excuses for the coaching staff. If Bowling Green and Toledo and Northern Illinois can beat teams from major conferences, then I don't understand how Notre Dame can't win.

I liked coach Davie. He was a great coach, and he gave me a chance. I wish he had just been more consistent in who he was. I didn't care whether he was a great guy or a jerk; I just wanted him to be consistent. When we were winning, he was great; when we weren't winning . . . he wasn't a great guy. I think he would have done a better job if he had just been more consistent.

That's why I think coach Meyer will be such a great head coach in college. He's consistent. He's always going to be in your face; there's always going to be discipline with him. I heard a lot of horror stories about coach Holtz, but the players responded and respected him.

Coach Meyer was tough on you on the field, but you always knew you could go talk to him about it. I talked to a couple guys from Bowling Green, and one guy said he was always there for the players. That's what you need. I don't know how the Utah players take all the cussing, but they're winning.

I can see [Meyer] being the head coach at Notre Dame. Hopefully he'll keep winning. That's all he knows how to do is win. If he ever comes to Notre Dame as a head coach, I'll be there in a second if he wants me to coach the receivers. I would love to come back to Notre Dame.

If there was a crowd favorite during the Bob Davie era at Notre Dame, it was 5'7", 175-pound flanker/kick returner Joey Getherall from Hacienda Heights, California.

Considered too small by hometown school Southern California, Getherall went on a mission to prove to the world that the size of the heart and the character of the man is more important that the size of the body. Although he never led the Irish in receptions in a season, he finished with 74 catches for 1,059 yards and eight touchdowns, while recording a 16.3-yard punt-return average to rank ninth in the country.

Getherall's most memorable moment came during his final season with the Irish when his reverse run for a touchdown gave Notre Dame a 34–31 overtime victory over Air Force. He also had a 76-yard punt return for a score against Nebraska in 2000.

ROCKY BOIMAN

1998–2001

I THINK I FIRST HEARD FROM NOTRE DAME when I was a junior in high school. You know the story. I had always wanted to go to Notre Dame ever since I was old enough to watch them on TV. I spoke with [offensive coordinator] Jim Colletto, who was recruiting me at the time. Bob Chmiel was the recruiting coordinator, and [receiver coach] Urban Meyer was involved as well. Everything just kind of fell into place for me.

What sold it for me was when I went up to the summer camp [in 1997]. They hadn't verbally made me an offer yet. I expressed to them how much I wanted to come to Notre Dame, and when they saw me run around a little bit, they really became interested. Coach Davie immediately went off to the side with me and worked a few drills for about 5 or 10 minutes, and a couple minutes later he comes up to me and says, "I'd like to offer you a scholarship to Notre Dame." I was probably at the camp for 15 minutes and coach Davie had offered me a scholarship. I had no idea how the process worked. I knew I had the athleticism and the things that it took to convince them. I was just fortunate that I got the opportunity to show them that day.

I was running track my senior year [1997] and I was 215 pounds and getting bigger, so I kind of knew I would move to linebacker once I got to Notre Dame. I made my first mark at Notre Dame on special teams as a freshman. Special teams were a way for me to show them that I was a football player and no matter what my job was, I was going to be a football player out there and make tackles and do whatever I could to help the team win. That was really the only opportunity I got my freshman year, and I wanted to make sure I took advantage of it. I was just excited to be one of the few freshmen that were playing. Most of the guys in my class were redshirted or sitting. So it was fun. It was my first opportunity to play in Notre Dame Stadium, and it was great.

I played behind Kory Minor, and then my sophomore year I started most of the games and shared time with Joe Ferrer. I ended up playing a little defensive end later in my career to help with the pass rush. I knew I might move to linebacker in college, but I never anticipated lining up in a three-point stance and rushing the passer! If you would have told me that, I wouldn't have believed it. It wasn't really my position so it wasn't my strongest attribute, but I did whatever I could in there, and I thought I did pretty well with it.

If I could put my finger on why we were so up and down record-wise while I was at Notre Dame, *I'd* be writing a book. I really don't know. It's one of those things, even now, that I still often think about. We had all these players. I had guys I played with who are in the [NFL] right now who are doing great, and it's like, "What was it? Why couldn't we get it together?"

The academic requirements that Notre Dame has . . . in today's era, kids are less drawn to Notre Dame. It's just one of those things. It's a great environment and a great place, but sometimes, if things don't mesh, it can be a tough place to win. There's great pressure to succeed, and you can get discouraged when things don't work out well.

342

I had some problems with some decisions that were made, especially my senior year when I was coming out of the lineup fairly frequently. I thought I was one of the best players on the team and one of the leaders, and I didn't know why I wasn't on the field more. But that's another subject. There were times I wondered whether Davie did a good enough job. I think it was just a combination of things. I don't want to put the blame on him because he did a lot of good things for the program, too.

Being named captain was really a special moment for me. It was announced to the team, and I remember it as being one of the greatest feelings in my life. It's something that nobody can take away from you, something I worked really hard to achieve because I felt like I really cared for Notre Dame as a place and a football institution. I had grown up loving it, and that honor was tremendous. I remember calling my dad from one of the phones in the Joyce Center. He and my mom were crying. . . . It was just a tremendous feeling. I took the honor very seriously in how I tried to lead the team.

Rocky Boiman made his mark on special teams as a freshman before emerging as a standout outside linebacker and quad-captain of the 2001 squad. *Photo courtesy of Matt Cashore/* Blue & Gold Illustrated.

Probably one of my strongest memories was the game against Nebraska my junior year [a 27–24 overtime loss in 2000]. That was crushing, but it was a great experience to be a part of. The day before you could feel the buzz around campus. I was a junior and starting to become a real prominent part of things. Then on game day, Jeff [Faine] came back from the field because he was out working with the quarterbacks early. He comes in and is like, "Dude, you won't believe it! It's all red out there! The stadium is red!" I had a really good game. That was the game where I felt like I had really arrived, and it was just such a shame to lose it. That crushed me for days.

The Fiesta Bowl loss [41–9 to Oregon State on January 1, 2001] was one of the lowest points of my career. To be truthful, I thought as a team we came out like deer in headlights. They were a flashy team, a talking team, and some guys on our team may have gotten intimidated. I just remember being so mad like, "These guys are just football players! We're better than these guys!" It was just very disappointing to be on that kind of stage and fail so miserably. We were intimidated, and they were on that night. They were extremely well coached, and I think they might have beaten anybody in the nation that night, so I give them a lot of credit.

344

The last year [5–6 in 2001], you could feel it coming with coach Davie. Not much was shared with us, but you could feel what was going on and that his job was in jeopardy. I think coach Davie was trying to prove that he could still do the job and run the team, but you could feel that he knew some things could be happening, just by some of the things he said. It was a shame for him, but my senior year [2001] you could feel the whole Notre Dame world coming down on him. I can't imagine all the stuff he went through dealing with that.

That was an unusual year anyway with 9/11. The whole country changed, and it definitely changed for us, too. We were preparing for Purdue when all that went down. We skipped a week, and that was just one of the crazy events that happened that year.

Then when we went to Purdue for the last game of the year, everybody was aware of [the possibility of Davie being fired]. In my personal situation, I had an injury and this was my last Notre Dame game, the last time I was ever going to put on the gold helmet. All the time growing up, wanting to put that helmet on, I wasn't going to let any of the outside issues get in the way of this final moment for me at Notre Dame.

I just told the team the night before, "Look, when we go out there tomorrow, we're not going to think about all the media issues and the outside issues that are going on. Let's win this game for Notre Dame, for what it means for the institution that is Notre Dame. All the great players and the great legacy that comes from this place, let's do it for Notre Dame and for ourselves." I was really happy that I could say we won my last game [24–18] as the Notre Dame captain.

Someone said this, and I think it's true. Someone said, "Notre Dame isn't always the greatest place to go to, but it's a great place to be from." You get a lot of compliments for being from Notre Dame once you've moved on. Sometimes when it's mid-February, and you're sitting in your dorm, and there's five feet of snow on the ground, and it's below zero, you're like, "What's going on here?" But my experience was great. I have three or four of the best friends in the world, a couple of whom weren't football players. Guys I had known from my dorm. Guys I still talk to every other day or so. Jeff Faine and Tommy Lopienski were two of my best friends from the football team. I had a lot of great times. I think I had a lot of success academically and athletically there. Overall I had a good experience.

I really enjoyed the times I spent speaking with [associate athletic director] George Kelly. As my years went by, I thought he was one of the last real hard-core Notre Dame guys. He came there in the sixties, I guess, and I liked listening to the stories he told. I really respected him because he was at Notre Dame when it was becoming legendary. I can't say that I spoke with him often. But I visited with him in his office a couple of times, and there was a great feeling after speaking with him.

345

Dr. Mickey Franco helped me out, especially my senior year when I was a captain and I was kind of struggling with why we weren't doing better. He offered me some advice, and I developed a good friendship with him. I don't know how the Notre Dame athletic department viewed him, but I thought he was great.

The Notre Dame experience was good for me. I wouldn't change any of my experience. I love the place. I had some issues with some coaches there. There were some things that went on that I didn't like but were motivation for me, both later in my time at Notre Dame and in the NFL. Notre Dame is still the greatest place. If I had to do it all over again, I'd do the same thing.

One of the most recognizable figures at Notre Dame at the beginning of the century was Rocky Boiman, whose flaming red hair matched his fiery determination on the Irish gridiron. Named captain of the 2001 squad (along with David Givens, Grant Irons, and Anthony Weaver), the Cincinnati native arrived at Notre Dame as a safety. He quickly developed into an outside linebacker who grew to 6'4", 240-pound proportions by his senior season. Boiman would eventually double as a pass rusher at defensive end.

Boiman spearheaded the 2001 defense, which ranked 14th in the country. He finished his career with 144 tackles and 8½ sacks. A fourth-round selection by Tennessee in 2002, Boiman remains a prominent part of the Titans' defense and special teams.

JEFF FAINE

2000–2002

Florida, Florida State, Miami, Nebraska, and Notre Dame were my top five schools coming out of high school. I took my visit to South Bend over the banquet weekend, and I really enjoyed the beautiful campus. Growing up, in my mind, when I pictured a college campus, I pictured Notre Dame. When I went to Florida, Florida State, and Miami, I didn't get that intimate feel. Not to take anything away from those schools, but they just felt like they were stuck in the middle of a city.

The magic of choosing a place like Notre Dame struck me pretty strongly when I realized that I'd be playing for the Blue and Gold. It still gives me chills down my spine thinking about running out of the tunnel. To be able to play with that gold helmet really helped me make my decision.

I didn't really get exposed to college football growing up because I was living in Hawaii until age 10 with my dad in the navy, so I didn't have any attachments to teams. My first memories of Notre Dame football were of Marc Edwards and Ron Powlus. I remember No. 44 [Edwards] busting through the line and scoring those touchdowns, and hearing how Ron Powlus was going to be an unbelievable hero.

In the end coming to Notre Dame was an easy decision, but it wasn't the clear choice from the beginning. Coming from Florida, there was a lot of pressure to stay in state. Before signing day it leaked out that I was going to Notre Dame. After I did my signing ceremony at my high school I found out that I had something like two dozen death threats. That shows you how serious people are about football down here. I didn't find out about the threats until about a month later because my high school coaches kept it from me.

Dealing with all that type of stuff was difficult, but in the end there was no way I could have picked any other school. It was Notre Dame. People who haven't played there or didn't have the opportunity to go to school there don't understand and won't ever understand that statement. Coming from Notre Dame is irreplaceable.

John Merandi was the starting center when I arrived, and I thought he was a pretty good one at the time. That year I was always the number six lineman, the first one to go in at any position if they needed me. The coaching staff wanted to save [a year of eligibility] so I could have the five years, but I wasn't used to losing. [Notre Dame was 5–7 in 1999.]

With Notre Dame coming off the Gator Bowl and losing a pretty good class with [Mike] Rosenthal and [Luke] Petitgout, [the 5–7 season] hit me hard. What hit me hardest was tearing my hamstring two weeks before camp. I couldn't participate in freshman practices to get ready. Then when the varsity got there, I was in a whirlwind. It's a possibility that I could have played that year, but missing three weeks really hurt me. I think the coaches wanted to save me anyway because they had a pretty good line already.

I knew after Merandi left that the center spot was mine to lose. All I had to do was prove to the coaches that I was worth what they thought I was worth. When it really clicked that I could start was during some one-on-ones that spring doing run blocking in front of the whole team. Coach Davie would call up the freshmen, and we could call out a teammate to block. Usually that was another freshman. Coach Davie called me up and I called out Lance Legree. Everybody went crazy because I called out a veteran who was going to be a fifth-year senior and is now starting for the New York Giants. So I'm taking this big step to call out a vet, I end up steamrolling him, and the whole team goes crazy. From then on I knew I was ready to start.

It's the Notre Dame in you that makes you want to fight for more. Even coming off the 5–7 season in 1999, we still felt like we were one of the best teams in the nation. Obviously we had some bad games, but we felt we could have won them, which was true. We proved some people wrong in 2000 [9–3].

As a Notre Dame football player, you never have to prove to yourself that you're worthy of the name. But in saying that, I went back to talk to the team in 2003, and I told them to make the alumni proud. I wear Notre Dame on my sleeve. I'm always proud to say I'm from Notre Dame, and I know other alumni are too. One thing guys coming up need to understand is that you don't have to prove it to yourself. That's the last person you should worry about proving it to. It's all the guys who have paved the way to make Notre Dame what it is today, those are the people you need to prove yourself to.

The buildup for that Nebraska game in 2000 [a 27–24 overtime loss] was unbelievable. The whole atmosphere . . . you knew it was going to be a huge game. Everybody was ready. The night before, the captains were speaking, and there was no doubt that we could beat them.

For most teams when they're playing the No. 1 team in the nation there might be a little doubt. There wasn't any for us. We knew we could beat those guys. I remember the overtime like it was yesterday, not being able to punch it in and then watching Eric Crouch come around the corner to punch it in. What haunts me still is seeing those fifth-year seniors like B. J. Scott passed out on the ground distraught. We had that game won, but we couldn't get it done. To this day that was probably one of my most hard-fought games.

A lot of the breaks that we didn't get in 1999 we got in 2000. A lot of those fifth-year seniors, they remembered the season before and didn't want another one like it. It was like 2002. I knew what it was like to lose, and I didn't want to do it again.

349

With the Fiesta Bowl being my first bowl game, I didn't know what to expect. I wanted it to be special, and I didn't take advantage of some of the activities that were going on because I was just sitting in my room trying to prepare, maybe overprepare. As a team, we were focused, and our coaches had us ready. You feel like you're ready, but then the ball is kicked off and you realize that you aren't. I don't know who to hold accountable for that. My opinion is that coaches don't lose the games, the players do. I have a real hard time with people blaming stuff on coaches. Players win and players lose. I guess you have to throw it on all 22 who played that night.

That game was embarrassing to be a part of [Notre Dame lost to Oregon State, 41–9], but I don't think the hangover of that game was what kept us from achieving success in 2001. I think the team trained hard and trained well and stayed together. We wanted to do it for ourselves, but the bounces didn't go our way. It's so ironic how a game is won on two or three huge plays. I really think that in so many of those games in 2001 things just didn't go our way.

While Irish teams were up and down during the early 2000s, one constant was eventual first-round NFL draft choice Jeff Faine (No. 52) at center. *Photo courtesy of Matt Cashore*/Blue & Gold Illustrated.

It was difficult to move on past Lincoln after we lost in the season opener [27–10 to Nebraska in 2001]. A lot of our two-a-days were structured around their option offense and their different style of defense. It was to the point where it seemed like we overprepared for that game. To have so much invested in playing one team and so much invested in one game and one night, and then to lose it the way we did, it just blew up in our faces. It was tough to leave that stadium because we invested two weeks in one game, and it wasn't even close.

Playing through 2001 with all the rumors about coach Davie, it really depended on who you were when it came to dealing with the situation. Some players didn't feel as strongly about the coaches as other guys. I loved playing for coach Davie and thought he was a good coach. Some players didn't. I loved [offensive line coach Dave] Borbely. I think he's singularly responsible along with me and [strength and conditioning coach] Mickey Marotti for preparing me to be a first-round pick and making it to the big leagues. I was pretty affected by those rumors because I didn't want the coaches to get fired. But in college football you have to produce results, the same as the pros. Everybody is on the hot seat, and in the pros the players are on the hot seat too. It's a cutthroat business. I think I was a little more involved with it than some of the other players because I was really let down when coach Davie was let go.

I was on the leadership board that helped in the process of getting a new coach, and I told the team that in this instance we had to be selfish and keep training for Notre Dame and keep training for ourselves and not worry about anything outside of that. When the whole fiasco happened with coach George O'Leary, it was unbelievable. I remember my mom calling me at 8:00 A.M. three or four days after we hired coach O'Leary, telling me that we had just fired our coach. She heard about it before I did.

351

From the players' perspective, we wanted a players' coach, someone who had an idea how to balance what the players want and what the players need and find a middle ground there. We wanted somebody who could keep us fresh on game day and keep us fresh at the end of the season. It's a huge deal how a coach prepares a team when it gets down to how much you hit and how much you run. It's a scary decision. I'd hate to have to make it. You want to work them hard, but you don't want to work them too much. That's hard to figure out.

Without a doubt it was a breath of fresh air when coach Willingham finally took over. People don't know how involved he is in the program. He'll do the workouts with you. When you see a coach being able to get it done, it makes you want to finish them too. To see the faces of my teammates and how much they changed over time, guys were so much happier. Not taking anything away from coach Davie, because I'm a big fan of his and I hope he gets back in coaching as a coordinator or as a head coach because he has a great defensive mind. But what that team needed was something different, a change and a breath of fresh air. That's what coach Willingham was.

Coach Willingham chooses his words very well and is an educated man. I respect him wholeheartedly. Everything he does is for the betterment of the team. He lets loose a little more than he does to the media. He's not as stone-faced as he is in public. I've had the opportunity to sit down with him a number of times, and he'll crack jokes, but you might not think it's a joke until he laughs to make sure you know he's joking. He's just a regular guy. I know he doesn't come off as a warm person, but he wants the team to know that you're going to get his best effort.

Now that I'm not playing for him it's a different story. Every time I go back it's a hug and, "It's so good to see you!" I never got that when I was there. He has to be tough to maintain the discipline and the respect that he requires from his team. But he's not stone cold all the time.

I knew we could beat Maryland to start out 2002 [a 22–0 victory]. That game was necessary to boost the morale of our team. It helped the young guys who were playing. Then coming back to my home state and playing Florida State, I thought about that game for two years going. Knowing that they had a real good defensive line with Darnell Dockett, it was unbelievable. Then we just blew them up [a 34–24 victory], just killed them. It was awesome.

352

After that game you got an example of coach Willingham being human and letting go of his guard. I remember getting back on the bus, and I don't remember what the song was, but my man was up at the front of the bus dancing like there was no tomorrow. He's still got some moves from when he used to be back in college. I'd never seen something like that out of him. It was almost like 1,000 pounds were lifted off his shoulders. Coach Willingham might not let me back into Notre Dame after telling that story.

Going into that stadium, beating coach Bowden and beating Florida State, I remember some of their assistant coaches asking me during recruiting why I was going to Notre Dame when I could go to a championship program in Tallahassee. To be able to shake that coach's hand after the game was a great feeling.

Going into the Gator Bowl [a 28–6 loss to North Carolina State], I knew that if I came out injury free that I was going to leave. I had gotten some good information before that game that I was going to go in the top two rounds. To be honest with you, I missed Notre Dame so much this past year. All the money in the world, playing in the NFL, having a nice house, driving a nice car, and all that jazz, I still I missed the 10-by-11 dorm room and going to the meal hall. To this day I still long for it.

I made the right decision. If I had the injuries in my senior year that I had as a rookie with the Browns, maybe I would have missed out on being a top pick. I know I made the right decision, but without a doubt I miss Notre Dame and would give anything to go through it again.

In the pros you're not playing for a team like you play for a team in college. When you're playing for your school you'll always be from Notre Dame. You'll always be Blue and Gold. I could be with three or four different teams before the end of my career. I play for the Cleveland Browns, and I sell out for the city of Cleveland, and I love being from here. It's a football city, and the fans are so passionate that it reminds me of Notre Dame. But every player in the NFL will agree that there's something more to playing for your school. There's a reason on Saturday afternoons and Saturday evenings we're sitting in front of the television rooting for our teams. It's important that our teams are successful, and we're proud of where we came from.

You go to Notre Dame as a teenager and you don't know what you're getting into or what to expect. But when you get done you walk out of there as a man, a woman, an adult. You really grow a lot. There are things that I take for granted that I learned at Notre Dame that people my age don't know. Guys talk about it all the time, and I'm not bragging, but I think I'm a little more mature than most people my age. I owe that to Notre Dame.

It's the whole bag there: the campus culture, the strong faith beliefs, the academics, the atmosphere of community. . . . You grow up with so many different people during those four years. There were nights I spent in the TV lounge with people from all over the country and all over the world. Those types of experiences are irreplaceable.

Center Jeff Faine is a throwback-type player who epitomized the tough, hard-nosed interior lineman upon which Notre Dame built its reputation. A shining star on a unit that never ranked higher than 76th in the country in total offense, Faine became known for his go-beyond-the-whistle approach to line play.

Faine was a second-team All-American in 2002 and a first-round draft choice (21st overall) of the Cleveland Browns, where he started as a rookie center for the 2003 squad.

NICHOLAS SETTA

2000–2003

NOTRE DAME WAS A SCHOOL THAT I KNEW about more than most, but I obviously had seen Michigan and Ohio State and a lot of those schools. When I went through the decision-making process, I didn't go into it with a specific favorite. Notre Dame wasn't having a great year [5–7 in 1999], so it wasn't like, "Oh my gosh, Notre Dame, national champions!"

But I actually never visited any other school. My mentality was that it didn't have anything to do with partying, it didn't have anything to do with nightlife. It had to do with whatever was going to be the hardest place to get through. I've always done things in terms of trying not to take shortcuts. I really believe that if you do the right things and you work hard and you do everything you can, you have no excuses.

One of the things I love about Notre Dame football is that we play one of the top schedules in the country every year. You have to play the best to be the best, in my opinion. If you play the best every week and you're mentally prepared and you're deserving, you'll win. It's as simple as that. So many people say Notre Dame can't win because of the schedule, Notre Dame can't win because of academics . . . I think those are reasons Notre Dame *should* win.

There are a lot of great schools out there, but there are a lot of schools where the players don't think, "I have to go to class and if I don't go to class, it's going to affect my play because it's showing the character of the person." They don't drill that into your head at other places. Here they drill in your head, "You're a student, just like anyone else here." That's why I really wanted to be a part of a place like Notre Dame.

I was frustrated not playing my freshman year. But I thought at the time, "If you leave Notre Dame, you'll regret it for the rest of your life." I'd rather lose at Notre Dame than win a national championship anywhere else. I just got back to work and tried to get better. People thought that my relationship with [punter] Joey Hildbold might be strained because we were in the same class and he won the punting job when we were freshmen. From high school to now, I've always done everything I can do to help my competitor for a position because I want everyone I compete against to be the best.

My freshman year, they had me change my punting style, but I never said to the coaching staff, "In high school, I had a 47.8-yard punting average, now you're going to make me change it?" That's what they wanted, they're the bosses, OK. There's enough bitching and moaning from everyone else out there. I made a commitment to Notre Dame. If I don't buy into what they say, we're never going to win. It's as simple as that. So I shut my mouth, did what I had to do, and I never had a problem with anyone on my team I was competing against.

I never considered myself as just a punter or a kicker or a kickoff guy. One of the pro scouts asked me, "What do you want to do [in the NFL]?" I said, "Kick, kick off, and punt. I want to do them all." I can understand why a coach would want you to focus on one thing, but you're a kicker. Why can't you do all the kicking? The problem is so many people can't maintain a work ethic to be successful at all facets of the kicking game.

As a kicker, you've got to be perfect at that moment. All that pressure is there, which was always the one thing that attracted me to being a kicker. It's the greatest feeling in the world. Why wouldn't you want that pressure as a competitor? It's the same thing as being a race car driver. I like to be driving. I've always wanted to be able to say, "Hey, if I miss this kick, blame me," because I know I can take that blame; I know it's not going to affect me either way. I can deal with success and I can deal with failure.

When I look back at the games while I was at Notre Dame, obviously, for a kicker, the most memorable moments are pretty well defined. The game-winner [a 38-yard field goal with no time left] to beat Purdue [23–21 in 2000]. The Maryland game in 2002 [a 22–0 victory] because I kicked five field goals, and the Washington State game in 2003 [a 29–26 overtime victory] because I kicked the game-winner.

I think coach Davie could have succeeded, but it's a matter of finding the right mixture of people. Davie is a smart coach and one of the greatest defensive coordinators in the country. It's a matter of getting the right people at the right time. Can coach Davie go somewhere else and win the national championship? I believe so. I mean, we went to the Fiesta Bowl [in 2000] and we lost to Nebraska in overtime and lost to Michigan State in the last two minutes. That's how close we were to winning the national title. You've just got to get the right mix of people, and you need things to just fall into place.

I felt like I had to prove myself all over again with a new coaching staff, so the first day I was out there with coach Willingham, I wasn't bashful to say, "Hey, Coach, let's try one from 60 yards. Now let's try one from 65." I'm not one to talk, but during those first few days, you want to make an impression. He learned early on from me that I had confidence I could make any kick he asked me to do.

I thought coach Willingham was an unbelievably great guy. He says all the right things and does all the right things. Most people will say the right things but they don't do the right things. That has an impact on the players. He just needs to get a group of guys who realize doing the right thing is the best thing to do. At Notre Dame, you can have great athletes who are extremely intelligent. That's what Notre Dame is built on. At other schools, you can have guys who are there just to play ball, but not at Notre Dame.

I wonder about coach Willingham's approach with some things. I think we need to do a better job with some communication things with the media. I had a pulled quadricep [in 2003], but the injury wasn't revealed, they said, because of the Privacy Act. All that did, however, was create rumors about me and my relationship with coach Willingham. My parents were like, "Are you going to get kicked out of school?" There was talk about trouble between coach Willingham and me. There was stuff said about me being racist toward coach Willingham. Coach Willingham and I had one of the best relationships on the team.

But if one simple statement had been made, "Nick Setta has a pulled quad," that would have been it. None of that talk would have happened. When I got hurt against Pittsburgh, I should have limped off. Then everyone would have known I was hurt. I was told I wasn't supposed to tell the media what my injury was, and half the time I felt like a jerk doing that.

An injury during the 2003 season left kicker/punter Nicholas Setta just five field goals short of Notre Dame's career record. *Photo courtesy of Matt Cashore*/Blue & Gold Illustrated.

I think [Willingham is] going to have to open up a little bit to the media. I understand the whole point of making the media work for a story. Some of the stuff is cute and everybody has his own way of expressing himself to the media. He's a great guy, but I'm not sure where he's coming from sometimes when it comes to things like that.

Notre Dame as a whole has affected me profoundly. It provides you with so much opportunity. [Athletic director] Kevin White was unbelievable. I was able to sit down and have dinner with Kevin White and his wife. How many people can say they had dinner with their athletic director? He really wants to understand who you are, what type of kid you are, and he's interested in the questions you have.

In terms of players, I think the guy I respected the most was [strong safety] Gerome Sapp. I respected him in the classroom. I don't think he got all *A*s or anything like that, but he really pushed himself. He was one of those guys who was accountable. There are very few people in the world who are accountable. I think you'll see him succeed in life. Jeff Faine is another guy like that. He's a mean SOB, but he's accountable.

Overall, it was the student body that made the experience so special. It was real easy to make it through school because of the support system, all the things that keep you going. I can't say enough good things about Notre Dame. I was fortunate to have parents who woke up at 5:00 in the morning to make me breakfast before I went to work out. They've always been there for me, and they've always cared. I leave Notre Dame feeling tremendously blessed.

Nicholas Setta, the 5'11", 185-pound kicker/punter from Lockport, Illinois, never met a pressure situation he didn't relish. An injury during the 2003 season prevented him from breaking John Carney's school record of 51 career field goals, but Setta finished his career 46 for 66 on 3-pointers while converting 104 of 105 extra-point attempts. He also doubled as Notre Dame's punter, taking over the job in 2003 upon the departure of four-year starter Joey Hildbold.

Setta's 248 points rank fifth in Notre Dame history, behind Allen Pinkett (320), Craig Hentrich (294), Autry Denson (282), and Louis "Red" Salmon (250).

COURTNEY WATSON

2000–2003

FOR ME, CHOOSING NOTRE DAME was a difficult choice because growing up in Florida, I didn't know a lot about Notre Dame. When I was growing up, we had Florida, Florida State, and Miami—three top 5, top 10 teams every year. I had a lot to learn about Notre Dame during the recruiting process.

I chose to visit Notre Dame basically from everything I had heard and learned about the place. Once Notre Dame started recruiting me, I learned more about the school from [receiver coach] Urban Meyer, who was recruiting the state of Florida for Notre Dame. He was a very intriguing person, and then there was the academic reputation of Notre Dame, which also intrigued me.

Believe it or not, it really came down to a decision between Notre Dame and Duke, as crazy as that sounds. The best chance I had with the three schools in Florida was with Florida. I wasn't recruited at all by Miami and not much by Florida State. The academic part was very important to me, so in the end I went with Notre Dame because of the academics and the football tradition.

I never played defense at all in high school, so that transition was pretty different. Quite honestly, it was a horrible transition because never in my entire football career had I been on defense. Not only was I now on defense, but I was expected to play behind Anthony Denman right off the bat, and Anthony was an All-American. If I had to step in then, I had to step in at a very high level.

So it was pretty tough. My first fall at Notre Dame, I split my time between running back and cornerback. Then that first spring when I switched to defense full time, that was very tough. It was hard for me to enjoy football at that time because it was like I was learning the entire game all over again, like starting from scratch. I had people tell me I might end up at linebacker, but I never really thought it would happen.

[Defensive coordinator] Greg Mattison broke the news to me. We were in the locker room and he said, "You're going to be with the defense. You're going to start working with coach [Kirk] Doll, with the linebackers." I thought to myself, "Is this really happening?" Looking back at it now, it was the best thing that ever happened to me.

My first start against Nebraska was very productive [18 tackles]. By no means did I think my transition was complete, but that really helped me feel good about myself making the transition to linebacker. Up until that point, I had not been battle tested. All I had really done was play linebacker in practice. So to go out against Nebraska, the No. 5 team in the country with the Heisman Trophy winner [quarterback Eric Crouch] . . . to be able to go out and play so well really gave me a lot of confidence. I started to believe that what the coaches were telling me was true. It was like, "The coaches know what they're talking about! I can play this position!" Yet I'm pretty sure that I probably did the wrong thing on more than half of those [18] tackles.

Through those first few games as a starter, I felt like I was learning so much every week with every game. I can remember what lessons I learned each step of the way. By the time I reached this past year, I felt really comfortable at the [Will linebacker] position. Plus I now felt very comfortable in our defensive philosophy.

Playing for coach Davie and then for coach Willingham was different, just because as soon as coach Willingham and his staff came in, we had such great expectations placed on us from the coaches. Then came the expectations from everybody on the outside because everybody on the outside saw what [Willingham] could do with what the media likes to say was talent that wasn't up to par.

When coach Davie was there, we kind of just took it week by week. When coach Willingham came in, it was like, "This is what I see from having prepared a team against you every year. And I think we can be a great team right now. Here are my reasons why we can do it right now."

To me it was obvious as a player that coach Willingham had more experience running a big-time program, setting goals and objectives, and letting everybody on the team know what those goals and objectives were. I think coach Davie had a problem communicating to the team what the goals were for the program. Not to say that he didn't have any goals or he didn't want to achieve any specific goals, but as a team we didn't really know what we were working toward. Obviously, at Notre Dame, your goal is always to win the national title, but I never really felt like we had a blueprint to achieve it. With coach Willingham, you knew what you wanted to get accomplished on this day, or in that meeting, or within this conversation.

[Willingham] definitely keeps you on your toes. I enjoy every conversation I have with him, even outside of football, because you will always take something away from it. Whether you agree with him or you don't, you will always take something away from it. You'll walk away from him and think, "That's kind of different. I never really thought that way about it."

I think the decision to hire coach Willingham was great for Notre Dame, great for him, and great for college football in general. For them to say, "We're not going to allow race to enter into this," is a great thing. They said, "We see a person we think can get us turned around and put us where we want to be, and we're going to go after him if he's black, if he's not a Catholic . . ." That was significant to me.

361

I had a great deal of pride in the university after what happened with the O'Leary situation. They took their time to make a very good decision. You look around now and a school or a program gets rid of a coach, and they feel the need to get another coach in there immediately. So they don't take the proper amount of time to find a coach, and that coach may not be a fit. I think Tyrone Willingham is a great fit for Notre Dame. That in itself gives me pride in Notre Dame, regardless of his race. For them to take their time to get it right, especially after the mistake that they made with the O'Leary situation, was great.

If you sit down and look at it statistically, I don't think there was a big difference from 2002 [10–3] to 2003 [5–7]. Our production on offense was similar. Our defense dropped down from where it had been, but it wasn't like we went from a top 25 defense to outside the top 100. I think you have to look at other factors, intangibles, such as a freshman quarterback, four new starters on the offensive line, losing several key senior leaders on our defense.

Losing Shane Walton, who had seven interceptions the previous year, was huge. [Strong safety] Gerome Sapp, who was a leader, and [defensive end] Ryan Roberts, who was a leader . . . you lose guys like that, and we just couldn't recapture the magic that we had early in the 2002 season.

We didn't get a lot of breaks, and when we did get breaks, we didn't always take advantage of them. Sometimes we didn't pick up a fumble and run it back like we did the previous year. We just fell on it. Or we'd drop an interception, or we didn't get a third-down stop when we had the momentum on our side in our own stadium. Instead, they got the first down and then went down and scored. I think it was more things like that than to say the team performed very poorly overall.

Another key thing was our special teams. That's one place you can look statistically and see the big difference from the previous year. It wasn't like we were coming out equal on special teams. We were coming out on the short side of things. When you're at Michigan and you've got a freshman quarterback and you start from your own 20 every series, that's asking a lot of him.

362

I don't know what happened to us from the end of the third quarter down at Doak Campbell Stadium against Florida State [a 34–24 victory in 2002] to the present. Maybe as a team, we took a sigh of relief and said, "Whew, we can do this!" Maybe we already wrote off the Boston College game [a 14–7 loss] and the USC game [a 44–13 loss].

Coach was angry at the end of the Florida State game, and I think a lot of the players were, too. What happened in those last 15 minutes was atrocious. It was humid that day, but we had guys playing in that game who hadn't played much who should have been excited just to be a part of a game like that. We were kicking the crap out of Florida State. My personal opinion was that at the end of that third quarter, as a team, we just let out a sigh of relief and said, "We've done it."

After we beat Florida State, all we heard about for the next seven days was 1993 when Boston College came in and beat Notre Dame after No. 2 Notre Dame had knocked off No. 1 Florida State. We were on an emotional roller coaster because we had just dealt with a team, Florida State, that probably had written us off, and now we were dealing with a Boston College team that we had probably written off. They were jacked just to have the opportunity to be a part of something special.

Linebacker Courtney Watson (No. 33) was a finalist for the Butkus Award in 2002 and paced the squad in tackles in each of his final two years with the Irish. *Photo courtesy of Matt Cashore*/Blue & Gold Illustrated.

In my opinion, Boston College didn't win that game; we gave it away to them. Offensively, they couldn't do anything, and that was with a running back [Derrick Knight] that came in averaging more than 100 yards rushing a game.

The one thing that helped the transition to [defensive coordinator Kent] Baer was the fact that coach Mattison was still there. Coach Mattison helped implement things, especially with terminology. Also, coach Willingham's staff weren't guys who were just coaches. They didn't just coach; they cared about us as people. They wanted to get a chance to know us. They weren't just people coming in who were going to tell us what to do. That made it a lot easier transition.

I had a very good relationship with coach Baer. We talked about a lot of stuff outside of football. That's the kind of person coach Willingham brought in. I think that helps you win in the long run. Not only did we see coach Baer as a coach, but as a person, and you know what he believes in as a person. You know his values, which makes it easier as a player to trust what he's telling you.

There's so much going on at Notre Dame as far as the type of people you meet and the things you can learn. It would have been really easy to go to school in Florida and just deal with kids from Florida. I wouldn't know half the things I know if I hadn't chosen to really broaden my horizons at Notre Dame. You have guys from Texas, California, Florida, and guys are jawing back and forth about who had the best high school, who had the best state for football . . . that was another way to bring us closer together as teammates.

If you go into [Notre Dame] with an open mind, knowing that you have an opportunity to meet new people and grow as a person, it enhances the experience. That's the approach I tried to have, which is why I enjoyed my time at Notre Dame so much. I went in with an open mind. I wanted to learn as much as I could about life, people, whatever. There are some people out there who have misconceptions about athletes. But I never had any run-ins with anyone where two years from now, I'll be telling a story about this guy or girl who didn't understand my perspective. That's another good thing about Notre Dame. You have people who are educated and therefore are pretty open-minded. Some people may say it's not a very open-minded place and there isn't a lot going on. But you have smart people who are open-minded. Maybe it's not the most liberal place where they have the most